From Welfare
to Work

A Manpower Demonstration Research Corporation Study

From Welfare to Work

Judith M. Gueron
Edward Pauly

with Cameran M. Lougy

RUSSELL SAGE FOUNDATION / NEW YORK

THE RUSSELL SAGE FOUNDATION

Russell Sage Foundation
112 East 64th Street
New York, NY 10021

Library of Congress Cataloging-in-Publication Data

Gueron, Judith M.
From Welfare to Work/Judith M. Gueron, Edward Pauly with Cameran M. Lougy.
    p.   cm.
Includes bibliographical references and index.
ISBN 0-87154-345-1 (hard)   ISBN 0-87154-346-X (soft)
1. Welfare recipients – Employment – United States. 2. Federal aid to public welfare – United States. I. Pauly, Edward. II. Title.
HV95.G843   1991
362.5'84'0973 – dc20

90-5603
CIP

The Manpower Demonstration Research Corporation's preparation of this volume was supported by the U.S. Department of Health and Human Services (HHS) and the Ford Foundation. The JOBS evaluation, of which this is a part, is funded by HHS under a competitive award, Contract No. HHS-100-89-0030. The findings and conclusions present-ed herein do not necessarily represent the official positions or policies of the funders.

Reproduction by the United States Government in whole or in part is permitted for any purpose.

The paper used in this publication meets the minimum requirements of American National Standard for Information Sciences – Permanence of Paper for Printed Library Materials, ANSI Z39.48-1984.

Cover and text design: Rowe & Ballantine

10 9 8 7 6 5 4 3 2 1

Contents

Tables and Figures

Tables

Figures

Preface

This book is the result of an extraordinary, long-term partnership between states and localities seeking to reform welfare and researchers attempting to assess the effectiveness of their efforts. In the late 1960s, Congress began to reshape Aid to Families with Dependent Children – the nation's largest cash welfare program – to encourage employment among the heads of families receiving welfare, most of whom were single mothers. As these initiatives got under way, starting in the mid-1970s, researchers at the Manpower Demonstration Research Corporation (MDRC) and other organizations, building on the approach successfully used in the earlier negative income tax experiments, began applying the tools of classical, random assignment field experiments to the key policy questions about these initiatives. Would they work? Could they reduce the welfare rolls? Would they cost or save money? Would they cause people to get good jobs and move out of poverty? This book summarizes and interprets research findings that help answer these questions. It thus provides a knowledge base for states as they make the critical choices that will turn the current welfare reforms, the Family Support Act of 1988, into a reality during the 1990s.

While this book was being written, the importance of this knowledge base came into sharper focus. The 1988 legislation offers states $1 billion a year in new federal money for welfare-to-work programs, but only if they put up matching state resources. States will be making these funding decisions in unusually harsh fiscal conditions, with many facing budget deficits and powerful competing claims on scarce funds. In such a climate, the reliable record of information on what works best for whom takes on added importance.

The legacy of the rigorous studies that have been completed, involving more than 65,000 people in scores of communities in 21 states, provides convincing evidence that, in many ways, these programs succeeded. Overall, they increased the earnings of poor families and saved money. However, they did not eliminate welfare or poverty. The challenge for the 1990s is to make such programs work better and to determine whether greater investments in education and training will pay off in higher skills and better jobs, in reducing long-term dependency, in strengthening families, and in improving outcomes for children.

The authors – MDRC's President and Senior Research Associate in education, respectively – had three main audiences in mind in writing this book: the state and local people on the firing line who fund, design, and implement the new reforms; the wider policy and academic community, which will shape public expectations for reform; and the U.S. Department of Health and Human Services (HHS), which will play a critical role in determining the agenda for future research, including the major evaluation of the new law that the authors and other staff at MDRC are conducting.

This volume reflects the work of many people. None of the information presented here could have been acquired without the active involvement of state administrators who put their programs under a magnifying glass, and the willingness of the staff in state and local agencies, in the midst of their harried work, to cooperate with the requirements of the research. We, and the community of practitioners and scholars committed to informed social policy, owe much to these individuals, only some of whom can be listed here. Among the administrators and staff who were involved in MDRC's completed welfare-to-work evaluations are: Rowena Bopp, John Burdette, Gregory Coler, Jerry Evans, Leon Ginsberg, Thomas Gunnoe, Kalman Hettleman, Richard Jacobsen, Ray Koenig, Larry Lockhart, William Lukhard, Ruth Massinga, Ronald McAtee, Linda McMahon, George Merrill, Jeffrey Miller, Douglas Patino, Walt Patterson, Michael Petit, Marion Pines, Frederick Pond, John Robbins, Ray Scott, Diana Scully, David Siegel, Sybil Stokes, and Linda Wilcox.

The book's greatest debt is to the staff at MDRC. While this volume summarizes the results from a substantial body of studies, those that form its core are the evaluations that made up MDRC's Demonstration of State Work/Welfare Initiatives, a multi-state field research project conducted between 1982 and 1988. The success of this undertaking depended on the entire study team: the many people who spent years designing the study, putting it in place, carefully collecting and processing the data, conducting the analysis, and reporting on the results. The Work/Welfare Demonstration was intensely collaborative, making this book a collective effort in the strongest sense of that phrase.

The staff working on this demonstration included economists and other social scientists, people with operational backgrounds, former welfare administrators, systems designers, and data analysts, with the senior author directing the research. The design and overall effort benefited from vigorous intellectual debate in which different perspectives and analytic styles merged and shaped the final products. Several people made critical contributions to that project and thus this book. Robert Ivry and Michael Bangser guided MDRC's work with the states and assisted in distilling the research findings. Barbara Goldman managed the research effort, was responsible for the study of participation, and contributed to all aspects of the project. Daniel Friedlander took the lead in the study of program impacts, David Long in estimating benefits and costs, and Karen Paget in overseeing the mammoth data collection effort. William J. Grinker, as president of MDRC when the project was conceived, helped shape its initial vision. Barbara Blum, who headed MDRC through most of the years of this project, brought a calm and sure hand to the implementation of a unique partnership in learning. Other staff who were instrumental to the success of this project were the late Joseph Ball, Gayle Hamilton, Darlene Hasselbring, James Healy, and Janet Quint. Major contributions were also made by George Cave, Gregory Hoerz, Marilyn Price, James Riccio, and Kay Sherwood.

Some of these people and others at MDRC also made a direct contribution to the preparation of this volume. Cameran Lougy had major responsibility for checking much of the detailed information in the book and made numerous substantive contributions. Daniel Friedlander both reviewed the manuscript and inspired some of the thinking that lies behind the book through his active collaboration with the senior author on a related project. Kay Sherwood contributed her insight on both the implementation of welfare reform and the details of the 1988 legislation in reviewing and critiquing the manuscript and responding to the many queries. Gayle Hamilton provided the authors with numerous suggestions and interpretations. Gordon Berlin, Robert Ivry, and John Wallace read many drafts and helped us sharpen our view of the critical choices facing program administrators. David Long reviewed the interpretation of cost data and wrote a special appendix on program costs. Patricia Auspos contributed to the project in its early stages.

This Preface began by acknowledging two partners: the states and the researchers. But the wherewithal to transform a mutual interest into actual knowledge came from the support of visionary funders. Throughout the last 17 years, the Ford Foundation stands out as the central force in creating the knowledge base that made this book possible. In 1974, the foundation initiated the National Supported Work Demonstration, which set a standard for future evaluations. In 1982, it provided the grant that led to the Demonstration of State Work/Welfare Initiatives, and did so under a unique challenge grant structure that reflected both an extraordinary vote of confidence in MDRC and the participating states and the willingness to take a risk for the sake of an unusual opportunity to learn. At the foundation, Susan Berresford has been the consistent voice making this work possible, and Prudence Brown and Gordon Berlin (then at the Ford Foundation) provided intellectual guidance and the flexibility and vision vital to the successful implementation of a complex, multi-year effort. The Ford Foundation's Project on Social Welfare and the American Future and its Urban Poverty Program also provided the resources that allowed us to transform our manuscript from its initial version into this book.

A major share of gratitude is also owed to many people at HHS. In late 1989, HHS awarded MDRC an eight-year contract to evaluate the Job Opportunities and Basic Skills Training (JOBS) Program, the welfare-to-work program that is at the core of the 1988 legislation. This book had its origin as a report written in 1990 under this contract. (The Introduction provides a detailed picture of this relationship as well as the rationale for the book's coverage and an overview of its contents.) In preparing this volume, we benefited directly from the review and assistance of people at HHS and also from the ongoing exchange that has shaped the agenda for the JOBS evaluation and thus the context for this book. Within the Office of the Assistant Secretary for Planning and Evaluation (ASPE), Canta Pian and Julie Strawn provided valued support, and they and their colleagues Michael Fishman, William Prosser, and Steven Sandell provided helpful comments on an earlier draft. In the Family Support Administration (FSA) – now the Administration for Children and Families – we particularly benefited from the counsel and critiques of several drafts by Howard Rolston, who over the past 10 years has been an insightful and valued reviewer of MDRC's work. The authors also gratefully acknowledge the assistance of the following other staff at FSA: Gary Ashcraft, Paul Bordes, Elizabeth Barnes, Nancye Campbell, Alan Yaffe, Penny Pendell, and Leonard Rubin.

Enduring thanks are due for the criticism, wisdom, and insights shared over the years by members of MDRC's Board of Directors and in particular its special Advisory Committee to the Demonstration of State Work/Welfare Initiatives. Chaired by Robert Solow, the committee included as its members Henry Aaron, Gary Burtless, David Ellwood, Frank Levy, Richard Nathan, Robert Reischauer, and Harold Richman.

Collectively and individually, the members of this committee inspired and shaped MDRC's work and the analysis that informs this book. Richard Nathan, Chairman of MDRC's Board and a member of this committee, stands out for the special contribution he made to the launching of the Demonstration of State Work/Welfare Initiatives and to MDRC's direction and evolution during these years. The volume also reflects the input of several people whose close reading of the manuscript proved highly useful: Gary Burtless, Mark Greenberg, Robert Greenstein, Lawrence Mead, and Kathryn Porter.

In preparing a volume that summarizes the completed and in-progress work of so many authors and organizations, we relied on the assistance of a number of colleagues. Stephen Bell at Abt Associates deserves special mention for his unstinting cooperation in discussing Abt's studies and reviewing the manuscript. George Falco of the New York State Department of Social Services, Demetra Nightingale of the Urban Institute, and Denise Polit of Humanalysis contributed much time and many suggestions. John Burghardt and Stuart Kerachsky of Mathematica Policy Research also provided assistance. Kathleen Nazar of the Pennsylvania Department of Public Welfare, Chris Hamilton of Abt Associates, Ellen Seusy of the Ohio Department of Human Services, and many others helped obtain documents.

Judith Greissman edited the book, always improving on our work. We also thank Suzanne Wagner for her care in editing the tables. Production of the text and tables of the many drafts owes much to the skills of Patt Pontevolpe, Stephanie Cowell, and Claudette Edwards. We are indebted to Rowe & Ballantine for the final design.

Finally, we thank the Russell Sage Foundation – and specifically Eric Wanner, the foundation's President, and Lisa Nachtigall, its Director of Publications – for its support and efforts as the book's publisher.

Judith M. Gueron
Edward Pauly

Abbreviations

ADC	Aid to Dependent Children
AFDC	Aid to Families with Dependent Children
AFDC-UP	Aid to Families with Dependent Children-Unemployed Parent
CEOSC	Comprehensive Employment Opportunity Support Centers (New York State)
CET	Center for Employment Training
CETA	Comprehensive Employment and Training Act (1973)
CWEP	Community Work Experience Program
DSS	Department of Social Services
ECCO	Expanded Child Care Options Demonstration (New Jersey)
EITC	Earned Income Tax Credit
EOPP	Employment Opportunity Pilot Project
EPP	Employment Preparation Program (San Diego and other sites in California)
ESL	English as a Second Language
ESP	Employment Services Program (Virginia)
ET	Employment and Training Choices Program (Massachusetts)
EWEP	Experimental Work Experience Program (San Diego)
FIP	Family Independence Program (Washington State)
FSA	Family Support Act of 1988
FY	Fiscal Year
GAIN	Greater Avenues for Independence Program (California)
GED	General Educational Development Certificate
HHS	U.S. Department of Health and Human Services
JOBS	Job Opportunities and Basic Skills Training Program
JTPA	Job Training Partnership Act (1982)
LEAP	Learning, Earning, and Parenting Program (Ohio)
MDRC	Manpower Demonstration Research Corporation
MFSP	Minority Female Single Parent Demonstration
MIS	Management Information System
NAEP	National Assessment of Educational Progress
OBRA	Omnibus Budget Reconciliation Act of 1981
OJT	On-the-Job Training
PSWP	Pennsylvania Saturation Work Program
REACH	Realizing Economic Achievement Program (New Jersey)
SES	Socioeconomic Status
SIME/DIME	Seattle-Denver Income Maintenance Experiment
SWIM	Saturation Work Initiative Model (San Diego)
WIN	Work Incentive Program
WRP	Work Registration Program (Pennsylvania)

From Welfare
to Work

Introduction

In 1988, Congress passed welfare reform legislation – the Family Support Act (FSA) – that affirmed an evolving vision of the responsibilities of parents and government for the well-being of poor adults and their dependent children. The new law left intact the basic entitlement nature of the Aid to Families with Dependent Children (AFDC) program, the nation's major federally funded cash welfare program, and even expanded it by requiring states to extend coverage to certain two-parent families. But in addition it sought to shift the balance between permanent income maintenance and temporary support toward the latter. Thus, the anchoring principle of FSA is that parents – both fathers and mothers – should be the primary supporters of their children and that, for many people, public assistance should be coupled with encouragement, supports, and requirements to aid them in moving from welfare to self-support. While placing a responsibility on welfare recipients to take jobs and participate in employment services, it places a responsibility on government to provide the incentives and services to help welfare recipients find employment. For noncustodial parents (usually fathers), this is reflected in a renewed emphasis on child support collection. For custodial parents (usually mothers), this means new opportunities for publicly supported child care, education, training, and employment services, coupled with new obligations to take a job or cooperate with the program.

The centerpiece of FSA is the Job Opportunities and Basic Skills Training (JOBS) Program, the vehicle for increasing poor families' self-sufficiency. JOBS provides new federal matching funds for state welfare-to-work initiatives but does not specify their design. Instead, it identifies a set of targeting and participation goals and a choice of service methods for achieving them and leaves it up to the states to transform these into a concrete program. JOBS' complex performance requirements offer states incentives and opportunities. At the same time, states face unfolding choices arising from the requirement that JOBS be implemented by October 1990 and the pressure to meet increasing performance goals through 1995.

Because JOBS, while building on earlier policies, represents an important new initiative, the legislation calls for an evaluation to determine the effectiveness of different approaches to assisting welfare recipients. The U.S. Department of Health and Human Services (HHS) contracted with the Manpower Demonstration Research Corporation (MDRC) to conduct a major, eight-year evaluation of the JOBS program. In considering its options for conducting this evaluation, HHS recognized the importance of the context in which JOBS would be implemented. First, while the extensive recent research on JOBS' predecessors – the Work Incentive (WIN) and WIN Demonstration programs – provides an important base of knowledge, federal and state policymakers face great uncertainty about the likely payoff of different JOBS implementation strategies. Second, over the next five years, the JOBS program will be evolving and is likely to vary substantially across the country, as states phase out WIN and design new programs to reflect available resources and perceived needs. Some state JOBS programs are in early stages of development, while others are relatively mature because they essentially expand and continue pre-JOBS program activities. In this environment, guidance on improving and shaping programs will be timely and useful. Third, to get the maximum potential knowledge from the JOBS evaluation, it should be designed and conducted not in isolation but within the framework of the numerous complementary studies.

As a result, HHS has requested that the JOBS evaluation be designed to build and expand upon two important bodies of knowledge: the recently completed large-scale studies of related programs operated during the 1980s, and the federal, state, and foundation-funded studies now under way that will be providing information during the period of the JOBS evaluation. It was hoped that with such a strategy the resources for the JOBS evaluation could be targeted to add new information to a growing knowledge base about the effectiveness of government employment and training services and mandates.

To meet this goal, MDRC was asked to produce a synthesis of what has been learned from past research on similar programs, what is likely to be learned from studies already funded, and what important gaps in knowledge will probably remain. This fit well with the charge contained in a joint grant MDRC had received from the Ford Foundation's Urban Poverty Program and its Project on Social Welfare and the American Future: to prepare a volume summarizing the lessons from selected welfare-to-work studies, including those conducted under MDRC's

Demonstration of State Work/Welfare Initiatives, a multi-state project funded through a challenge grant from the Foundation. With support from these two sources, at MDRC Judith Gueron (President) and Edward Pauly (Senior Research Associate) took on the task of writing this book, which also reflects the input and work of many of their colleagues. In preparing the volume, the authors sought to identify the primary research questions that should form the basis for the JOBS evaluation. But there was a broader goal as well: to inform administrators, policymakers, and the concerned public of what past studies suggest is and is not known about the trade-offs involved in the critical JOBS design choices. Decisions on JOBS are being made and will be rethought over the coming years, and the considerable research record can provide important guidance.

This synthesis covers a specific domain of programs and services and addresses a particular group of questions. It summarizes what is known and will be learned from completed and current studies about the impact and cost-effectiveness of welfare-to-work programs and the different approaches used in these programs, in varied local contexts and for important groups of AFDC recipients. It reflects the existing state of knowledge about different program components (job search, work experience, training, and education), administrative strategies (case management, monitoring, and sanctioning), and support services (child care). It covers both what the authors call broad-coverage (mostly mandatory) programs and selective-voluntary (mostly smaller-scale, more expensive) programs. It discusses program effectiveness for different groups in the AFDC caseload, particularly long-term and potential long-term recipients and other AFDC subgroups given prominence in the JOBS legislation. The synthesis focuses on program impacts, rather than operational feasibility or program implementation, although this further body of findings (including information on participation rates) is summarized briefly when it is directly relevant to the literature on impacts.

In conducting this review, the authors placed primary emphasis on studies that used an experimental design. In these studies, people in the research sample are assigned to an experimental group (targeted for the welfare-to-work program) or a control group (not eligible for services provided through the program but eligible for all other employment and training services in the community, as well as for basic welfare benefits). Crucially, assignment is by a random process, resulting in the creation of directly comparable research groups. The employment and welfare experiences of the two groups are then followed over time; the performance of the control group serves as a benchmark against which to compare the performance of the experimental group. These designs are generally considered to be more reliable than available alternatives,[1] and FSA specifies their use in the JOBS evaluation.[2]

Thus, this review draws primarily on the growing number of studies that use this type of design. Also included is information from selected other evaluations. Because there are previous research reviews that cover earlier non-experimental studies,[3] this discussion emphasizes relatively recent ones that evaluated treatments comparable to those in the experimental studies and that are directly relevant to the JOBS program.

The synthesis focuses on two distinct types of impact and cost-effectiveness questions. The first is whether welfare-to-work programs and particular services are effective. This is a *net impact* question and is the usual bottom line of an evaluation. The second is whether certain welfare-to-work services (or different ways of organizing such services) are *more* effective than others. This is a *differential impact* question and has rarely been addressed with the same rigor in prior evaluations because it requires a random assignment design that is more complex and demanding to implement.

Because this book examines a large number of studies in considerable detail, many readers will find it useful to begin with an overview of the book's main findings. Therefore, Chapter 1 sets forth the central conclusions and policy implications from the completed welfare-to-work studies of the 1980s. Later chapters present the analysis on which these conclusions are based and the lessons of the research. Chapter 2 briefly reviews the evolution of state welfare-to-work programs and the distinctive features of the JOBS legislation. It then provides a framework for both the JOBS evaluation and this volume by identifying the dimensions of a welfare-to-work program and the local context that can affect program impacts. It concludes with the discussion of some of the issues

---

[1] For example, two recent panels established to examine the record of alternative approaches – i.e., non-experimental designs – used in numerous evaluations of employment and training programs funded under the Comprehensive Employment and Training Act (CETA) highlighted the problematic results of those studies and urged greater use of classical, random assignment field experiments. See Betsey, Hollister, and Papageorgiou, 1985; Job Training Longitudinal Survey Research Advisory Panel, 1985.

[2] Family Support Act of 1988, Title II, Sec. 203.

[3] See, e.g., Goodwin, 1977; Gordon, 1978; Gueron and Nathan, 1985; Malone, 1986.

that arise in estimating program impacts and making comparisons across evaluations. Chapter 3 describes the data base for this synthesis, identifying the nature and status of the range of available studies. Chapters 4 and 5 contain the core of the analysis: They outline the findings (and the forthcoming studies) on each of the key welfare-to-work program dimensions and impacts, overall and for relevant subgroups. These chapters contain the lessons of research for JOBS policymakers. Based on this summary, Chapter 6 identifies major gaps in knowledge that constitute the challenge for future research in this area.

By summarizing what is known about the effectiveness of welfare-to-work programs, this book focuses on one major element of all recent proposals to redesign welfare with the goal of encouraging self-support and reducing long-term welfare receipt: requiring people on welfare to participate in employment-directed services. Programs and proposals have varied in their emphasis on carrots or sticks, but the basic vision of recent reforms is to change AFDC from a means-tested entitlement (where benefits depend only on income and assets) toward a reciprocal obligation. This would require welfare recipients to seek employment or participate in some form of employment-directed service, or risk losing some or all welfare benefits; at the same time, government agencies would be responsible for providing welfare-to-work services designed to help people get jobs.

While this new vision of a social contract has been a central element of reform proposals since the late 1960s, the recent proposals also reflect another concern: Even if they meet their goals, welfare-to-work programs may simply move families on welfare into the ranks of the working poor, rather than getting them out of poverty. This has raised the issue of the value of complementary policies specifically designed to reduce poverty by providing alternative sources of income that increase the returns from part- and full-time, low-wage work. Examples of suggested reforms designed to "make work pay" include: strengthening the child support collection system (a key element in FSA); having the federal government guarantee child support payments if fathers do not pay (the Child Support Assurance concept); instituting a children's allowance or a refundable tax credit for families with children; further increasing the Earned Income Tax Credit (EITC), which was raised substantially in the Omnibus Budget Reconciliation Act of 1990; expanding health insurance and child care subsidies to the working poor; increasing the minimum wage; and providing guaranteed jobs for welfare recipients who cannot find unsubsidized work (usually proposed in conjunction with a limit on the length of time people can receive welfare).[4]

This book assesses what past studies suggest about the potential and limits of programs such as JOBS that seek to restructure AFDC to move people from welfare to work. While the broader context of the problems of the working poor is not specifically addressed, it remains a critical backdrop to understanding the challenges that have faced administrators implementing welfare employment programs. Viewed this way, the other reforms mentioned above represent important complements that may increase the effectiveness of JOBS programs by strengthening the payoff of work.

---

[4]See, e.g., the proposals in Garfinkel and McLanahan, 1986; Ellwood, 1988; Ford Foundation, 1989.

Chapter 1

The Findings in Brief

Across the nation, states are implementing the many provisions of the Family Support Act. As they make the funding and design choices that will determine the size and shape of the JOBS program, policymakers can benefit from studies of earlier programs, for there is an extensive and reliable record of the accomplishments of pre-JOBS efforts to move welfare recipients into employment. The public can also join in debates on JOBS, aided by information from the record of completed welfare-to-work studies. However, translating this evidence into decisions about how JOBS programs should be structured, and what should be expected of them, is difficult. The abundance of findings, the lack of evidence regarding some new JOBS features, and the urgency of the policy task are apparent. Nevertheless, the pre-JOBS record points to three key lessons: (1) Different services and program models have different payoffs for particular groups within the welfare population, so targeting to get resources where they are likely to count most is central to JOBS planning. (2) There may be trade-offs in meeting program goals – notably, in both reducing welfare expenditures and maximizing the earnings of the people served in welfare-to-work programs. (3) Understanding the magnitude of possible effects of JOBS, and how such effects are achieved, is essential to resource allocation decisions. To provide the details of these themes and assist JOBS policymakers, this volume summarizes the lessons from some of the major recent studies, pointing out what is and is not known about critical JOBS choices. This chapter presents an overview of the book's main conclusions.

For the past 25 years, AFDC has been criticized for failing to sufficiently reduce poverty among children and for discouraging poor parents from leaving welfare for work. With the creation of the WIN program in 1967, Congress directed the states to reorient welfare toward work. But WIN, the vehicle for imposing requirements and mustering employment-directed services, was judged inadequate for not delivering on the promise of change.

During the 1980s, several factors increased confidence in the potential of welfare-to-work programs and helped shape the JOBS legislation.

First, in response to new flexibility in federal rules, and despite shrinking federal funding, states demonstrated that they could design and implement programs that reflected their priorities and resources. Second, studies of a number of these state programs gave convincing evidence that a variety of approaches in a range of conditions could both benefit welfare recipients and produce budget savings that exceeded the initial investment. But these studies also suggested that the low-cost programs predominant during this period had modest effects and did not usually increase the employment of the most disadvantaged. In addition, JOBS reflected the research on welfare dynamics which showed that, while the majority of people used public assistance for only short-term support, a substantial minority remained poor and on welfare for long periods.

The evidence of strong programs and positive results prompted Congress to establish the JOBS program, which makes available increased funding to the states; to expand the population that could be required to participate in JOBS programs (to include women with preschool children); and to continue to encourage state diversity. The evidence of limited impacts and concentrated dependency also influenced the legislation. It prompted provisions in JOBS that set priorities and incentives intended to boost overall program impacts and lead to greater success with long-term welfare recipients. These included: an emphasis on education and other intensive employment-directed services following an initial assessment; a focus on long-term recipients and those with high probability of remaining on welfare (such as young adults without high school diplomas and young custodial parents); and (through other titles of FSA) in-program and transitional support services. In response to criticisms of WIN, Congress also linked enriched JOBS funding for states to their meeting program performance standards.

As a result, JOBS simultaneously pushes states in two directions. On the one hand, it emphasizes human capital development and investing to increase the employability of long-term recipients. This suggests more expensive services. On the other hand, it establishes the concept of monthly participation standards and extends a participation mandate to a much-enlarged share of the AFDC caseload. This suggests serving more people.

The early JOBS experience indicates that states are responding to the legislation's incentives by replacing the relatively simple programs of the 1980s (typically a fixed sequence of activities beginning with mandatory job search) with more complex initiatives. These programs place greater emphasis on assessing service needs, offering choices, using counseling and case management, focusing on those who volunteer for services, reaching long-term recipients, and providing education and training (usually through coordination with the education and Job Training Partnership Act [JTPA] systems). However, this early experience also shows that many states, facing serious budget problems and competing pressures to fund other FSA provisions, are not putting up the funds required to draw down their entire federal matching allotment or to build JOBS programs of a scale to meet the full ambition of the legislation. Thus, budget constraints (even when mitigated through effective linkages with the education and training systems) suggest that, while the states face a requirement, in principle, to serve all adult recipients with children 3 years of age or older (the new "non-exempt" caseload), no state will have the resources to provide comprehensive services to everyone in this group; for most, it is even doubtful that resources will enable them to provide low-cost services for the full non-exempt JOBS caseload. State administrators will have to choose how to allocate their resources. Regardless of the size of their budgets, they will have three potential responses:

- **Option 1:** Operating a program that emphasizes low-cost services (primarily job search assistance) for a large portion of the caseload.

- **Option 2:** Targeting more intensive, higher-cost components and case management on a smaller, more narrowly defined group and leaving the rest unserved.

- **Option 3:** Designing a mixed strategy, with low-cost services for certain groups and higher-cost services for others, and reaching a share of the caseload in between those reached by the other two options.

The JOBS legislation leads states toward Option 3 – the mixed strategy – and focuses state administrators' choices on *how* to target and structure more intensive, higher-cost services as well as the role of lower-cost components in a varied program. Making these choices requires critical decisions about the basic goals of the JOBS program in each state, including the relative emphasis on investing to improve job skills versus maximizing immediate job entries, and on raising earnings versus reducing welfare costs. Even after their initial JOBS program designs are in place, states will have to revisit these trade-offs several times as the phased-in provisions of the legislation take effect, resources change, and implementation lessons accumulate.

An Overview of the Findings from Pre-JOBS Programs

In an effort to inform federal and state policy decisions about JOBS and to clarify the agenda for further evaluation, this volume synthesizes completed and in-progress studies that examine total welfare-to-work programs or components of them. In presenting the results, it makes a critical distinction between clear findings that a program was or was not effective and uncertainty owing to the lack of a reliable study to determine its effectiveness. It also points out the ways in which JOBS may differ from the earlier approaches, qualifying the application of their results. Throughout, the emphasis is on programs serving single (generally female) parents, who head more than 90 percent of all AFDC families.

The main findings from studies of pre-JOBS programs are:

- A range of welfare-to-work programs – those that emphasize immediate job placement as well as those that provide some more intensive services – can produce sustained increases in employment and earnings for single parents on welfare and a clear payoff on the public's investment.

- Analysis of the response of subgroups of the AFDC population to programs that provided primarily low-cost services showed that the most job-ready have not been helped; earnings gains have been concentrated on a middle group; and most of the welfare savings (and smaller and less consistent earnings gains) have come from a more disadvantaged group. The lessons for program targeting thus depend on whether the objective is increasing earnings or producing welfare savings.

- Programs that have produced increases in earnings have not always succeeded in reducing welfare expenditures, while those that have achieved welfare savings have not always produced net income gains for those whose welfare receipt was reduced. Thus, different program goals will affect how states use the available evidence to structure their program models.

- While substantial evidence shows that moving women from welfare to work is feasible, it also suggests that expectations should be modest. Caseload reductions have not been dramatic and increases in people's standard of living have been limited. This suggests (1) that it is important to learn in future studies whether programs that focus on increasing welfare recipients' human capital – such as their educational and occupational skills levels – can produce better results, particularly for potential long-term recipients, and (2) that policies directed at providing income to the working poor are likely to play an important role if the goal is not only to decrease welfare receipt but also to make a meaningful reduction in child and family poverty.

- The knowledge base is limited for comparing programs that offer more intensive versus less intensive services. This is because there are no completed studies of large-scale programs emphasizing education or skills training. However, findings from a Baltimore demonstration and from San Diego's Saturation Work Initiative Model (SWIM) – both of which combined job search and work experience with some education and training – augmented by results from small-scale tests of voluntary on-the-job training and subsidized employment point to the potential of mixed-strategy JOBS programs. There are indications that such programs can produce larger impacts on earnings and get some people into higher-paying jobs. The results also suggest that programs that begin with job search (either as the only service or followed by other activities as part of a mixed strategy) produce greater welfare savings per dollar spent on the program.

- Among large-scale programs directed at a cross section of the eligible welfare caseload, San Diego SWIM was unusual in providing education and training following job search and work experience and in its strong enforcement of a participation requirement. It showed the potential of welfare-to-work programs to make a more substantial difference than had previously been demonstrated, including for the first time increasing the earnings of men in two-parent cases. Results were particularly impressive for single parents already on welfare (a more disadvantaged group than the people who came on the rolls during the study period); their average earnings increased by $889 a year (or 50 percent) and average welfare payments decreased by $608 (or 13 percent). Since these averages include everyone who was required to be in the program – many of whom did not participate, receive any services, or obtain a job – the actual earnings gains of those who worked were much higher.

Together, these results suggest that, within a given budget, JOBS administrators may face a trade-off in meeting different potential program objectives: getting people into better-paying jobs, maximizing welfare savings, and increasing the self-sufficiency of potential long-term recipients.

- Providing mandatory job search to large numbers of people may maximize welfare savings and job-holding, but by itself usually will not get people better-paying jobs or benefit the more disadvantaged. Providing mainly higher-cost, more intensive services to a selected population can get people jobs with somewhat greater earnings, but will produce lower welfare savings per dollar invested. (It is not clear whether the more intensive services will be effective for very disadvantaged people because few programs of this type have been tested and only one has focused on this group.) Strategies that mix higher-cost and lower-cost services may offer an opportunity to partially meet all of these objectives.

In addition to producing these findings, the studies of past welfare-to-work programs point to several areas where recurring uncertainties suggest caution for JOBS planners. There is very limited evidence on the effectiveness of key JOBS innovations: the expanded investments in education and skills training or the focus on teen mothers and other potential long-term recipients. (It is possible, for example, that these programmatic and targeting changes could avoid the potential trade-off suggested by earlier findings.) There is also little knowledge about the relative impacts of voluntary versus mandatory programs, in part because the operational differences between voluntary and mandatory approaches are often cloudy, rather than representing a clear dichotomy. The effects of different methods of managing program caseloads and determining which people should receive which services – potentially important to JOBS' effectiveness – are also not clear. Further, welfare-to-work programs serving adults in two-parent AFDC families (usually the fathers) do not have a record of success comparable to those for single mothers: Only a few studies included such families, and the results were mixed. Finally, there is also uncertainty on whether JOBS can elicit the gubernatorial and state ownership, commitment, and funding that may have been critical elements in the success of the earlier WIN Demonstration programs, which were explicitly state initiatives.

Studies conducted in the 1980s have provided a strong basis for action by resolving a major issue: whether welfare-to-work programs can produce positive results. The answer is clearly yes, and Congress acted on that answer by creating JOBS. But the question of whether JOBS will go beyond past successes sets a compelling agenda for research in the 1990s. To address this, future studies should seek to determine: Will welfare-to-work programs that incorporate JOBS' new goals and services produce greater impacts, particularly for subgroups of the welfare population that were not usually helped by prior efforts? What are the most effective ways to design and target welfare-to-work programs? Can the budget savings achieved in some of the programs of the 1980s be maintained while more money is spent in JOBS for certain subgroups? Or, if JOBS results in lower returns to the taxpayer in welfare savings, will these be balanced by greater gains in employment and earnings for the welfare recipients who are targeted for larger investments? After describing the studies and their results, this chapter concludes with a discussion of the major open questions facing policymakers and researchers as they confront the choices that JOBS poses.

The Studies of Welfare-to-Work Programs

A substantial number of studies examine the effectiveness of welfare-to-work programs. A good starting point for interpreting them is the extensive research on welfare dynamics, which shows that many people leave welfare – sometimes because of employment, more often because of marriage and other reasons – with no special program assistance. This underlying caseload turnover, which varies with local labor market conditions, AFDC grant levels, caseload characteristics, and the extent of existing community services, makes it very difficult to determine whether a new welfare-to-work program is making a difference. Uncertainty about how much caseload turnover is normal and how much is attributable to the welfare-to-work program – combined with consistent evidence that funding is inadequate to serve all eligible people – has prompted policymakers increasingly to demand program evaluations that are based on random assignment field experiments in which, using a process similar to a lottery, potential program participants are placed in the program or in a control group. (Control group members are not eligible for special program services, but they are eligible for all other employment and training services in the community, as well as for all basic welfare benefits.) The activity of the control group shows the employment and welfare behavior of people in the absence of the program; the program (or experimental) group shows the behavior with it; and the difference reliably isolates the effect or impact of the welfare-to-work program itself.

A growing number of evaluations have used this approach, and the authors of this synthesis focused on them in summarizing what is known about program effectiveness. This volume reviews 45 completed and in-progress studies that directly inform JOBS implementation. This chapter, however, centers on 13 completed studies of programs operated primarily during the 1980s because they illustrate most clearly the choices that JOBS decisionmakers face.

Table 1.1 presents the characteristics, costs, and impacts of those 13 programs as studied (but omitting the AFDC two-parent component present in several of them). The studies are ranked by average net cost (i.e., in most cases, the operating agency's average cost per enrolled experimental minus any costs it incurred for controls) and are further grouped into two basic categories that are fundamental to interpreting their findings: those examining broad-coverage programs that encompassed entire service delivery systems and those focused on selective-voluntary programs, each of which was the equivalent of a program component within a broader system.

- **Studies of service delivery systems**. One group of program evaluations included not only particular service components or providers but also administrative activities (such as intake, orientation, assessment and referral, case management, monitoring, and deregistration from WIN) that affected the coverage and allocation of services throughout the WIN or WIN Demonstration program. Together these services and administrative activities made up a service delivery system. Because the systems studied were intended to reach a wide range of AFDC eligibles, without selection or screening, they are referred to here as **broad-coverage programs**. Almost all of the completed studies in this category were of mandatory programs that, to varying degrees, required people to participate in order to receive their full welfare grants.

- **Studies of program components**. Another group of program evaluations did not encompass full systems but, in most cases, looked at small-scale demonstrations of a component (or potential component) of a much larger, broad-coverage program. All

TABLE 1.1 AFDC WELFARE-TO-WORK PROGRAMS: CHARACTERISTICS, COSTS, AND IMPACTS

Program (Ordered by Increasing Net Cost)	Program Activities and Study Characteristics	Coverage/ Mandatoriness	Net Cost Per Experimental	Annual Impacts for All Years of Follow-Up		
				Outcome	Experimental-Control Difference	Percent Change Over Control Group Level
Broad-Coverage Programs						

Arkansas WORK Program	Sequence of group job search and (for a few) unpaid work experience; low-grant state; highly disadvantaged population; evaluation began in 1983	Mandatory; targeted AFDC applicants and recipients with children 3 or older; few sanctions; 38% ever participated in job search or work experience during 9-month follow-up	$118	Earnings
				  Year 1
				  Year 2
				  Year 3
				
				AFDC payments
				  Year 1
				  Year 2
				  Year 3
					$167**
					223
					337**
					
					-$145***
					-190***
					-168***
						33%
						23
						31
						
						-13%
						-19
						-18

Louisville WIN Laboratory Experiment-Individual Job Search	Individual job search; low-grant state; evaluation began in 1978	Mandatory and voluntary; targeted AFDC applicants and recipients with children of any age; 55% ever participated in individual job search during 8-month follow-up	$136[a]	Earnings
				  Year 1
				  Year 2
				  Year 3
				
				AFDC payments
				  Year 1
				  Year 2
				  Year 3
					$289**[b]
					456**[b]
					435**[b]
					
					-$75*[b]
					-164**[b]
					-184**[b]
						18%
						20
						18
						
						-3%
						-8
						-10

Cook County WIN Demonstration	Sequence of individual job search and unpaid work experience; program provided little direct assistance, mainly monitored and sanctioned those who did not participate; medium-grant state; highly disadvantaged population; evaluation began in 1985	Mandatory; targeted AFDC applicants and recipients with children 6 or older; many sanctions; 39% ever participated in any activity during 9-month follow-up	$157	Earnings
				  Year 1
				
				AFDC payments
				  Year 1
					$10
					
					-$40
						1%
						
						-1%

(continued)

15

TABLE 1.1 (*continued*)

Program (Ordered by Increasing Net Cost)	Program Activities and Study Characteristics	Coverage/ Mandatoriness	Net Cost Per Experimental	Outcome	Annual Impacts for All Years of Follow-Up	
					Experimental-Control Difference	Percent Change Over Control Group Level
Louisville WIN Laboratory Experiment-Group Job Search	Group job search; low-grant state; evaluation began in 1980	Mandatory and voluntary; targeted AFDC applicants and recipients with children of any age; 65% ever participated in group job search during 6-month follow-up	$230[a]	Earnings Year 1	$464**[c]	43%
				AFDC payments Year 1	–$40[c]	–2%
West Virginia Community Work Experience Program (CWEP)	Open-ended unpaid work experience; rural labor market with very high unemployment; low-grant state; highly disadvantaged population; evaluation began in 1983	Mandatory; targeted AFDC applicants and recipients with children 6 or older; few sanctions; 24% ever participated in work experience during 9-month follow-up	$260	Earnings Year 1	$16	4%
				AFDC payments Year 1	$0	0%
Virginia Employment Services Program (ESP)	Sequence of individual or group job search, unpaid work experience, and some education or job skills training (but only slightly more than controls received on their own); medium-grant state; disadvantaged population; evaluation began in 1983	Mandatory; targeted AFDC applicants and recipients with children 6 or older; few sanctions; 58% ever participated in any activity during 9-month follow-up	$430	Earnings Year 1 Year 2 Year 3	$69 280** 268*	5% 14 11
				AFDC payments Year 1 Year 2 Year 3	–$69 –36 –111**	–3% –2 –9

Program	Description				
San Diego I (Employment Preparation Program/ Experimental Work Experience Program [EPP/EWEP])	Sequence of group job search and unpaid work experience; substantial program assistance provided; high-grant state; less disadvantaged population; evaluation began in 1982	$636	Earnings 　Year 1 AFDC payments 　Year 1	$443*** -$226***	23% -8%
San Diego Saturation Work Initiative Model (SWIM)	Sequence of group job search, unpaid work experience, and education and job skills training; high participation and ongoing participation requirement; high-grant state; less disadvantaged population; evaluation began in 1985	$919	Earnings 　Year 1 　Year 2 AFDC payments 　Year 1 　Year 2	$352*** 658*** -$407*** -553***	21% 29 -8% -14
Baltimore Options Program	Choice of services, including individual or group job search, education, job skills training, unpaid work experience, and on-the-job training; program constrained to serve 1,000 enrollees per year; medium-grant state; less dis-advantaged population; eval-uation began in 1982	$953	Earnings 　Year 1 　Year 2 　Year 3 AFDC payments 　Year 1 　Year 2 　Year 3	$140 401*** 511*** $2 -34 -31	10% 17 17 0% -2 -2

(continued)

TABLE 1.1 (continued)

Program (Ordered by Increasing Net Cost)	Program Activities and Study Characteristics	Coverage/ Mandatoriness	Net Cost Per Experimental	Annual Impacts for All Years of Follow-Up		
				Outcome	Experimental-Control Difference	Percent Change Over Control Group Level
Selective-Voluntary Programs						

New Jersey On-the-Job Training (OJT) Program	Subsidized on-the-job training; enrollees quite disadvantaged in terms of prior welfare receipt and recent work histories, but had relatively high levels of GED attainment; medium-grant state; evaluation began in 1984	Voluntary; targeted selected AFDC recipients over 18 with children of any age; 40% participated in employment with OJT (84% ever participated in any WIN or JTPA activity) during 12-month follow-up	$787 [$439][d]	Earnings
				  Year 1
				  Year 2
				
				AFDC payments
				  Year 1
				  Year 2
					N/A[e]
					$591*[e]
					
					-$190**[e]
					-238*
						N/A
						14%
						
						-6%
						-11

Maine On-the-Job Training (OJT) Program	Sequence of employability training, unpaid work experience, and subsidized on-the-job training; enrollees quite disadvantaged in terms of prior welfare receipt and recent work histories, but had relatively high levels of GED attainment; medium-grant state; evaluation began in 1983	Voluntary; targeted selected unemployed AFDC recipients on rolls for at least prior 6 months, with children of any age; 90% ever participated in any activity during 12-month follow-up	$2,019 [$1,635][d]	Earnings
				  Year 1
				  Year 2
				  Year 3
				
				AFDC payments
				  Year 1
				  Year 2
				  Year 3
					$104
					871**
					941*[f]
					
					$64
					29[f]
					80[f]
						8%
						38
						34
						
						2%
						1
						4

AFDC Homemaker-Home Health Aide Demonstrations	Job skills training and subsidized employment program; varied population; low-, medium-, and high-grant states; evaluation began in 1983	Voluntary; targeted selected AFDC recipients on rolls for at least 90 days who were not employed as home health aides during that time; 84% participated (i.e., entered training)	$9,505 ($5,957-$12,457 across states) [$5,684][d]	Earnings		
				Year 1	$2,026[g]	N/A
				Year 2	1,347[g]	N/A
				Year 3	1,121[g]	N/A
				AFDC and Food Stamp benefits		
				Year 1	-$696[g]	N/A
				Year 2	-855[g]	N/A
				Year 3	-343[g]	N/A
National Supported Work Demonstration	Structured, paid work experience; targeted extremely disadvantaged AFDC recipients; low-, medium-, and high-grant states; evaluation began in 1976	Voluntary; targeted selected AFDC recipients on rolls for 30 of prior 36 months, with children 6 or older; 97% participated (i.e., showed up for their program jobs)	$17,981[a] [$9,447][d,h]	Earnings		
				Year 1	$6,402***[i]	327%
				Year 2	1,368***[i]	36
				Year 3	1,076***[i]	23
				AFDC payments		
				Year 1	-$2,200**[i]	-39%
				Year 2	-1,165***[i]	-26
				Year 3	-401**[i]	-10

SOURCES: Data from the reports listed at the end of this chapter and additional MDRC estimates.

NOTES: The cost estimates reported in this table are the net costs of these programs. These include all expenditures incurred specifically for the programs under study by the operating agency, plus any expenditures by other organizations for services that were an essential part of the program treatment, minus costs to the operating agency or other organizations of serving members of the control groups. See Appendix A for further discussion.

Net costs and annual impacts are in nominal dollars except where noted.

[a]The net cost is adjusted to 1985 dollars.

[b]The impact is adjusted to 1985 dollars. Year 1 begins with the quarter of random assignment. The annual earnings impact for year 3 is based on one quarter of follow-up. The annual AFDC payments impact for year 3 is based on three quarters of follow-up. Statistical significance was not calculated for year 3. However, since the quarterly impacts are statistically significant, the annual impacts are assumed also to be significant.

(continued)

TABLE 1.1 (continued)

[c] The impact is adjusted to 1985 dollars. The annual earnings impact is based on two quarters of follow-up. Statistical significance was not calculated. However, since the quarterly impacts are statistically significant, the annual impact is assumed also to be significant. The annual AFDC payments impact is based on four quarters of follow-up.

[d] The bracketed figure excludes wage subsidy payments for participants, whereas the other figure includes them.

[e] A year 1 earnings impact is not available in New Jersey for the same sample as the year 2 impact and is therefore not shown. The annual earnings impact for year 2 is based on three quarters of follow-up. Statistical significance was not calculated for year 2. However, since the earnings impact for quarters 5-7 is statistically significant, the annual impact is assumed also to be significant. Similarly, the quarterly AFDC payments impacts for quarters 2, 3, and 4 of year 1 are statistically significant, so the annual impact is assumed also to be significant.

[f] Annual earnings and AFDC payments impacts for year 3 are based on three quarters of follow-up. Statistical significance was not calculated for year 3. However, since the quarterly earnings impacts are statistically significant, the annual earnings impact is assumed also to be significant.

[g] Cross-state annual impacts are estimated from state-specific impacts presented in Table 5.2, so statistical significance and experimental and control group means are not available. Year 1 is defined by the original researchers as the number of months from random assignment until the typical experimental left subsidized employment. Year 2 is defined as the 12-month period following the time when the typical experimental left subsidized employment. Year 3 is based on all months in the follow-up period after year 2. Average annual impacts for each year were calculated by multiplying the average monthly impacts for that period by 12. Total earnings of the experimental group include both demonstration and non-demonstration earnings. Since the Homemaker-Home Health Aide Demonstrations offered up to a year of subsidized paid employment, earnings and consequently reduced AFDC and Food Stamp benefits during the first two years partly reflect wages earned in the program, and not post-program impacts. In year 2, there were statistically significant gains in monthly earnings in all seven states and welfare savings in six. In year 3, there were significant gains in monthly earnings in five of the seven states and welfare savings in four.

[h] Supported Work projects generated revenues of $4,352 per experimental (in 1985 dollars), which offset part of the cost reported here.

[i] The impact is adjusted to 1985 dollars. Since Supported Work offered up to 18 months of subsidized paid employment, earnings and consequently reduced AFDC payments during the first two years partly reflect wages earned in the program, and not post-program impacts. The annual earnings and AFDC payments impacts for year 3 are based on quarter 9, the last quarter for which there are common follow-up data for all recipients who responded to the final survey. AFDC payments impacts include impacts on General Assistance, Supplemental Security Income, and other unspecified cash welfare.

*Denotes statistical significance at the 10 percent level; ** at the 5 percent level; and *** at the 1 percent level.

of the completed studies are of programs that encouraged but did not require participation by a subset of the AFDC population and that could be "selective" in one or two ways: Eligible people could select whether or not to enroll, and program operators could select among eligible applicants. Because of these recruitment practices, in this document these are called **selective-voluntary programs or demonstrations**.

While it is too early to tell the extent to which state JOBS programs will correspond to these categories (or to a third that combines features of both), the two types of studies already provide lessons applicable to JOBS. Nine recent evaluations of broad-coverage, mandatory programs are of the greatest relevance. They assessed total WIN or WIN Demonstration systems (either at full or smaller scale) and supply information on impacts for a cross section of the then-mandatory (under WIN) caseload. The programs reflected the range of budget constraints likely to face states implementing JOBS. The average gross costs of operating these programs ranged from $162 to $1,545 per targeted eligible person, among the five broad-coverage programs for which data were collected on the costs borne by outside agencies as well as by the welfare agency itself. (The former include, for example, Job Training Partnership Act agencies, which provided some employment and training services to people referred by the welfare programs.) The net costs, shown in Table 1.1, were lower, because they did not include two items: the costs to the administering agency of processing and serving members of the control group and any outside agencies' costs for provision of services that were not an integral part of the program model.

With the variations noted in Table 1.1, seven of the nine broad-coverage programs represented an Option 1 budget allocation – i.e., low-cost services for a large portion of the targeted eligible caseload. Typically in these programs, participation was more or less required of all eligible AFDC applicants and recipients with school-age children. The services generally consisted of relatively low-cost group or individual job search, sometimes followed, for those who did not find a job, by assignment to three months of unpaid work experience ("workfare"). Two of the broad-coverage programs reflect an Option 3 allocation – a mixed strategy combining low-cost services for most of the eligible individuals and higher-cost services for some – and thus came closer to meeting the vision expressed in the JOBS legislation. These two multi-component programs also reflected the main JOBS alternatives for deciding how to allocate and target intensive services. In Baltimore, a process of assessment, which incorporated case manager and recipient preferences, determined how people were assigned to a variety of employment-directed services (including job search, work experience, education, or training). In San Diego's Saturation Work Initiative Model (SWIM), services were provided in a fixed sequence, with education and training required and reserved for those who did not find employment as a result of job search and, following that, work experience.

The four studies of selective-voluntary demonstrations described in Table 1.1 provide information relevant to JOBS' new emphases on targeting and intensive services. They included several more intensive on-the-job training and subsidized employment approaches that could be part of an Option 2 or 3 allocation strategy. The demonstrations were targeted to particular groups of AFDC recipients, who were motivated to seek out services and (usually) were screened on specific eligibility criteria. Two of these – the subsidized on-the-job training (OJT) program in New Jersey and the sequence of services (including OJT) in Maine – while relatively small, operated at a scale that was consistent with traditional WIN programs, given their selection and screening practices. The simpler New Jersey model is most relevant to future programs because it tested a straightforward OJT component, which is a JOBS option and can feasibly be afforded. The others – the Supported Work and Homemaker-Home Health Aide demonstrations – were multi-site demonstrations of activities that are less likely to be affordable and prevalent in JOBS programs. The former provided structured, paid work experience; the latter, training and subsidized employment. None of the four studies examined the effectiveness of education or classroom training in the forms encouraged by JOBS.

These 13 studies constitute a major body of knowledge on the effectiveness of employment programs for welfare recipients. But, for several reasons, it is difficult to use them to reach firm conclusions about the relative impact and cost-effectiveness of various broad-coverage and selective-voluntary approaches in order to design successful JOBS programs. In particular, this volume argues for caution in comparing results from these two categories of studies because of fundamental differences in the program and evaluation designs. Broad-coverage, mandatory programs are intended to spend resources and have impacts on participants through (1) their receipt of education and employment services, job placement, and other direct services, and (2) monitoring, counseling, and the threat or reality of monetary sanctions. However, broad-coverage programs also monitor, counsel, and sanction (or threaten to sanction) nonparticipants, whose behavior the program is thereby expected to affect as well. In contrast, selective-voluntary programs are intended only to affect people who actually participate in program services. (Throughout this volume, the words "participant" and "participation" refer to persons who actually attended the program's employment, education, or training activities. This is distinct from other members of the experimental group who took no part in the program whatsoever or who attended only WIN registration, program orientation, assessment, or counseling, but did not actually spend time in a program component.)

This distinction is mirrored in the way the two types of programs are typically assessed. Evaluations of broad-coverage programs study people who are actually subject to the program's mandate, even if they do not participate in employment-directed services; evaluations of selective-voluntary programs focus on participants. Thus, the measured impacts of broad-coverage programs provide information on the effect of a system (not just its employment-directed services) on the diverse people subject to its requirements, only some of whom participate. In contrast, estimates of the impacts of selective-voluntary programs reflect how a particular component of the system (i.e., a service or set of services) affects the subset of the caseload who volunteer, most of whom participate.

This evaluation design difference is important to JOBS decisionmakers who are trying to use research results to guide program design choices. The studies generally show larger average impacts for selective-voluntary than for broad-coverage programs, but that does not necessarily mean that the former's employment-directed services were more effective. Instead, the impact differences may reflect other factors, e.g., higher participation rates or targeting a subgroup that was more likely to benefit from services. Such factors are often overlooked in summaries of the lessons from the studies discussed in this volume.

An additional caution to JOBS decisionmakers concerns comparisons across sites: The group of 13 programs operated under widely varying conditions – different labor market and AFDC caseload characteristics, as well as AFDC grant levels and alternative community services. Further, there are particular problems in contrasting the costs of programs in the two categories of studies, since the higher costs for the four selective-voluntary programs reflected, in part, the inclusion of subsidized wages that may have led directly to offsetting AFDC savings. The costs of Supported Work are particularly difficult to compare to those of the other programs. Inflating the mid-1970s estimates may have produced some distortion. In addition, Supported Work not only spent the most on participants' wages but also incurred substantial expenses that were subsequently offset by revenues received from the sale of program services, reducing the net budget cost below that shown in Table 1.1.

Finally, none of the 13 programs specifically tested key JOBS and FSA innovations, such as the emphasis on education or the provision of continued support services (child care and Medicaid) to welfare recipients who go to work and leave welfare. These issues point to the need for additional studies, including those specifically designed to facilitate direct comparisons of different welfare-to-work program approaches.

The Results of Key Studies

Findings on Participation

The broad-coverage programs provide benchmarks for participation rates in JOBS. But there are two major caveats: None of the programs operated under JOBS' monthly participation standards, and none of the evaluations measured participation according to JOBS' criteria.

- **Welfare-to-work programs proved capable of serving a substantial share of the caseload in broad-coverage programs, some of which were large-scale.**

In the nine broad-coverage programs, between 38 and 65 percent of all targeted people took part in a specific employment-directed activity (excluding orientation, assessment, or counseling) within six to twelve months after applying for welfare or registering with the program. To achieve these rates, staff had to work with a much larger share of the caseload, many of whom did not participate in employment services because they subsequently left welfare, were no longer eligible, or were deferred from participating.

In programs that provided a fixed sequence of services, participation was two to three times higher in the first than in subsequent components, as a result of normal welfare caseload dynamics and job placements from the initial activity. The two more intensive broad-coverage programs – Baltimore and San Diego SWIM – involved roughly a fifth of eligibles in education or training. The mandatory program with the highest monthly participation and the greatest proportion of those who ever participated in an activity – San Diego's SWIM program – was also the one with the most consistent and, generally, the highest impacts.

The studies also showed that a surprisingly large number of people in both the experimental and control groups participated in education and training services on their own, so that the net increase in those services (and the net cost shown in Table 1.1) was often substantially below the total service level (and the gross program cost).

- **None of the broad-coverage programs would have met the participation standards that have been established by the JOBS legislation and regulations.**

To obtain full federal matching funds under JOBS, states must have an increasing share – reaching 20 percent in fiscal year 1995 – of JOBS eligibles participating in certain allowable activities during each month. SWIM provides the most relevant data on the likelihood of programs meeting the JOBS participation standards. There are several reasons for this. First, among the mandatory, broad-coverage programs studied, SWIM had the highest *longitudinal* participation rate – 64 percent of eligible individuals participated within 12 months of registering for the program. Second, SWIM required a cross section of the AFDC caseload to participate in various program components on a *continuing* basis. Third, the study was explicitly designed and funded to help establish expectations about maximum feasible *monthly* participation rates. The SWIM study found that monthly participation rates averaged 22 percent if only program-arranged activities were counted, 33 percent when self-initiated education and training were added, and 52 percent if part-time work was also included. The evaluation concluded that these rates were close to the maximum possible for the SWIM approach. While these monthly rates appear very high, the numerous differences be-tween what is included in the numerator and denominator of the SWIM participation rate and the standard established for JOBS make it hard to predict what the rates would have been had the JOBS rules been applied during the SWIM demonstration. Moreover, it is impossible to judge how San Diego program administrators would have changed the SWIM model and daily program operations had they been striving to meet the JOBS participation standards. It is very likely, however, that SWIM as it operated in the pre-JOBS era would not have met the JOBS standard, principally because most SWIM activities did not offer services for at least 20 hours per week, which is a major determinant of who qualifies as a "countable" JOBS participant.

Impacts on Employment and Earnings

- **Almost all of the welfare-to-work programs studied led to earnings gains. This was true for both low- and higher-cost programs and services, and for broad-coverage and selective-voluntary programs.**

The studies of AFDC welfare-to-work programs provide a remarkably consistent record. Seven of the nine broad-coverage programs led to increases in average annual earnings, ranging from $268 to $658 in the last year of follow-up. Depending on the program, this was 11 to 43 percent above the annual earnings of people in the control group. The smaller-scale, selective-voluntary programs increased average annual earnings by $591 to $1,121 – 14 to 34 percent above the control group's earnings. (See Table 1.1.) These earnings gains take on greater significance because they are averages for all people eligible for or enrolled in the program, including those who did not work and did not actually receive any services. While the studies did not look behind the averages to determine the distribution of earnings gains, the findings suggest that gains were much more substantial for some people and minimal for others.

- **Earnings impacts for both low-cost job search and higher-cost programs were sustained for at least three years after program enrollment.**

Job search programs are designed to have an immediate impact on employment; in contrast, education and training programs make an up-front investment in anticipation of larger future returns. Surprisingly, these studies show that short-term impacts from lower-cost programs were sustained over at least three years. This is also the case for the broad-coverage programs that included some higher-cost components, and for the selective-voluntary programs. The Baltimore program, one of the few to include education and training services, suggests that these may have a different time path of impacts, with low initial gains increasing markedly during the second and third years after enrollment. (See Table 1.1.) Completed studies do not address the five- or ten-year results of these approaches, findings that will be important in judging their ability to meet JOBS' goal of reducing long-term dependency.

- Broad-coverage programs that began with mandatory job
  search increased both employment rates and average earnings, but usually did not get people higher-paying jobs. There
  is limited and inconsistent information on the effect of unpaid work experience. Selective-voluntary programs that
  provided higher-cost or more intensive services appeared to
  get people into jobs with somewhat higher earnings, but did
  not make a consistent difference in the proportion of people
  employed. Broad-coverage programs that included some
  higher-cost services had greater average earnings impacts
  than those that did not.

Earnings impacts result if programs cause a change in the number of
people working, the number of hours people work, or their hourly
wages. Completed studies suggest that different program approaches
act differently on these three earnings components. Studies of broad-
coverage programs provide compelling evidence that job search alone
and the job search/work experience sequence produce modest, but
nonetheless relatively long-lasting, impacts on employment rates and
earnings. These services almost always led to more people working, but
they did not seem to increase the amount people earned while employed.
Because job search was the first and most used component in the studies
of a job search/work experience sequence, it probably produced most of
the programs' impacts. (Several of the studies examined whether unpaid work experience had an independent effect. One, in West Virginia,
found that it did not, and another, in San Diego, showed positive but
not robust results.)

In contrast, findings on the four selective-voluntary programs point
to the potential of more intensive approaches for getting people into jobs
with somewhat higher wages or hours. In fact, they had most of their
effect through augmenting the earnings of those who would have
become employed without the program, and relatively little through
increasing employment rates. Taken together, these studies also suggest
a relationship between program cost and average earnings gains, with
higher impacts for the Supported Work and Homemaker-Home Health
Aide demonstrations than for the two lower-cost programs that
emphasized on-the-job training. Importantly, Supported Work also
showed that carefully structured, subsidized employment could produce
sustained and relatively large impacts for very disadvantaged, long-term
recipients.

There is very limited information on the relative effectiveness of welfare-to-work systems that did and did not contain some higher-cost components. None of the programs focused specifically on education, a key JOBS activity. However, the research suggests that including higher-cost, more intensive components (usually education and skills training) in broad-coverage programs that provided mainly job search and work experience led to larger absolute earnings gains per person in the study. As Table 1.1 shows, average annual earnings impacts in San Diego SWIM and Baltimore were somewhat higher than those in the lower-cost broad-coverage programs.

The contrasting patterns of impacts described above are echoed in these two mixed-strategy, broad-coverage programs, one of which was more mandatory and began with up-front job search (SWIM) and the other of which was more voluntary and referred some people to education and training as a first activity (Baltimore). The SWIM program produced relatively large increases in earnings, most of which were a result of an increase in the number of people working. Baltimore had a smaller effect on long-term employment rates, but did improve the earnings of those working. The difference was reflected in the two programs' impacts on the earnings distribution of people who got jobs: SWIM increased the number of people with relatively low as well as relatively higher earnings and did not change the overall earnings distribution, whereas the employment increase in Baltimore was concentrated in the higher earnings category. In these two different ways, and possibly because they provided some added education and training, both programs increased the percent of people earning more substantial amounts. In Baltimore, there was a 3.8 percentage point increase (compared to the control group) in the share of people earning more than $6,000 a year; in San Diego SWIM, there was a 4.6 percentage point gain in the proportion of all program eligibles who earned $5,000 a year or more and a 3.2 percentage point increase in the share of AFDC recipients (a more disadvantaged group than AFDC applicants) who earned $10,000 or more a year. However, these are only two studies, and the results may have been due to other elements: for example, SWIM's strict enforcement of an ongoing participation requirement and its relatively high sanctioning rate, Baltimore's implementation at a relatively small scale, or the extensive experience and capacity of the administering agencies in both places.

- **Employment and earnings impacts did not occur when resources per eligible individual were too low to provide employ-**

ment-directed assistance or when programs were operated in a rural, very weak labor market.

For states assessing whether to spread resources thin to increase program coverage or to concentrate them to increase service intensity, the studies provide a mixed message. Some very low-cost approaches (Arkansas and the two Louisville programs) did have positive employment impacts. However, the lack of success from the Cook County (Chicago) program may suggest that there is a threshold in this trade-off. When resources are so limited that staff can only process and sanction cases and provide virtually no direct assistance, even in the job search component, a program may have no effect on earnings. (While these four programs had similar costs, Cook County probably had the fewest real resources and used them more for monitoring and processing people than for providing direct services.)

The other program without employment and earnings impacts was implemented in West Virginia, a rural state with extremely high unemployment. This pure work experience program achieved its planners' goal of providing useful public services and work in exchange for welfare, but it did not lead to an increase in unsubsidized employment.

Impacts on AFDC Payments and Receipt

- **Average welfare savings were smaller than earnings gains. The inclusion of more intensive, higher-cost services did not assure welfare impacts.**

Earnings gains were not always accompanied by welfare savings, and there was no consistent relationship between the size of the earnings and welfare impacts. Three very different programs and conditions produced moderate reductions in the share of people receiving welfare at the end of follow-up: a decrease of 7 percentage points compared to controls in low-grant Arkansas, high-grant California (San Diego SWIM), and the multi-site Supported Work Demonstration. The other programs had a smaller or no effect on this measure (not shown in Table 1.1; see Chapters 4 and 5). In these same three programs, welfare payments declined by an average of $168 or 18 percent, $553 or 14 percent, and $401 or 10 percent, respectively, in the last year of evaluation follow-up. Some of the other programs also produced welfare savings. (See Table 1.1.)

Broad-coverage programs emphasizing relatively low-cost, up-front job search led to fairly consistent welfare savings, but the savings were often small because not all of the jobs moved people off welfare. The two broad-coverage programs that also included some higher-cost components had the largest earnings impacts, but they produced very different welfare results: San Diego SWIM had the largest savings and Baltimore had none. The Maine study also did not translate relatively large earnings impacts into any significant welfare savings. The researchers did not pin down the reason for the lack of welfare impacts in Baltimore and Maine, but they concluded that the programs may have led to higher-paying jobs for people who (as shown by the control group) would have obtained work and moved off welfare anyway or they may have increased the time on welfare for people involved in lengthy education or training activities (offsetting savings for others who were assisted in finding employment).

Impacts on Different Groups Within the Caseload

- The impacts of broad-coverage programs were not equal across all groups in the caseload. The most consistent and largest earnings gains were made by the moderately disadvantaged. The largest welfare savings were achieved for the more disadvantaged. There were usually no impacts – on earnings or welfare receipt – for the most job-ready. The lesson for targeting services to different groups within the welfare population thus depends on the relative importance placed on increasing earnings or reducing welfare costs.

Studies of broad-coverage programs are of unique value for determining programs' effectiveness for subgroups of AFDC recipients because all members of a subgroup – and all targeted subgroups – are required to participate and are therefore present in the research sample. In contrast, subgroup estimates from selective or voluntary programs do not apply to the many subgroup members who were not selected or did not volunteer and are therefore not included in the research sample. A study of five such programs (excluding San Diego SWIM but including Baltimore) showed that the most employable people (e.g., women who were first-time welfare applicants and had recent work experience) had little or no gain over the benchmark established by similar people in the control groups. Even without special assistance, many of these women stayed on welfare for relatively brief periods. In contrast, a middle group (e.g., people who had received AFDC before and were reapplying, sometimes following their employment in a job with some limited earnings) had the most consistent earnings impacts from these programs, with gains averaging between $450 and $850 a year after the first nine months of follow-up, compared to similar people in the control group. The more disadvantaged – those already on welfare, including longer-term recipients with no recent employment – did not show consistent or large earnings gains, but they produced a major share of the welfare savings. Even modest reductions in the number of longer-term recipients can produce substantial welfare savings because their relatively lengthy periods of welfare receipt account for the bulk of AFDC expenditures. This phenomenon is apparent during the three-year follow-up period for the evaluations.

- **San Diego SWIM produced earnings and welfare impacts for AFDC recipients – who are more disadvantaged than individuals applying for AFDC – that exceeded those of other broad-coverage studies and equaled the levels achieved in much smaller, selective-voluntary programs.**

The SWIM program's success with AFDC *recipients* is particularly impressive. Overall, this group is more disadvantaged than AFDC *applicants*, and recipients did not benefit consistently from the other broad-coverage programs. During the second year of follow-up, the average AFDC recipient targeted by SWIM was earning $889 (or 50 percent) more than the average for the control group and had $608 (or 13 percent) less in welfare benefits. These earnings gains compared favorably with the average impacts of the smaller, selective-voluntary programs, even though SWIM's impacts were averaged across the full spectrum of mandatory recipients – nonparticipants as well as participants, and the most disadvantaged as well as the more job-ready. The welfare savings were the highest found in a broad-coverage welfare-to-work program and exceeded those found in the selective-voluntary programs.

It is unclear which features of SWIM accounted for its greater success with recipients than the programs that provided primarily job search and Baltimore's mixed strategy. Possible explanations include: the service sequence (up-front job search and work experience, followed by education and training), the strong enforcement of a continuous participation requirement, the extensive experience of SWIM program managers, or other characteristics of the San Diego environment and caseload. Moreover, since impact findings for subgroups of recipients

are not yet available, it is not clear whether these positive results extended to the most disadvantaged recipients. However, the magnitude of the
impacts suggests that they are unlikely to have been limited to the more
employable recipients.

- **JOBS encourages states to serve people who are likely to
  become long-term welfare recipients. The research record is
  not strong as to whether intensive services can be more successful with this group than lower-cost services, particularly
  in producing earnings gains.**

In contrast to the strong evidence that low-cost services can produce
consistent impacts for a moderately disadvantaged group, only one study confirms that welfare-to-work programs can succeed with the least
job-ready: very long-term welfare recipients with little or no prior
employment. Supported Work specially targeted this group and served
women who averaged 8.6 years on welfare. This program demonstrated
that 12 or 18 months of paid, carefully structured work experience could
produce sustained effects on earnings and welfare receipt for this group.
But Supported Work was among the highest-cost programs studied.
(See Table 1.1.) In light of Supported Work's large investment, it is particularly important to determine whether SWIM did indeed benefit long-
term welfare recipients (this study is under way). The other selective-voluntary programs had positive impacts on selected AFDC recipients, but it
is not clear whether they reached particularly hard-to-employ populations.

Other Impact and Cost-Effectiveness Findings

The cost-effectiveness results show a complex picture for different
welfare-to-work approaches. Typically, in a benefit-cost analysis, key
questions include: Who benefits – program participants and/or the public at large? By how much? At what cost? Together, answers to these questions provide information on the level of public investment associated
with varying returns to different beneficiaries. Because the programs of
the 1980s sometimes produced gains in earnings without associated
welfare savings, and because of the variation in the magnitude of program results and resources, when impacts and costs are compared, the
net benefits can point in different directions. This volume also presents
other measures of cost-effectiveness that go beyond these more familiar
indicators. For example, policymakers might consider the return provided
to welfare recipients or the public per dollar invested in a welfare-to-work

program. These different perspectives on the 13 broad-coverage and selective-voluntary programs underlie the cost-effectiveness results presented here.

- **Welfare-to-work programs usually benefited AFDC eligibles, but generally led to only modest increases in their measured income.**

Table 1.1 indicates that, for both broad-coverage and selective-voluntary programs, although the extra earnings from increases in work effort were often substantially offset by reductions in AFDC payments, there were modest increases in average combined income from the two sources. When estimated reductions in other transfer payments – e.g., Medicaid and Food Stamps – and increases in taxes were also considered, benefits to welfare recipients usually continued to outweigh losses, although the net benefits were small. Only the Supported Work study measured the program's impact on the proportion of participating families living below the poverty level, and found no statistically significant long-term change, despite the relatively large earnings gains.

As a result, the findings indicate that, while this range of welfare-to-work programs modestly improved people's income, they proved unlikely to move many people out of poverty. This suggests the limited potential of these programs to help most welfare recipients obtain jobs with substantially higher wages, at least within the three years of follow-up, and points to the importance of determining whether programs that make a more conscious investment in increasing human capital can do better. It also suggests that, if reducing poverty is the goal, other types of policies directed at providing more income to the working poor will be important complements.

- **Welfare-to-work programs usually had a positive impact on government budgets. Public investments in a range of programs were more than returned in increased taxes and reductions in transfer payments.**

Extensive benefit-cost analyses show that, while welfare-to-work programs require an initial investment, this is usually offset by subsequent savings in transfer payments and increased taxes. For seven of the nine broad-coverage programs, the payback period was rapid: two to five years. In some cases, budget savings were substantial: e.g., every dollar spent on San Diego SWIM saved the government $3.

Taxpayers benefited less consistently from the higher-cost, selective-voluntary programs. Two of these – the Maine and Homemaker-Home Health Aide demonstrations – incurred net costs. The New Jersey and Supported Work programs produced net savings for the government, the former within three years and the latter over a substantially longer period.

- **Measured in terms of impact per dollar invested, low-cost job search/work experience programs produced larger earnings gains and, to some extent, welfare savings than programs that emphasized higher-cost components, suggesting the existence of diminishing returns.**

In addition to the traditional evaluation measures discussed above (average impacts and net benefits), JOBS administrators may be interested in cost-effectiveness as measured by a program's impact per dollar invested. A comparison of the average cost and final-year impact findings in Table 1.1 shows that, as long as service levels exceed the threshold level suggested by the Cook County program, earnings gains and, somewhat less consistently, welfare savings per dollar outlay tend to decrease as program costs increase. For example, the annual earnings impact per dollar invested was $2 or more in the last year of follow-up in the low-cost Arkansas and Louisville job search programs; 50 to 75 cents in Virginia, San Diego I, SWIM, Baltimore, and New Jersey; and substantially less in Homemaker-Home Health Aide and Supported Work.

- **Evaluation results on welfare-to-work programs for AFDC-UP eligibles are limited. Available studies show welfare savings but do not always show earnings gains.**

FSA requires all states to implement a public assistance program for two-parent families: the AFDC-UP (Unemployed Parent) program. It also calls on states to involve (with eventual very high participation rates) at least one parent in these families in JOBS activities that emphasize work. (For young parents who have not completed high school or its equivalent, education may be substituted.) In contrast to the strong record from numerous studies of pre-JOBS programs for single parents on AFDC (primarily women), there are few data on programs for fathers, usually the adult involved in AFDC-UP work programs, and none that allow a clear comparison among alternative program approaches.

Only the two San Diego evaluations had sufficiently large samples to measure accurately the impacts of broad-coverage programs targeted at

AFDC-UPs. The study of the San Diego I program for applicants showed no statistically significant employment and earnings impacts. Average welfare savings of $374 were attained in the first year of follow-up. The San Diego SWIM study showed a consistent pattern continuing into the second year of follow-up, when the AFDC-UPs in SWIM were earning $454 (or 12 percent) more than the average for the control group and had $551 (or 12 percent) less in welfare benefits. Both programs produced budget savings, but the men in the SWIM study only broke even, with their earnings gains about matching their losses from AFDC, other transfers, and tax payments. The men in the San Diego I study incurred net losses.

Policy Trade-Offs

- Within a given budget, administrators may face a trade-off in meeting different JOBS objectives – producing more substantial earnings gains for some individuals, maximizing welfare savings, or reducing long-term dependency. Providing mandatory job search to large numbers of people may maximize welfare savings and job-holding, but by itself usually will not get people better-paying jobs or benefit the more disadvantaged. Providing mainly higher-cost, more intensive services to a selected population can get people jobs with somewhat greater earnings, but will produce lower welfare savings per dollar invested. It is not clear whether high-cost programs will be effective for very disadvantaged people because few programs of this type have been tested and only one has focused on this group. Administrators seeking to balance the JOBS objectives may favor a mixed strategy that combines higher-cost and lower-cost services.

The JOBS program has multiple objectives, and administrators will differ in the importance they attach to particular ones. Some will aim to produce earnings gains that are large enough to substantially improve the well-being of families. Others will focus on maximizing overall welfare savings. Still others may emphasize reducing long-term welfare dependency. The three resource allocation strategies identified at the beginning of this chapter represent routes to meeting these varied objectives, in the context of JOBS' participation standards and targeting objectives. Table 1.2 summarizes what past evaluations suggest about the strengths and limitations of the different options.

TABLE 1.2   RESULTS FROM COMPLETED EVALUATIONS
            OF WELFARE-TO-WORK PROGRAMS[a]

**Evidence on Option 1: Results of Low-Cost, Broad-Coverage Programs
(Primarily Mandatory Job Search)**

- Consistent and sustained increases in employment and earnings

- Rapid payoff – relatively large welfare savings per dollar spent

But

- Earnings gains mostly from increases in the number of people working and not from increases in earnings for those employed (i.e., not from improved job quality)

- Modest increases in welfare recipients' total income – many remain in poverty and on welfare

- Not all groups benefited. Little or no impact on the most job-ready; earnings gains concentrated in a middle group; most of the welfare savings concentrated among the more disadvantaged, who showed no consistent earnings gains

**Evidence on Option 2: Results of Higher-Cost, Selective-Voluntary Programs
(Primarily Subsidized Employment)**

- Consistent and sustained increases in employment and earnings

- Some improvement in job quality – earnings gains mostly from increases in hours or wages and less from increases in the number of people working

- Supported Work found to be successful with long-term recipients

But

- Slow payoff – relatively small welfare savings per dollar spent

- Except for Supported Work, little information about success with the most disadvantaged

- Many remain in poverty and on welfare

- No completed studies of programs emphasizing education or skills training

**Evidence on Option 3: Results of Mixed-Strategy Programs
(Combining Higher-Cost and Lower-Cost Services)**

- Can meet diverse objectives: some improvement in job quality, relatively large earnings gains, and, in one of the two programs tested (San Diego SWIM), substantial welfare savings and success with the more disadvantaged

NOTE: [a]In this table, increases, gains, and savings refer to differences between the experimental and control groups in the studies.

Administrators whose main goal is to maximize welfare savings may favor Option 1 (serving a large number of people with low-cost, primarily job search services), which will also enable them to produce some earnings gains. They can find support in the findings of sustained welfare and earnings impacts and cost-effectiveness from the broad-coverage programs of the 1980s. The Option 1 strategy would allow a state to serve large numbers of people and (as long as the program exceeds the service threshold suggested by the Cook County study) to produce the largest welfare savings and earnings gains per dollar invested and thus the highest aggregate impacts. (Aggregate impacts are the sum of impacts for all individuals exposed to the program.) However, evaluations showed that such programs did not usually help the most disadvantaged, and that those people who did become employed did not get higher-paying jobs.

Administrators whose main goal is to get people into higher-paying jobs may consider Option 2 (which would provide mainly intensive services). Those favoring this strategy anticipate that, in contrast to Option 1, their approach may also be effective with more disadvantaged individuals and with those who would remain unemployed and on welfare if offered only job search assistance. Administrators weighing this option could find support for it in results showing that programs providing more costly, intensive services can get people into jobs with somewhat higher earnings (through higher wages, longer hours, or both). Most of the evidence for these findings can be found in the studies of selective-voluntary programs. Option 2, however, also has limitations: There is no experience with such programs operated on the scale required to meet JOBS participation levels. Further, resource constraints virtually assure that only a small percentage of eligibles could be served, and (judging from studies of past programs) welfare savings per dollar outlay may be relatively low.

Those interested in meeting all of these JOBS goals – improving job quality, achieving welfare savings, and reducing long-term dependency – might favor Option 3, the mixed strategy. This strategy – by providing low-cost services (to assure immediate welfare savings) and more expensive, carefully targeted services (to benefit long-term recipients and get people into higher-paying jobs) – could allow states to serve a relatively large share of the welfare population and to target the most disadvantaged, both explicit goals of FSA. Available evidence from the mixed-strategy, broad-coverage SWIM program – and to a lesser extent the Baltimore program – provides support for this approach. Compared to the findings from programs that provided mainly lower-cost services, results from these programs suggest that providing some higher-cost services can lead to greater average earnings impacts per person targeted, and also (especially in Baltimore) get some people jobs with higher earnings. Both programs led to an increase in the percent of people with somewhat higher earnings (those earning more than $6,000 a year). As noted previously, the San Diego SWIM model stands out for the magnitude of its impacts and (in contrast to Baltimore) both its success with welfare recipients (a group that is, on average, more disadvantaged than new applicants) and its relatively large impacts on both earnings and welfare savings. By combining low-cost job search services for the majority of participants with education and training services for some, SWIM produced gains that appear to have been more widely distributed among all categories of people on welfare than the gains of programs following the Option 1 approach. But here, too, there are drawbacks: Obviously, for the same budget, fewer people can be served in a mixed strategy than under the low-cost Option 1 approach (possibly limiting aggregate welfare savings). At the same time, fewer people will receive more enriched services than under the Option 2 model.

Unfortunately, the nature of the trade-off in reaching different policy objectives, and its applicability to current JOBS program models, remains highly uncertain. The completed studies of broad-coverage programs focused on approaches that were often different from those emerging under JOBS. The completed studies of selective-voluntary programs concentrated on intensive work experience and on-the-job training. Importantly, there is very little evidence of the effects of education for welfare recipients, which JOBS stresses. Also, follow-up was limited to at most three years, not an adequate time to determine the long-term effect of more intensive services, or to see whether the impacts of high- or lower-cost services increase or decrease over time. Moreover, there is very limited evidence on program effectiveness for women with young children, and on whether any large-scale component, even higher-cost ones, can succeed with very disadvantaged groups. In addition, there is uncertainty about the point at which any trade-off among program objectives would be affected by program scale; it is possible (although there is no evidence on this) that diminishing returns may set in if particular welfare-to-work services are provided to an expanded share of the caseload. Finally, the relative cost-effectiveness of low- and high-cost services may not be the same under FSA as it was in the pre-JOBS period. One potentially major factor is the introduction of a year of transitional child care and Medicaid for people who leave welfare for a job. This may reduce the total savings that might otherwise have accrued from people taking low-wage jobs.

Critical Unanswered Questions

The knowledge summarized here is the product of rigorous field experiments on pre-JOBS welfare-to-work programs. However, the Family Support Act and its JOBS title confront administrators with new choices and challenges. They are simultaneously urged to build more complex programs, reach a larger share of the caseload, succeed with new and more disadvantaged populations, provide more intensive services (including some that are untested in the welfare-to-work context), and offer expanded in-program and transitional support services. To deliver on JOBS' promise of increased effectiveness, they need new information that will guide them in matching services to people, and in allocating resources between employment-directed activities and case management and oversight.

If mixed-mode program designs will predominate in the welfare-to-work environment of the 1990s, then JOBS administrators will need information to help them determine the optimal mix for their diverse caseloads, labor markets, AFDC benefit levels, and communities, within their particular JOBS resource constraints, and given their individual policy preferences.

Providing this information requires a new generation of studies that build on the existing lessons and refine the answers to a fundamental question: What works best for whom? Under JOBS, both the "what" and the "whom" have changed, with the new emphasis on education and training, for example, and incentives to serve more disadvantaged groups. Indeed, the understanding of what "best" means may well change under JOBS, too; a major impetus for the Family Support Act was the policymakers' hope that the welfare system, with more resources, could do better at moving AFDC recipients into employment and self-sufficiency. Fortunately, more than 20 studies are currently under way that will address some of the open questions highlighted here. (These studies are described in later chapters.) The JOBS evaluation, funded by the U.S. Department of Health and Human Services (HHS), is being structured to answer others. The most critical unanswered questions include:

- **Will greater investments in education and training lead to larger impacts? Will additional gains justify the expanded outlays?**

In deciding how to respond to JOBS' pressure to both reach more people and provide more intensive services, the most critical uncertainties facing administrators are the unknown impacts and cost-effectiveness of providing education and other intensive services for long-term welfare recipients. State JOBS programs are placing larger numbers of welfare recipients in education components, based on a belief that poor reading and computation skills prevent people from getting jobs that pay enough to support a family. The goal is to provide the most disadvantaged welfare recipients with enough education to help them obtain good jobs and move out of poverty. What will be the result of these efforts?

Although there is a great deal of cross-sectional research (mostly on the non-welfare population) showing that those with higher education levels have higher earnings, there is very little evidence on the key cause and effect question – i.e., will the expansion of educational activities for welfare recipients help them leave welfare? Completed studies examine only a relatively narrow range of outcomes and do not even address the question of whether broad-coverage programs that emphasize education are able to improve participants' educational achievement levels. The evaluations of the SWIM and Baltimore programs – which provided substantial amounts of both education and training – offer the most reliable information currently available on the longer-term impact of adding these more intensive services to broad-coverage welfare-to-work systems. While these studies were not designed to provide separate estimates of the effectiveness of the education and training components, their sizable overall earnings impacts, compared to programs that did not offer education and training, provide some basis for encouragement.

Given the remaining uncertainty, results from an ongoing evaluation of California's broad-coverage welfare-to-work program, Greater Avenues for Independence (GAIN), will be highly relevant, since the program places an unusually heavy emphasis on education. The GAIN study will be the first to assess the impact of a broad-coverage program on educational achievement as well as on a wide range of economic and non-economic outcomes. In another study, the selective-voluntary Minority Female Single Parent (MFSP) Demonstration, initial findings from the four service providers were mixed. The providers, which differed substantially in their services and service delivery, offered relatively intensive education and training to low-income minority women. During months 10 through 12 after program enrollment – when some people were still in the program, forgoing work and "investing" in education and training in anticipation of future returns – experimentals' employment and earnings already exceeded those of controls at one site and had caught up with controls at the other three. (It will be important to see whether longer-term follow-up for the full MFSP sample confirms the initial reports on the early program entrants, which suggest that the differing site impacts may persist 30 months after program enrollment.) The MFSP researchers offer a number of possible explanations for the greater early success at one site: job skills training that was integrated with remedial education and open to all (regardless of educational skills), greater operating experience and higher-quality services, stronger links to employers, local labor market conditions, and the availability of high-quality on-site child care. They note that it is impossible to isolate the influence of any one of these factors because of the study design, the limited number of sites, and the short-term nature of the findings.

Given the small number of studies examining large-scale welfare-to-work systems that emphasize education and training for a cross section of welfare recipients determined to need these services, there remains a clear need for further evaluations. These should include studies of programs using various education and training approaches and levels of service intensity to understand the benefits and costs of developing welfare recipients' human capital in this way. Evaluations that directly compare this approach to programs that do not emphasize education and training have not yet been carried out, and are greatly needed. In these studies, long-term follow-up will be important (particularly given the Baltimore finding of increasing impacts over time), since education represents a substantial up-front investment that is unlikely to show a payoff within a short period of time.

- **Can programs for young mothers prevent long-term welfare receipt? Can program impacts for the most disadvantaged welfare recipients be improved, and will services for these**

groups be cost-effective? Will JOBS be successful for mothers with younger children?

A major policy thrust of the Family Support Act is to prevent long-term welfare receipt. This objective is reflected in several key JOBS provisions that specify target groups and establish participation requirements. States are required to meet expenditure goals for service to the most disadvantaged groups; in some cases, the type of service (primarily education) is prescribed.

JOBS' establishment of a school requirement for young custodial parents is an innovation based on as yet untested assumptions. Ongoing studies of Ohio's Learning, Earning, and Parenting (LEAP) program (which requires attendance in school programs leading to a high school diploma or in a General Educational Development [GED] program and provides child care and other support services) and HHS's Teenage Parent Demonstration (which requires participation in education and/ or training, and provides life skills instruction, job search assistance, and support services) test mandatory programs for teen parents that combine services with financial sanctions and, in the case of LEAP, financial incentives in the form of increased monthly assistance payments for regular school attendance. It is not yet clear whether other states' approaches to mandatory education for young people will resemble these programs.

A very different vision of how to prevent long-term welfare receipt among teenage mothers is examined by studies of selective-voluntary programs offering more intensive services. Among these, the New Chance and JOBSTART demonstrations will yield information on dropout recovery programs for young women on welfare. New Chance provides participants with comprehensive education and training, and employability, life management, and parenting instruction (along with child care). JOBSTART offers volunteers a non-residential program loosely modeled on the Job Corps, and including education, training, job placement assistance, and support services. JOBSTART's initial results show large impacts on GED attainment. In addition, the completed study of Project Redirection (which offered services intended to help dropouts and potential dropouts to complete their education, increase their parenting and life management skills, and enhance their employability) showed promising results for young pregnant and parenting teens receiving AFDC, some of whom were still in school when they enrolled in the program. Even more than programs that emphasize education for adults, those for young people will require evaluations that use long-term follow-up to measure the delayed benefits (if they exist) of investing in education to improve employment and earnings and to shorten the length of time public assistance is received.

Regarding long-term welfare recipients, in those welfare-to-work programs of the 1980s that included them, the results were mixed. Supported Work was effective in increasing the employment and earnings of this group, but at a cost probably beyond the resource capacity of most JOBS programs (at least for implementation at any substantial scale). Low-cost programs beginning with job search were sometimes effective in reducing the welfare receipt of the most disadvantaged segment of their caseloads, but not generally at improving their earnings. The pertinent results from the mixed-strategy SWIM program are not available yet. Thus, the unanswered question for JOBS is whether there are service components or programs for long-term recipients that are feasible and affordable at scale, and that can help them achieve both earnings gains and welfare reductions.

Finally, JOBS' extension of a participation requirement to women with younger children is another untested innovation. This population, which spans the full range of employability characteristics from very disadvantaged to job-ready, has been studied almost exclusively in programs for which they volunteer. Early evidence on programs for women with children 3 to 5 years old will come from the evaluations of Florida's Project Independence and the selective-voluntary Minority Female Single Parent Demonstration.

- **What are the effects of different processes for determining who gets which JOBS services and for managing the caseload?**

JOBS puts new emphasis on assessment as a means to match people to services. It also permits states to offer case management services. Past studies provide almost no guidance on the relative effectiveness of different approaches to matching clients to services and managing JOBS caseloads.

Regarding assessment, almost all of the earlier broad-coverage programs used a fixed service sequence that relied on a job search activity to determine which clients were immediately employable and which needed more intensive services. Only the Baltimore program employed an assessment approach and emphasized client choice. While the experience of selective-voluntary programs has the potential for illuminating the process of screening welfare recipients for a particular JOBS component, these programs offer few lessons for a multi-component JOBS program. The "labor market screen" (i.e., up-front job search) approach of the broad-coverage programs has not been directly compared to the "up-front assessment" model, although choosing between these may be a key resource allocation decision for JOBS administrators.

Welfare-to-work programs currently use a wide range of case management approaches. In some localities, tasks associated with assessing, assisting, motivating, monitoring, and brokering services for program participants have been divided between welfare agencies and other service providers and, within these agencies, between case managers and other staff. Alternatively, a single case manager may be responsible for every aspect of participation for those assigned to him or her. Caseload sizes and the emphasis of case management activities – e.g., on counseling versus monitoring and enforcing participation – vary as well, and may affect program impacts.

The studies of California's GAIN, Florida's Project Independence, Massachusetts' ET (Employment and Training) Choices, and New Jersey's Realizing Economic Achievement (REACH) program should provide initial information on the effects of JOBS-relevant program structures and management approaches. The substantial share of JOBS resources that will probably be devoted to these activities and the central role given this function in some state programs highlight the importance of further understanding the cost-effectiveness of different case management strategies.

- **Are mandatory welfare-to-work programs more or less effective than voluntary ones?**

Some people argue that mandatory programs are likely to have larger impacts than voluntary ones, primarily because they reach people who can benefit but would not opt to participate on their own and because they reach more people overall. Deterrence and sanctioning effects can also contribute to mandatory programs' impacts. Others claim that voluntary programs are likely to be more successful because they enroll people who are more predisposed to take advantage of services and who therefore attend activities more regularly, saving the program "compliance costs." Partly for this reason, these people argue, voluntary programs are easier to administer. The JOBS legislation calls for states to give first consideration to volunteers among the program's target groups. But it allows for a participation mandate for the full non-exempt caseload. As was also observed in the 1980s WIN and WIN Demonstration environment, states are implementing programs that run the gamut from all-volunteer programs to mandatory ones that pay a great deal of attention to compliance, with many programs arrayed between these poles.

Unfortunately, past studies do not provide clear guidance on this design choice. The data for the broad-coverage programs in Table 1.1 suggest no evident relationship between either sanctioning or participation rates – both possible proxies for the extent to which a program was mandatory – and program impacts. There have been studies that found positive results for both broad-coverage mandatory and smaller voluntary programs, but there are no rigorous studies that allow a direct comparison of the impact and cost-effectiveness of mandatory and voluntary broad-coverage programs or of programs that are more or less stringent in imposing program requirements. A comparison of the pattern of findings for SWIM (with its distinctive, strictly enforced continuous participation requirement, which began with job search) and Baltimore (with a much less mandatory design, which began with an assessment) may inform the mandatory/voluntary issue as well as the question of how to match people to services. Both programs had relatively large earnings impacts. SWIM had uncommonly large impacts on earnings and welfare payments, primarily driven by an increase in employment rates for the more disadvantaged two-thirds of the caseload. Baltimore, in contrast, was more likely to produce higher earnings (i.e., higher wages or longer hours) for people who would have worked but earned less without the program. Baltimore's earnings impacts increased with time, while the program had little effect on welfare payments and did not generally benefit the more disadvantaged share of the caseload.

If states are unable to meet the participation standards specified for JOBS programs in the law and implementing regulations, the choice of methods for encouraging program participation may rise to the top of the JOBS agenda. The question for administrators might then be: Can programs switch from voluntary to mandatory policies, or vice versa, and still achieve the desired impact results?

- **What works for the (usually male) participants from two-parent welfare families?**

As noted earlier, the JOBS legislation contains special provisions for the small segment of the welfare caseload in the AFDC-UP program, which call for involvement primarily in work programs, with an option of education for young fathers who have not completed high school. They set eventual participation standards that are much higher than those for single parents. The dilemma administrators will face when these standards take effect between 1994 and 1998 is how to design programs that are effective and meet the standards, without targeting a disproportionate share of JOBS resources to AFDC-UP cases. Prior research is scanty and has not found effects for work-only models. However, SWIM's sequence of activities produced both earnings gains and welfare savings for AFDC-UP recipients and the GAIN evaluation will provide evidence on an education-oriented model.

- **What are the nature and duration of JOBS' economic and non-economic impacts on welfare recipients and their children?**

Underlying FSA are critical assumptions about the impact of particular services on AFDC mothers and their children. The emphasis on education and other intensive services comes from a conviction that these are more likely to lead to better jobs, stable employment, and reductions in poverty, and thus to meet JOBS' goal of reducing long-term welfare dependence. The extension of JOBS' participation requirements to mothers of preschool children, FSA's extensive provisions for in-program and transitional child care, and the involvement of mothers in education programs that may improve not only skills but also self-esteem and parenting practices are based on an implicit assumption that a mother's participation in JOBS and subsequent employment can have a positive effect, or at least not a negative effect, on her children.

Testing these assumptions will require that data from future studies go beyond those collected for prior ones. Information on a wider range of outcomes will be essential, including (for AFDC parents) wages and job quality, educational achievement, family income and poverty, family functioning and parenting, and health status, and (for the children of JOBS enrollees) cognitive, social, emotional, and physical development. Knowledge about this wide range of outcomes will sharpen policymakers' understanding of how JOBS programs achieve their effects.

Future studies will also need to follow people for longer periods. The completed studies showed that the impacts of low-cost services start quickly and last for at least the three years measured in some studies, while those of more intensive services start more slowly and last for at least the same period. To quantify the trade-off between different JOBS approaches, follow-up data will be needed that are adequate to determine whether larger investments deliver greater long-term benefits, to measure changes in the impacts of high- and low-cost services over time, and to estimate the effects of JOBS on the average length of stay on welfare and on the rate at which people who leave welfare subsequently return to the rolls.

- **Will JOBS programs be able to achieve the scale needed to meet participation standards and yet maintain the successes demonstrated in smaller or simpler pre-JOBS models? Will the results of JOBS programs depend on the strength of local labor markets?**

There are numerous open feasibility questions for JOBS that also have implications for program impacts. For example, while most of the broad-coverage evaluations examined large-scale programs in real-world conditions, the JOBS legislation – if implemented as envisioned – would increase program scale. It is not clear whether the measured impacts of these earlier programs would be replicated if the approaches studied are expanded and extended to a much greater share of the caseload. Similarly, when JOBS programs utilize components that resemble those tested in selective-voluntary demonstrations, but at a larger scale, it will be important to see whether the same results are achieved, and how these components function within broad-coverage programs. Finally, JOBS programs that involve multiple components, numerous decision points, and coordination among many agencies will face formidable management challenges: They will have to work very hard to route clients to the correct component, and to keep clients from dropping out between components and between agencies. These implementation problems multiply the difficulty of managing the JOBS caseload; they can also lead to delays and reduced participation levels. Few program operators have much experience with these complex management issues; thus, the feasibility of the new programs is yet to be determined.

A related unanswered question is the extent to which the effectiveness of JOBS – particularly when it is operated at large scale – will depend on local and national economic conditions. Positive evaluation results in sites with a range of unemployment levels and other labor market characteristics (but not confronting highly depressed local economies) suggest that these programs can have impacts in relatively strong or weak labor markets and in improving or deteriorating economic contexts. However, the West Virginia study suggested that welfare-to-work initiatives may not succeed in rural areas with very weak labor markets. Extreme cyclical variations in the economy may also affect the size of program impacts or the relative effectiveness of different JOBS approaches in ways that are currently unknown.

The JOBS legislation's call for specific participation levels suggests that these programs will be larger than those in past studies and also raises other issues. The participation targets are elaborated by regulations that focus on the hours of activity by JOBS participants. The legislation also calls for future outcome-based performance standards. While the WIN and Job Training Partnership Act experiences suggest both the power of focusing staff on performance outcomes and the importance of doing it in a way that supports program goals, it is not at all clear how these issues will play out in JOBS. Past research points to some of the challenges in designing JOBS' performance standards, but further study is important for understanding the feasibility and impact of alternative approaches.

- **What are the impact and cost-effectiveness of child care and Medicaid benefits that are provided to welfare recipients who leave the rolls to work? What are the effects of different administrative and funding arrangements for in-program child care?**

The impact of subsidized child care on participation in welfare-to-work services and on subsequent employment have not yet been measured. This is true of both in-program child care and that offered as a transitional, or post-program, service. Expenditures on child care are certain to rise under JOBS; consequently, information on the kinds of child care arrangements and subsidy levels that will contribute to the effectiveness of welfare-to-work programs will be particularly valuable. A few current studies – including an especially relevant one (the Expanded Child Care Options Demonstration) that compares the impacts of three levels of child care funding – will partially address these questions. Other issues regarding the relationship between child care and work for welfare recipients will require a range of research designs.

Regarding the transitional child care and Medicaid provided for in FSA, key questions include: What is the take-up rate for these services? Do they help people enter employment, increase job stability and retention, and reduce the rate at which people return to welfare? Do they boost the impacts of either low-cost "labor market attachment" or higher-cost "human capital investment" program models, or both? Do they change the relative cost-effectiveness of different JOBS approaches, e.g., of programs that tend to place people in lower- or higher-wage jobs? The challenge facing future studies that focus on transitional benefits and child care is to expand the knowledge base in ways that are useful to states seeking to improve the quality and effectiveness of their JOBS programs.

* * * * *

During the past 15 years, state and federal policymakers, foundations, and community-based service providers made a remarkable commitment to learning in a systematic and rigorous way whether different approaches could be effective in increasing the self-sufficiency of single parents on welfare. This produced a substantial body of experience and knowledge on which JOBS is already building.

While JOBS administrators can benefit from the past, their tasks are no less formidable than those faced by people who designed and implemented the initiatives of the last decade. The challenges, however, are different. In the 1980s, the goal was to learn whether investments in welfare-to-work programs had a clear payoff. This threshold question has been answered. The challenge for JOBS – both for those wrestling with the key operational issues and for researchers – is to do better: to improve on the performance of past programs and to advance the state of knowledge.

The JOBS legislation embodies lessons from the past, but it also reflects optimism about untried ways to achieve results that go beyond the accomplishments of the first round of welfare-to-work programs. The research planned for JOBS, and the large number of relevant studies already under way, can inform the choices JOBS administrators will face in the years to come as they apply their experience and program designs to the new vision of welfare reform.

Sources for Table 1.1

AFDC Homemaker-Home Health Aide Demonstrations
Bell, Stephen H.; Enns, John H.; and Orr, Larry L. 1986. "The Effects of Job Training and Employment on the Earnings and Public Benefits of AFDC Recipients: The AFDC Homemaker-Home Health Aide Demonstrations." Draft. Paper presented at the Annual Research Conference of the Association for Public Policy Analysis and Management, Austin, Texas.
Orr, Larry L. 1987. *Evaluation of the AFDC Homemaker-Home Health Aide Demonstrations: Benefits and Costs.* Cambridge, Mass.: Abt Associates Inc.

Arkansas WORK Program
Friedlander, Daniel; and Goldman, Barbara. 1988. *Employment and Welfare Impacts of the Arkansas WORK Program: A Three-Year Follow-Up Study in Two Counties.* New York: MDRC.
Friedlander, Daniel; Hoerz, Gregory; Quint, Janet; and Riccio, James. 1985b. *Arkansas: Final Report on the WORK Program in Two Counties.* New York: MDRC.

Baltimore Options Program
Friedlander, Daniel. 1987. *Maryland: Supplemental Report on the Baltimore Options Program.* New York: MDRC.
Friedlander, Daniel; Hoerz, Gregory; Long, David; and Quint, Janet. 1985a. *Maryland: Final Report on the Employment Initiatives Evaluation.* New York: MDRC.

Cook County WIN Demonstration
Friedlander, Daniel; Freedman, Stephen; Hamilton, Gayle; and Quint, Janet. 1987. *Illinois: Final Report on Job Search and Work Experience in Cook County.* New York: MDRC.

Louisville WIN Laboratory Experiments (Group and Individual Job Search)
Goldman, Barbara. 1981. *Impacts of the Immediate Job Search Assistance Experiment.* New York: MDRC.
Wolfhagen, Carl. 1983. *Job Search Strategies: Lessons from the Louisville WIN Laboratory.* New York: MDRC.

Maine On-the-Job Training (OJT) Program
Auspos, Patricia; Cave, George; and Long, David. 1988. *Maine: Final Report on the Training Opportunities in the Private Sector Program.* New York: MDRC.

National Supported Work Demonstration
Grossman, Jean Baldwin; Maynard, Rebecca; and Roberts, Judith. 1985. *Reanalysis of the Effects of Selected Employment and Training Programs for Welfare Recipients.* Princeton, N.J.: Mathematica Policy Research, Inc.
Hollister, Robinson G., Jr.; Kemper, Peter; and Maynard, Rebecca A., eds. 1984. *The National Supported Work Demonstration.* Madison, Wis.: University of Wisconsin Press.
Kemper, Peter; Long, David A.; and Thornton, Craig. 1981. *The Supported Work Evaluation: Final Benefit-Cost Analysis.* Princeton, N.J.: Mathematica Policy Research, Inc.

New Jersey On-the-Job Training (OJT) Program
Freedman, Stephen; Bryant, Jan; and Cave, George. 1988. *New Jersey: Final Report on the Grant Diversion Project.* New York: MDRC.

San Diego I (Employment Preparation Program/Experimental Work Experience Program [EPP/EWEP])
Goldman, Barbara; Friedlander, Daniel; and Long, David. 1986. *California: Final Report on the San Diego Job Search and Work Experience Demonstration*. New York: MDRC.

San Diego Saturation Work Initiative Model (SWIM)
Hamilton, Gayle; and Friedlander, Daniel. 1989. *Final Report on the Saturation Work Initiative Model in San Diego*. New York: MDRC.

Virginia Employment Services Program (ESP)
Friedlander, Daniel. 1988a. "An Analysis of Extended Follow-Up for the Virginia Employment Services Program." Unpublished internal document. New York: MDRC.
Riccio, James; Cave, George; Freedman, Stephen; and Price, Marilyn. 1986. *Virginia: Final Report on the Employment Services Program*. New York: MDRC.

West Virginia Community Work Experience Program (CWEP)
Friedlander, Daniel; Erickson, Marjorie; Hamilton, Gayle; and Knox, Virginia. 1986. *West Virginia: Final Report on the Community Work Experience Demonstrations*. New York: MDRC.

Chapter 2

The Context for Evaluating
Welfare-to-Work Programs

In analyzing research relevant to JOBS, it is important to identify what is distinctive about the JOBS approach and to understand the factors and program dimensions that potentially can affect program impacts. To address these two issues, the chapter begins with a brief review of the evolution of welfare-to-work programs, the new features contained in the JOBS legislation, and the context of federalism in which JOBS will be implemented. This is followed by the presentation of a framework or conceptual structure for summarizing how different features of JOBS and the local context can influence the behavior of AFDC recipients and affect program impacts. The chapter ends with a discussion of some of the challenges this framework implies for determining the impacts of different welfare-to-work approaches.

The Evolution and Distinctiveness of JOBS

From Welfare to Work

This country's 25-year welfare reform debate reflects widespread dissatisfaction with the design of the nation's public assistance system and its ability to solve fundamental problems of poverty and dependence. Aid to Dependent Children (ADC) – subsequently replaced by Aid to Families with Dependent Children (AFDC) – was enacted as part of the Social Security Act of 1935 to provide for the needs of poor children in single-parent households. The program was expected to be small, and its goal was to provide poor widows with the opportunity to stay at home and care for their children in accordance with prevailing norms for women.

Since the 1930s, however, a number of developments have prompted discontent with the program. First, close to 90 percent of AFDC cases are now headed not by widows but by mothers who are separated or divorced or were never married; welfare for families with absent fathers who are not supporting them has never been popular. Second, enthusiasm for the welfare system has been eroded further by the change in women's work patterns. In recent years, employment rates for all women – including single parents and women with very young children – have increased dramatically. With the majority of mothers working at least part-time and often from economic necessity, it became difficult to defend the equity of supporting a sizable number of poor mothers who are not employed. This is particularly true since research does not show any clear link between a mother's employment status and the well-being of her children.[1] Third, contrary to original expectations, AFDC caseloads and costs grew rapidly in the 1960s and early 1970s.

Finally, although recent research confirms that most people use welfare for only short-term support, it also identifies a substantial minority who remain poor and receive assistance for very long periods and consume a disproportionate share of welfare expenditures (Bane and Ellwood, 1983; Ellwood, 1986). The current debate has focused on these families because of both the high cost of supporting them and the assumed negative effects of long-term welfare receipt on these mothers and their children.

In addressing these concerns, federal reform efforts – culminating in the Family Support Act – have reflected increasing support for a different view of public and individual responsibilities. The key elements are that parents should be the primary supporters of their children and that government should provide incentives and assistance to welfare recipients to find employment. This has meant greater enforcement of child support collections from absent fathers and new obligations on welfare mothers to cooperate with such efforts. It has also meant requiring mothers to take a job or participate in activities designed to enhance their employability, and a renewed emphasis on the government's responsibility to assist them in this process.

---

[1] See Garfinkel and McLanahan, 1986; Wilson and Ellwood, 1989; Brooks-Gunn, 1989. For example, Garfinkel and McLanahan, 1986, report that, while some negative effects on adolescents have been associated with maternal employment, positive effects on younger children have also been found. For the most part, these positive effects disappear when income is taken into account, suggesting that higher income (rather than the mother's working) may be the reason for the beneficial effects. They also point to studies that suggest a possible "modeling effect," i.e., the mother's employment can affect the career aspirations of older daughters. In summarizing their review of research in this area, they conclude: "At present we cannot say with certainty that the mother's working has no negative consequences for children. However, there is good reason to believe that the effects on children of preschool and elementary school age are neutral to positive. The . . . negative effects for high school sophomores and seniors, however, make this less certain for adolescents" (p. 37).

Since 1971, state Work Incentive (WIN) programs have explicitly required adults in single-parent (usually female-headed) AFDC households without preschool-age children or specific problems that keep them at home – and one adult (usually the male) in two-parent AFDC-UP (Unemployed Parent) families – to register and participate in a welfare-to-work program or risk grant reductions or termination. After WIN's initial years, its emphasis shifted to direct job placement.[2] However, because of administrative issues and resource constraints, participation was often limited to registering welfare recipients without actually involving them in program activities. The program lost credibility as it failed to meet its operational objectives and could provide no reliable evidence of cost-effectiveness.

Congressional action in the early 1980s gave states new flexibility in assisting and requiring welfare recipients to work. States could mandate Community Work Experience Programs (CWEP) – where people would work in exchange for their welfare benefits in what are often called "workfare" positions – or expand job search requirements. Under the WIN Demonstration provisions, they could end dual agency oversight and shift full responsibility for administration to the welfare agency. Despite simultaneous sharp funding cutbacks, these changes increased state ownership, prompting a number of states and localities to implement innovative programs and breathing new life into a scaled-down WIN program. During the early and mid-1980s, almost all of the states picked up on at least one of the new provisions, implementing programs that were usually low- or moderate-cost and that imposed short-term job search or workfare requirements on part of the caseload. Usually, this was limited to some or all adults in two-parent households and single parents with school-age children, and to only certain areas of the state. (See U.S. Congressional Budget Office, 1987; U.S. General Accounting Office, 1987b; Nightingale and Burbridge, 1987.)

More recently, a number of states have instituted more far-reaching changes. Some states, such as Massachusetts in its Employment and Training (ET) Choices program and Washington in its Family Independence Program (FIP), have emphasized voluntary participation and offered welfare recipients a choice of services. Others, such as

---

[2]For a summary of the history of the WIN program, its modification by the provisions of the Omnibus Budget Reconciliation Act of 1981, and congressional actions on work requirements in the AFDC program, see Malone, 1986; U.S. Congressional Budget Office, 1987; Mead, 1986; Rein, 1982.

California in its Greater Avenues for Independence (GAIN) program, adopted in 1985, require mandatory up-front education for many. Still others, such as New Jersey in the Realizing Economic Achievement (REACH) program, started in 1987, have required participation based on the results of an assessment and have included mothers with younger children. Thus, flexibility, decentralization, and reduced funding transformed WIN by the late 1980s from the relatively uniform federal program of the 1970s to state initiatives of varied cost, coverage, design, and goals.

Disenchantment with the AFDC program and concern about the high rate of poverty among children, combined with the widely accepted evidence from studies on the cost-effectiveness of state initiatives, built support for expanding welfare-to-work programs. While there appeared to be agreement on the underlying concept of a reciprocal obligation between the AFDC recipient and the state, this masked continued disagreement over the goal, and thus the tools, of reform. Some argued that welfare recipients want to work but lack the education and skills to obtain jobs that assure self-sufficiency and a decent standard of living. They saw reductions in poverty as the primary reform goal and favored programs that serve volunteers first, offer choices, provide education and training, and do not require people to take low-wage jobs. Others argued that jobs were available and believed that welfare recipients were either unwilling to work or too discouraged to try. They saw reducing welfare dependence as the primary objective and favored programs that set clear expectations, require participation for those not already employed, provide low-cost job placement assistance rather than expensive training, and mandate workfare for those who remain on the rolls.

The JOBS Program

JOBS – the centerpiece of FSA – replaces the Title IV-C (WIN) and Title IV-A work programs authorized by the Social Security Act with a newly expanded and consolidated welfare-to-work program. JOBS allows states flexibility in designing future initiatives but establishes mandates and incentives to move state programs in new directions. JOBS goes substantially beyond WIN in its emphasis on education; in extending a participation mandate to women with no children under age 3 (age 1 at state option); in instituting a school requirement for young custodial parents; in setting minimum participation standards; in emphasizing service to potential long-term welfare recipients; and in its funding, under another title of FSA, for child care.[3] JOBS thus seeks to reduce welfare receipt through elements of both views of welfare reform: participation mandates, strengthened work incentives and supports, and investments to improve the capacity of AFDC mothers to obtain jobs and possible self-sufficiency.

The complex funding structure and the many – sometimes contradictory – visions within JOBS mean that future programs are likely to vary substantially across states. States can be expected to choose both different program designs within the framework of JOBS requirements and different levels of investment in JOBS, since the law states that many requirements are to be met "to the extent that resources permit." For AFDC recipients, the key features of JOBS include:

- **Services.** States have flexibility in program design but must provide educational activities (high school education and/or its equivalent, basic and remedial education, and education in English as a second language [ESL]); job-readiness activities (including pre-employment training in job skills); job skills training (training in technical job skills); and job development and job placement. They must also offer at least two of the following: group and individual job search, on-the-job training (OJT), work supplementation (grant-diversion-funded OJT), and community work experience or other work experience. JOBS gives states an option to allow participation in self-initiated education or training at a post-secondary institution or vocational or technical school.

  The JOBS statute emphasizes education by requiring that it be offered to any adult JOBS participant who lacks a high school diploma or does not demonstrate basic literacy, unless the employability plan for the individual identifies a long-term employment goal that does not require a high school diploma (or its equivalent). (To support the education requirement, JOBS provides federal funding for certain educational activities.)

---

[3]Key non-JOBS provisions of FSA strengthen child support enforcement, authorize funding for in-program child care for JOBS participants, require states to provide benefits to unemployed parents, and provide for a year of transitional child care and Medicaid for individuals leaving welfare for employment.

However, the program-design flexibility granted states by the statute suggests that they will differ in their emphasis on different components, including education, and the sequence of activities. JOBS promotes intensive services, particularly because the regulations define program participation based on the number of individuals who, on average, participate in activities scheduled for 20 hours per week. (States may count individuals in programs with more and less than this number of hours to reach the 20-hour average.)

JOBS also introduces a new requirement that, with few exceptions, custodial parents under age 20 who have not completed high school or its equivalent must participate in an educational activity or risk having their welfare benefits reduced (the "learnfare" provision).

- **Targeting.** The JOBS legislation contracts the definition of who is exempt from participation in welfare-to-work activities, thereby extending the coverage of these activities to AFDC applicants and recipients who have children 3 to 5 years of age (1 to 5 years of age at state option) and who are not otherwise exempt. To avoid a reduction in federal matching funds, states must spend at least 55 percent of JOBS funds on families in which the custodial parent is under age 24 and has no high school diploma (or equivalency) or has had little or no work in the last year, the youngest child is within 2 years of ineligibility for AFDC, or the family received AFDC during 36 of the prior 60 months.

- **Management, Monitoring, and Mandatoriness.** JOBS requires that states conduct an initial assessment (the form is not specified, and it may follow a brief job search) and develop an employability plan. It gives them an option to develop a case management system. While JOBS specifies that the welfare agency take overall responsibility for the program, the agency may subcontract for a wide range of activities and is required to coordinate with the Job Training Partnership Act (JTPA) and education systems.

While JOBS requires participation, and sets monthly participation standards, which increase from 7 to 20 percent over time, it calls on states to give first consideration, in determining priority for services, to those people within the JOBS target groups who volunteer to participate.

- **Support Services.** To mandate participation in JOBS, states must provide child care and pay for transportation and other expenses. A separate title of the Family Support Act (Title III) allocates funds for in-program care for participants' children. Child care purchased for JOBS participants must meet applicable standards of state and local law, and states must coordinate JOBS child care with early childhood education programs.

In addition, FSA requires that all states provide cash assistance to AFDC-UP (two-parent) families as of October 1, 1990. While states that had an AFDC-UP program as of September 26, 1988, must continue operating programs that provide benefits for 12 months per year, other states can choose to limit AFDC-UP benefits to as few as 6 months in any 12-month period. Tied to this, JOBS establishes special participation rates for parents in AFDC-UP families, which increase from 40 percent in 1994 to 75 percent by 1998. The state must require at least one parent in the family to participate in one of the following: a work supplementation program, community work experience, on-the-job training, or a state-designed work program approved by the Secretary of Health and Human Services; for parents under age 25 who have not completed high school or its equivalent, the state may require participation in an educational activity directed toward that end. In most cases, the parent(s) must participate for at least 16 hours per week; however, in states that choose to require education for AFDC-UP parents who are under age 25 and lack a high school or equivalent education, individuals will be considered as meeting participation requirements if they make satisfactory educational progress.

The new features of JOBS simultaneously push states in two directions. The emphasis on human capital development, intensive weekly participation, and the importance of investing to increase the employability of long-term recipients suggest more expensive services. The establishment of monthly participation standards and the extension of a participation mandate to a much-enlarged share of the AFDC caseload suggest serving more people. Combined, these encourage states to develop more complex programs than the job search/work experience sequence typical of the early and mid-1980s.

States will be designing JOBS programs in response to the regulations, state and local conditions and resources, and their existing welfare-to-work programs. Because of the highly varied experience of the 1980s, states will be launching JOBS from very different positions: Some have virtually no program in place and very limited likely state (and thus federal) funds; others have already made major investments in JOBS-like programs and are committed to a particular model and service delivery strategy. JOBS is less a single federal "program" than a federal/state partnership. The law establishes a set of incentives (i.e., enhanced federal funding) and requirements that encourage states to move in particular directions, but states will probably respond very differently. It is hard to predict the extent to which JOBS will be broad-coverage and mandatory, reach long-term welfare recipients and young mothers, and in fact change the tone and message of the welfare system. The most likely scenario is great cross-state variation in the cost, quality, and type of services; the extent and nature of coordination across major delivery systems; the form of assessment and case management; the extent to which participation is mandatory or voluntary for different groups in the caseload; the scale of the program; and the reality of educational innovation. The most critical uncertainty is the likely state response to the JOBS funding incentives. FSA establishes the maximum federal matching funds available to states. To draw down these funds, states must commit substantial resources of their own, and at an overall less favorable matching rate than that required under the earlier WIN program. The scale of the JOBS program will, therefore, depend on the response of state legislatures, acting at a time when many face large budget deficits and simultaneous pressure to fund other priorities, including several other provisions of FSA.

The early JOBS experience confirms the variation and the shift in focus, as well as the funding uncertainties. States are replacing the relatively simple programs of the 1980s with more complex initiatives that place greater emphasis on assessing service needs, offering choices, using counseling and case management, focusing on those who volunteer, reaching long-term recipients, and providing education and training (usually through coordination with the education and JTPA systems).[4] Many states are also experiencing budget deficits that are threatening the scale of their new JOBS programs.[5]

---

[4]See, e.g., American Public Welfare Association, 1990.

[5]A study of early JOBS implementation (American Public Welfare Association, 1990) indicates that states are not putting up the funds required for them to receive their full allocations of federal JOBS funds (their "capped entitlement").

A Framework for Understanding the Effects of State JOBS Programs

On the surface, the basic approach of welfare-to-work programs would seem to be simple and direct: Increase participants' employment and earnings and thereby reduce welfare receipt and expenditures. In fact, many forces shape employment and welfare behavior, making successful intervention a complex challenge. This section lays out a framework that is used in the rest of this synthesis for understanding the ways in which welfare-to-work programs can affect behavior and for discussing past research designs and findings.

Our starting point is to group the forces shaping program implementation and impacts into two categories: (1) those defining the external context in which the program intervention is implemented, which determine the underlying pattern of welfare dynamics, and (2) those defining the nature and strength of the program intervention.

The extensive recent research on welfare caseload dynamics (Bane and Ellwood, 1983; Ellwood, 1986) provides a critical background for understanding past studies and assessing the impact of welfare-to-work programs. Any effort to reduce welfare receipt and increase self-sufficiency must start with a recognition that many people leave welfare – some to employment – with no program assistance. The underlying pattern of welfare dynamics (including the usual length of welfare receipt, caseload turnover, and case reopenings or recidivism owing to a return to welfare) is represented by the behavior of the control group in the impact analyses of welfare-to-work programs. Bane and Ellwood's work has highlighted the fact that most people receive public assistance for a relatively short time, while a smaller group receives assistance continuously for an extended period. The JOBS legislation reflects the implications of this research in its emphasis on targeting certain subgroups of AFDC recipients in an effort to reduce long-term dependence.

The nature and strength of the program intervention determine the extent to which the labor market, income, and family experiences of those in the experimental group rise above the base level represented by the control group. Program impacts are estimated by comparing the experiences of controls (who do not receive services from the welfare-to-work program) to those of experimentals (who are served by the program). This framework for understanding the determinants of program impacts is summarized in Figure 2.1.

**FIGURE 2.1   FACTORS AFFECTING THE IMPACTS OF WELFARE-TO-WORK
PROGRAMS**

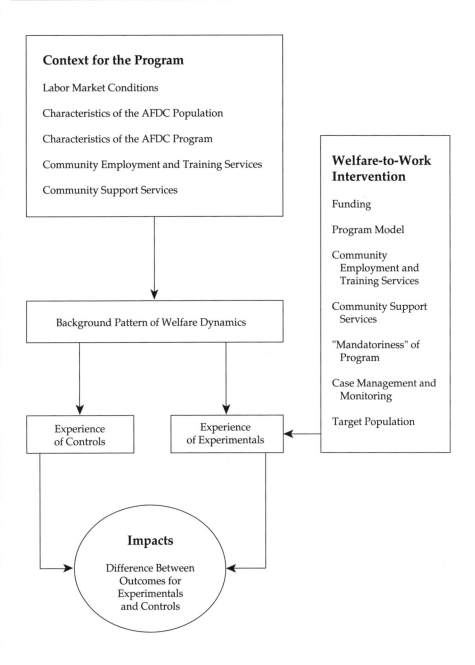

Contextual Factors That Affect the Underlying Pattern of Welfare Dynamics

Past research and experience have identified several key contextual factors that influence welfare dynamics.

Labor Market Conditions and Area Characteristics. Labor market conditions influence welfare dynamics in two ways: They affect the ability of recipients to find work and leave welfare, and they also more subtly influence the characteristics of the remaining public assistance caseload. When labor demand is strong, relatively job-ready individuals – who might apply for welfare in a poor economy – may find employment and never receive public assistance, or, if they do become recipients, they may leave the rolls more rapidly. Thus, a strong labor market will result in a less job-ready caseload, although its effect on program impacts is less certain.[6]

Characteristics of the AFDC Population. A number of studies have used national data to identify characteristics that help predict duration of AFDC receipt (Bane and Ellwood, 1983; O'Neill et al., 1984; Ellwood, 1986; Maynard et al., 1986).[7] This research has found several characteristics to be associated with longer welfare receipt: Marital status, race, work experience, education, mother's age, and the age of the youngest child are important predictors of the likely duration of welfare receipt.[8] For example, mothers with younger children are likely to have longer stays on welfare and increased repeat spells. Lower levels of education were also found to be associated with longer AFDC receipt. A negative relationship was also found between extent of work experience and probability of greater welfare dependence.

This research (Ellwood, 1986) also identified a group most likely to become long-term recipients: young women who have never been married and who begin to receive assistance when their child is less than 3 years old. Over 40 percent of this group will receive welfare for ten years or more. Dividing the welfare population by race, work experience, and education has been found to yield other important subgroups.

---

[6]See, e.g., the discussion in Goldman, Friedlander, and Long, 1986.

[7]See Interagency Low Income Opportunity Advisory Board, Executive Office of the President, 1988, for a useful summary of this research.

[8]These correlations are calculated with other characteristics not held constant. Since targeting strategies for programs would identify individuals by a few simple characteristics with other characteristics not held constant, this concept of correlation is the relevant one for this discussion. (See Ellwood, 1986.)

Recent evaluations of state welfare-to-work programs support these conclusions. For controls, length of prior welfare receipt, prior earnings, and educational attainment all were important predictors of long-term welfare receipt (Friedlander, 1988b).

Characteristics of the AFDC Program. State AFDC grant levels affect welfare dynamics and program impacts by influencing the characteristics of the program-eligible population and the relationship between employment and welfare receipt. At low grant levels, AFDC recipients tend to be more disadvantaged than those of similar-size families receiving higher grants. In addition, with low grants, even modest earnings lead to case closure, whereas people can combine work and welfare more easily in high-grant states. Finally, differences in the design and grant levels of state programs for two-parent households can be expected to affect the characteristics and turnover of the AFDC-UP caseload.

Other elements of the AFDC program, such as the FSA provisions offering a year of transitional Medicaid and child care to people who leave welfare for a job, may also affect welfare dynamics by making it more or less attractive to apply for (or to leave) welfare. Factors in the welfare-to-work program itself may similarly influence AFDC entry and exit rates by changing the climate for welfare receipt: e.g., reducing or increasing the stigma associated with welfare, or changing the perceived total benefit package. Recent studies have not focused on estimating entry effects, but instead on determining whether the programs have impacts of any magnitude on those who apply for AFDC, which would appear to be a precondition to their attracting substantial numbers of additional applicants.[9]

Existing Community Employment and Training Services. The existence of employment-related services that are separate from the welfare-to-work program also influences welfare dynamics. Some communities have a wide array of organizations providing education, training, job search assistance, and other employment services, which will presumably benefit everybody in the area, including members of the control group. One of the surprising findings in studies of 1980s welfare-to-work programs was the high rate of self-initiated participation in these types of community programs by members of the experimental and control groups.

---

[9]An exception is the non-experimental study by O'Neill, 1990, which sought to capture both entry and exit effects in estimating the impact of Massachusetts' welfare-to-work program on the size of the welfare caseload.

Existing Community Support Services. The availability and quality of child care and other support services can affect participation in employment-related programs, work patterns, and, hence, welfare dynamics.

Factors Defining the Nature and Strength of Welfare-to-Work Interventions

Seven factors, shown in the right-hand box of Figure 2.1, are likely to shape the strength or effectiveness of the welfare-to-work intervention. These dimensions – some of which reflect different program philosophies and competing claims for resources – represent the major choices facing states as they design welfare-to-work programs. While these factors are discussed separately, specific state programs will be multi-dimensional, reflecting decisions in each of these areas. Together, these will determine participation rates, the nature and quality of employment and support services, and possible deterrence to continued welfare receipt – all of which, when combined with the contextual factors, will affect outcomes for people targeted to receive JOBS services (the experimental group) and through this determine the program's net impact. (See Figure 2.1.) A primary task of this synthesis is explaining what is currently known– and likely to be learned from funded studies – about the importance of each of these factors: that is, about what works best for whom.

Funding for the Program. While states face a theoretical requirement to serve all adult recipients with children 3 years of age or older, budget constraints suggest that no state will have the resources to provide comprehensive (or even low-cost) services to everyone in this group. The level of available funding will strongly influence the number of people served and the intensity of services (including employment-directed services, support services, and oversight and case management). Regardless of the size of their budgets, program administrators will have three potential responses. In simplified terms, they are:

- **Option 1**: Operating a program that emphasizes low-cost services (primarily job search assistance) for a large proportion of the caseload.
- **Option 2**: Targeting more intensive, higher-cost components and case management on a smaller, more narrowly defined group and leaving the rest unserved.

- **Option 3**: Designing a mixed strategy, with low-cost services for certain groups and higher-cost services for others, that reaches a share of the caseload in between the other two options.

Consequently, the amount of funds available will play an important role in determining how a JOBS program plan is translated into participation in substantial employment-related services for a significant portion of the caseload.

Program Model. The design of state welfare-to-work programs will reflect available resources and an underlying implicit focus on certain presumed causes of welfare receipt, with a resulting recommendation of certain types and ordering of services. Program approaches will differ in program goals (e.g., the relative emphasis on reducing welfare receipt or increasing earnings and reducing poverty), services provided (e.g., job search, community work experience, education, or training), techniques used to deliver these services, and the sequence and duration of activities.

Other Community Employment and Training Services. Within any given WIN or JOBS budget, more AFDC recipients can be served and more intensive activities provided in communities where there are many other independently funded education and training services and well-developed interagency coordination. In this situation, welfare agencies can refer recipients to the appropriate agency, monitor their progress once referred, and arrange new placements if the initial service plan does not prove satisfactory.

For this reason, the budget trade-off is more complex than suggested in the section on "Funding for the Program." All JOBS expenses will not in fact compete for the same budget dollars. Some services (e.g., case management) will typically be paid for directly with JOBS funds, while others will be funded by other delivery systems. The legislation's emphasis on coordination across the welfare, job training, and education systems means that the welfare agency's real budget constraint depends to an important extent on the services provided by these other agencies. This is particularly the case for education, since services provided by local school districts, regional vocational-technical centers, and community colleges may limit the costs paid by JOBS, making this the intensive service that can most feasibly be provided to substantial numbers of enrollees.

Community Support Services. FSA guarantees child care for all program-eligibles who need it in order to participate in approved activities (unless their children are age 13 or over). Further, no one can be required to participate in such programs unless child care is available. Thus, the availability and quality of child care in the community assume special importance, and serious supply constraints could lower participation and hence program impacts.

The Degree of "Mandatoriness" of the Program. Participation in program activities can be voluntary or mandatory, with the choice reflecting basic differences in states' assumptions about the causes of poverty and thus appropriate program approaches. (See the discussion of program philosophies in the first section of this chapter, "The Evolution and Distinctiveness of JOBS.") Mandatory programs will probably draw participants with a wider range of "job-readiness" than would voluntary programs, though the evidence is unclear. In addition, mandatory programs can have impacts on people who never participate in required activities if they change their behavior to avoid the increased "hassle cost" of the program requirement: Individuals may leave welfare or never apply (i.e., be deterred), or they may initiate education, training, job search, or employment on their own outside the program, anticipating that a participation requirement will soon be applied to them. Still others may be sanctioned for failure to comply with participation requirements. The impacts of voluntary programs, on the other hand, are primarily limited to those who participate in program activities.

Prior research suggests that mandatory and voluntary labels obscure great variation in the extent to which a participation requirement is actually enforced and in the nature of the mandate. The degree to which a program was, in practice, mandatory depended on procedures for granting exemptions and deferrals and on the extent to which staff followed up on and, ultimately, sanctioned people for noncompliance.[10] Under JOBS, this distinction is likely to be even more complex than under WIN, since the Family Support Act leaves up to states the question of how much emphasis should be placed on recruiting volunteers versus enforcing participation obligations. While certain individuals are

---

[10]Thus, a more mandatory program involves more frequent tracking of clients' activities and status, more narrowly defined deferrals issued for shorter periods of time, frequent communications to clients concerning the fact that program participation is mandatory, and adequate but not drawn-out conciliation procedures for individuals who fail to comply with program participation requirements. The extent of a program's mandate also depends on other program design choices: e.g., what individuals are required to do, whether they are given a choice, and the length of the requirement.

theoretically exempt and others are "required" to participate, the message of a program will be determined by the balance between serving people in the two groups and the extent to which the program actually enforces a participation mandate on people in the non-exempt group.

Case Management and Monitoring Capacity. Participants do not automatically link up with needed support services and program activities. In the single-component or short-term, fixed-sequenced approaches of the early and mid-1980s, managing and monitoring the caseload to assure program participation was relatively straightforward. In more complex JOBS programs – particularly those that involve extensive cross-agency referral and coordination – case management and assessment practices and reliable management information systems are likely to be important factors in determining whether welfare recipients actually show up and receive program and support services.

The Target Population for the Program. Past research has found that impacts vary substantially for different AFDC subgroups and are more consistent for women on AFDC than for men in AFDC-UP cases (e.g., Friedlander, 1988b; Grossman, Maynard, and Roberts, 1985). In an environment of limited funding, states may choose to target more intensive services – or even the entire welfare-to-work program – on certain groups of recipients rather than attempt to reach the full non-exempt caseload.

The Range of Potential Program Impacts

The impacts themselves are the final element in Figure 2.1. Welfare-to-work programs can have a wide range of direct and indirect effects on AFDC recipients and their families. These include impacts on work and income (earnings, employment rates, total income, and poverty rates), receipt of public transfers (AFDC, Medicaid, Food Stamps, and other benefits), family formation, health status, educational attainment and achievement, family functioning and parenting, and the well-being – along a number of dimensions – of children in AFDC families.[11] Chapter 3 discusses the range of impacts measured in different program evaluations; Chapters 4 and 5 present what has been learned; and Chapter 6 points to the major gaps in knowledge about certain types of impacts.

---

[11]See Wilson and Ellwood, 1989; Brooks-Gunn, 1989; Cherlin, 1989, for a review of the direct and indirect mechanisms through which JOBS programs can affect children in AFDC families.

Estimating Program Impacts

The framework in Figure 2.1 points to several challenges in estimating the impacts of welfare-to-work programs. These issues underlie the discussion of studies and evidence in Chapters 3 to 5.

The Distinction Between Outcomes and Impacts. Administrators operating welfare-to-work programs typically have information on the behavior of people who participate in a program: e.g., whether they take jobs or leave welfare (the job placements or case closures of people in the experimental group, as indicated by the "Experience of Experimentals" in Figure 2.1). The framework in this chapter indicates that these "outcomes" – sometimes called "gross impacts" – will always overstate program achievements. This is because they count all positive changes as program accomplishments and do not identify the extent to which any changes in status actually result from the welfare-to-work program, rather than the underlying welfare dynamics, where people constantly enter and leave the rolls of their own accord (as indicated by the "Experience of Controls" in Figure 2.1).

As illustrated in Figure 2.1, the correct measure of a program's success is its "net impact"– the change in an outcome (e.g., in the employment rate) that results only from the program. The challenge in estimating this is to distinguish accurately between program-induced changes and the normal dynamics of welfare turnover and labor market behavior represented on the left-hand side of Figure 2.1. This requires a precise estimate of what would have happened to people in the program in the absence of the intervention.

The Role of Random Assignment Field Experiments. A number of recent studies and advisory panels point to the difficulty of developing a control group that accurately mimics the behavior of program enrollees. They urge the value of classical experiments using random assignment as a way to obtain accurate and unbiased estimates of the behavior of people with and without a program, and thus of the program's net impact. For example, a National Academy of Sciences panel concluded:

> Our review of the research . . . shows dramatically that control groups created by random assignment yield research findings about employment and training programs that are far less biased than results based on any other method. . . . Future advances in field research on the efficacy of employment and training programs will require a more conscious commitment

to research strategies using random assignment.[12]

Of course, using a random assignment design does not assure valid inferences. As with non-experimental studies, the design must be implemented carefully and must be relevant to the key questions the study hopes to answer. Recognizing this, the same National Academy of Sciences panel recommended

> the following conditions as necessary but not sufficient for quality research: (1) the use of random assignment to participant and control groups and to program variations; (2) reasonable operational stability of the program prior to final assessment of effectiveness; (3) adequate sample coverage and low rates of sample attrition; (4) outcome measures that adequately represent the program objectives, both immediate and longer term; and (5) a follow-up period that allows adequate time for program effects to emerge or decay.[13]

While a social experiment can provide an unbiased estimate of the impact of adding a program to the existing array of services in the community, it is important to correctly interpret the resulting net impact. It does not show the *total* effect of the program, but only its effect *over and above* the services received by members of the control group. To the extent that controls receive some services on their own – and many of the studies suggest that this service receipt can be substantial – it is a conservative estimate of the total effectiveness of the experimental treatment. Moreover, caution is called for in extrapolating the results to other conditions, e.g., to programs implemented at greatly expanded scale,[14] in

---

[12]Betsey, Hollister, and Papageorgiou, 1985, pp. 18, 30. See also Job Training Longitudinal Survey Research Advisory Panel, 1985; Burtless and Orr, 1986; Ashenfelter, 1987; Lalonde and Maynard, 1987. For a different view, see Heckman and Hotz, 1989.

[13]Betsey, Hollister, and Papageorgiou, 1985, p. 32. See also Burtless and Orr, 1986, for a detailed discussion of the methodological challenges facing both experimental and non-experimental studies.

[14]While extrapolating findings from small-scale tests of programs intended for much larger-scale replication poses clear problems, this issue is minimized in some of the recent experiments that, as discussed in Chapter 3, for the first time evaluated full-scale, mandatory WIN and WIN Demonstration programs under real-world conditions. Because welfare-to-work programs have never been entitlements (i.e., programs with adequate resources to serve all eligibles), it proved possible in these large-scale studies to implement random assignment without reducing program scale. While, as a result, these studies avoided many of the concerns about extrapolation, potential threats to external validity exist, e.g., it is possible that the creation of a control group caused the program to follow up on and serve a somewhat different group of people. See Gueron, 1985, for a discussion of the factors that contributed to the successful implementation of these large-scale social experiments that tested full WIN and WIN Demonstration programs.

different economic or administrative conditions, or with different recruitment practices.

Net Versus Differential Impacts. Almost all prior random assignment field experiments have compared the outcomes for individuals in one experimental and one control group. The resulting net impacts reflect the changes brought about by the full program, including decisions on all seven of the dimensions noted above. In many ways, these programs represent a "black box," in that it is not possible, with the precision of the experimental design, to determine either what factors in the welfare-to-work model are responsible for the program's success or the relative effectiveness of different services.[15] Such comparisons have to be made across sites and programs, with all the problems of competing explanations and a small number of sites.

An alternative approach is to use a more complex random assignment design to determine the relative effectiveness of different welfare-to-work programs. This requires that the random assignment design go beyond what is typical in most evaluations and involve the assignment of program eligibles to several different treatment options (as well as to a control group, if there is also an interest in measuring the net impact of each approach). This design is known as a "differential impact" study. If this could be successfully implemented, it would provide more compelling evidence on the relative payoff of different program approaches: e.g., programs that emphasize education compared to those that stress immediate job placement and labor force attachment.[16]

Estimating Impacts for Broad-Coverage and Selective-Voluntary Programs. In this synthesis, we distinguish between two types of studies: those that evaluate welfare-to-work delivery systems (which we call "broad-coverage programs") and others that assess individual components (or potential components) within these systems (which we call "selective-voluntary demonstrations or programs" because of their

---

[15]For example, Heckman, 1990, argues that "to use the experimental method to evaluate a wide menu of proposed policies requires one randomization for each relevant policy variation. Since most proposed social programs have a large variety of potential options, the experimental method entails one randomization for each option" (pp. 12-13).

[16]The success of differential impact designs depends on (1) disciplining random assignment and program operations to minimize crossovers (i.e., experimentals or controls receiving inappropriate services), and (2) the actual implementation of the two or more experimental treatments. As discussed in Chapters 3 and 4, these more complex experimental designs have been used – with mixed success – in studies of welfare-to-work programs in Virginia; Cook County, Illinois; and San Diego and Riverside, California.

recruitment practices). These two categories differ in their targeting, screening, selection, and participation rates, and these differences must be understood if evaluation results are to be accurately interpreted and compared. Chapter 3 defines these two types of programs and studies at length. This section focuses on the methodological implications of this distinction for interpreting program impacts.[17]

Welfare-to-work programs like WIN or JOBS are usually targeted at a broad group in the caseload: e.g., all AFDC applicants and recipients whose youngest child is at least 3 years old. If the program is mandatory, people in the eligible group can be affected directly by actually participating in program services or indirectly by the threat (or reality) of sanctions for not participating. (That is, nonparticipants can be deterred from continuing to apply for or remaining on welfare by the prospect of required participation or the actual application of sanctions.)

In evaluations of broad-coverage, mandatory programs where the structure and goals suggested that there might be indirect effects, researchers have estimated impacts across the full caseload that was actually subject to the participation mandate, including people who might never have gotten their grants approved or received program services.[18] So that this could be done, random assignment occurred at either the welfare intake office or the office of the welfare-to-work program. The resulting experimental group included many people who went through intake, orientation, and specific service components, but there was typically a dropoff at each step – significantly reducing the participation rate in the actual service components – owing to a variety of factors such as normal welfare caseload dynamics, deterrence of nonparticipants, and temporary or permanent deferrals because of illness, child care problems, or part- or full-time employment. Evaluations of broad-coverage programs such as these show the impact of the entire welfare-to-work (WIN or JOBS) *system* on the caseload targeted for services. They answer the question: How is the average (targeted and/or enrolled) mandatory AFDC applicant or recipient affected by the existence of the WIN or JOBS program?

---

[17] For a more detailed discussion of these methodological issues, and of the uncontrolled variables that suggest caution in comparing results across studies, see Friedlander and Gueron, forthcoming.

[18] As discussed in Chapter 3, there were some differences across studies in who was included in the research samples.

This is a very different kind of question than that addressed in evaluations of particular voluntary employment and training components within welfare-to-work delivery systems. (Since studies of particular service components have only been conducted for voluntary activities, we call these "selective-voluntary demonstrations or programs.") These programs are designed to affect only people who directly participate in services. As a result, to assess the impacts of such programs, random assignment is most appropriately located after program enrollment and ideally just at the point where participation in services is about to begin,[19] so that impacts are estimated for an experimental group with very high or even universal participation. Evaluations of these programs show the impact of a specific employment-directed service on self- and program-selected volunteers. They answer the question: How is the average welfare applicant or recipient who gets into the program component affected by the services provided?[20]

This methodological distinction is critical to the discussion of "broad-coverage" and "selective-voluntary" studies in Chapters 3 to 5. Because of it, impacts from these two types of studies are not directly comparable, even when both use experimental designs. One provides information on the effectiveness of a system that manages and offers services to a diverse caseload, some of whom participate; the other provides information on a particular component of the system for a subset of the caseload, most of whom participate.

The distinction between broad-coverage and selective-voluntary studies is complicated by the fact that the completed studies are for programs that differed along three dimensions:

- a focus on the full service delivery system or on a (potential) component within that system;

---

[19]Random assignment at this point is most appropriate to estimating the impact of the employment services; earlier random assignment would provide information on the percentage of eligibles who actually participate in the component and would facilitate generalizability to the broader AFDC caseload.

[20]As an artifact of the timing of random assignment, however, some percentage of experimentals in these studies may not actually receive services. Thus, in some evaluations of selective-voluntary programs (e.g., the National Supported Work Demonstration), almost all experimentals actually received program services. In others, random assignment occurred earlier, and participation was less than universal, e.g., 89 percent of experimentals received program services in the JOBSTART Demonstration (Auspos et al., 1989), and 77 percent in the Minority Female Single Parent (MFSP) Demonstration (Gordon and Burghardt, 1990). See Chapter 3 for a description of these projects.

- inclusion of the full eligible caseload (or a cross section of the full caseload) or of a subset of screened and selected eligibles; and

- the mandatory or voluntary nature of participation in the program.

The contrast between what we have called broad-coverage and selective-voluntary studies on the last two dimensions can be seen in the matrix below. Completed studies fall only in cells A (broad-coverage and mandatory) and D (selective and voluntary), although it is possible to operate and evaluate programs falling in cells B and C.[21]

Dimensions of Program Design

	Mandatory	Voluntary
Wide range of eligibles, without screening	A	B
Self- and program-selected eligibles	C	D

Examples of programs that fit in different cells in this matrix are discussed in the next chapter: San Diego SWIM and most other broad-coverage programs fall in cell A, Massachusetts ET Choices is in cell B, and the Homemaker-Home Health Aide Demonstrations and other selective-voluntary programs are in cell D. While no current program fits into cell C, this combination is also possible. For example, in some states, the initially selective-voluntary New Chance program for young mothers (see Chapter 3), while remaining small-scale and selective, can

---

[21]This distinction between program types sharpens our understanding of reality, but it does so by simplifying reality to some extent. First, while broad-coverage programs included a cross section of the eligible population (not just selected or motivated people), they did not always include all people required to register with WIN, nor will present ones always include all of those who can be required to participate in JOBS. While some of the broad-coverage studies include all people found to meet the mandatory criteria during the period of the study, others are broad-coverage only for certain categories within the caseload (e.g., new applicants or young custodial mothers). Second, as discussed earlier in this chapter, the distinction between a mandatory and voluntary program is often a matter of degree. It should not be assumed that, because a program is mandatory, all those who participate do so under duress. In fact, people who take part in such programs represent a wide variety of levels of motivation, from those who would have volunteered for the program to those who are there only because of the threat of a reduction in their welfare grant. (In addition, the enforcement activities of mandatory programs vary in intensity.) Conversely, while voluntary programs obviously enroll people who at some time elect to participate, volunteers' motivation does not remain constant over the course of their stay in the program.

fulfill JOBS' mandatory participation requirement for out-of-school teen mothers.

Figures 2.2 and 2.3 compare the scope of these two kinds of studies. Figure 2.2 shows the flow of clients in studies of broad-coverage programs. The area enclosed by dashed lines represents the program activities whose effects are measured by evaluations of these programs. Two illustrations of broad-coverage programs are given, depicting a fixed-sequence model (such as San Diego SWIM) that starts with job search, and an up-front assessment model (such as Baltimore Options) that permits client and caseworker discretion regarding clients' activities. Figure 2.3 shows the flow of clients in studies of selective-voluntary programs (such as the New Jersey OJT program, which was operated as a component within a larger, broad-coverage program – a likely scenario under JOBS). Note that in these studies the area enclosed by dashed lines contains only the activities of persons who were screened and chosen to enroll. (Persons who were screened out of the selective-voluntary program, or who did not volunteer for it, may have been included in the activities of a broad-coverage program.)

Because random assignment occurs early in the flow of people into services in studies of broad-coverage programs (as shown in Figure 2.2), the average measured impact – as well as the net cost per person – is spread across a larger number of individuals, only some of whom are affected by the programs' services or requirements. Thus, a finding of lower average impacts per experimental in broad-coverage programs would not necessarily mean that these programs provided less effective employment-directed services than selective-voluntary programs. Instead, it might simply reflect lower participation or the focus on a broader group of welfare recipients, including subgroups less likely to benefit from services. (See Maxfield, 1990, for an example of a recent summary that does not consider these issues in summarizing what past random assignment studies tell us about the relative effectiveness of different service approaches.)

As a result, in assessing the results from prior studies, JOBS planners and administrators should focus on findings for comparable populations, and be cautious in reaching conclusions about the relative effectiveness of alternative service approaches and sequences by comparing results across these two different categories of studies.

The Need for Adequate Follow-Up. Different employment-directed services can be expected to produce their impacts over different periods

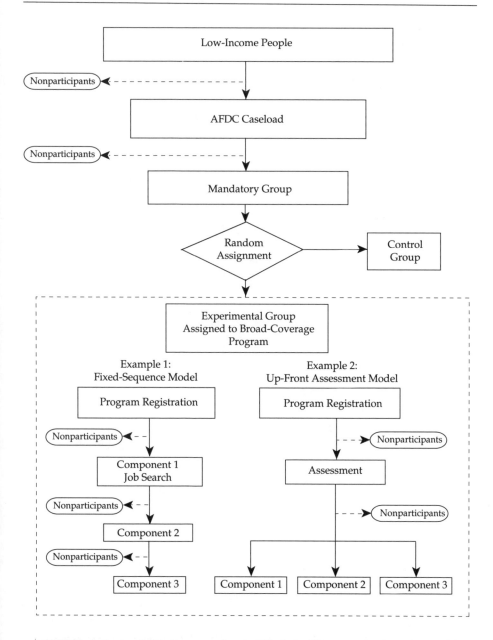

NOTES: The bottom part of the figure – enclosed within dashed lines – represents program activity captured in evaluations.

In some studies, random assignment occurred at the welfare office prior to program registration, as shown here. In others, random assignment occurred at the welfare-to-work program office.

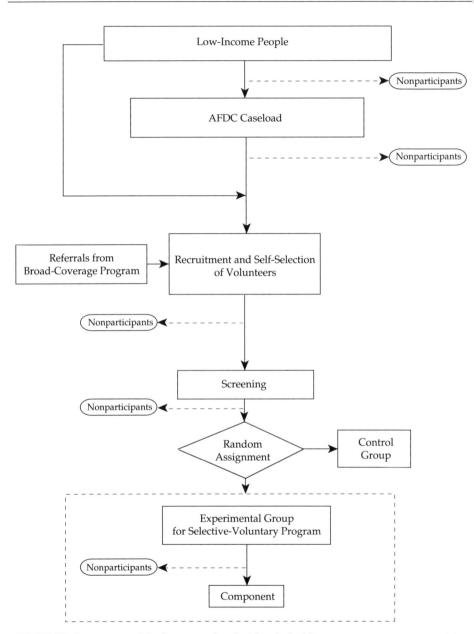

NOTES: The bottom part of the figure – enclosed within dashed lines – represents program activity captured in evaluations.

In these studies, random assignment occurred at the selective-voluntary program office after screening, as shown here.

of time. For example, low-cost job search programs are intended to place people rapidly in jobs, with the hope that the initial placement will lead to a subsequent job and to some sustained impact on employment. Higher-cost education and training services anticipate making a larger up-front investment – at the expense, in the short term, of delaying entry into the labor force and serving fewer people – in anticipation that the new skills and "human capital" will ultimately allow the participants to obtain better and more stable employment. As a result, in the short run, it can be expected that a job search program will appear more successful than a human capital investment approach. A critical question is whether, as is often assumed, the impacts of more intensive services are ultimately greater and more long-lasting. Long-term follow-up (possibly five years or more) is essential to determining whether higher investments deliver greater eventual benefits, and the extent to which the impacts of different services increase or diminish over time.

Estimating Entry and Macroeconomic Effects. To date, field experiments of broad-coverage systems have placed random assignment at the income maintenance or welfare-to-work program office (see Figure 2.2). When well-executed, these studies provide a reliable estimate of the impact of a welfare-to-work program on the rate at which people who receive or apply for AFDC benefits (the group randomly assigned) leave welfare as well as the impacts on their employment behavior. In other words, they capture the program's effect on welfare exits, i.e., on people delaying or speeding their departure from welfare as a result of the program's mandates and services. This is the first-order issue of whether a welfare-to-work program impacts those directly involved in its activities and subject to its requirements.

It is possible, however, that welfare-to-work programs affect caseloads by another route: by changing the rate at which people apply for welfare. For example, if JOBS administrators publicize the program's opportunity for education and training, this could attract people onto welfare; if they emphasize program obligations, this could deter people from applying. Since the JOBS message (and word-of-mouth publicity) is likely to vary across states and localities, the magnitude and direction – positive or negative – of any net effect on AFDC entries is unclear. Capturing these effects would require a different type of research design.[22]

---

[22]See Moffitt, 1990, for a discussion of the potential of FSA's enriched services to encourage welfare applications and of possible research designs for measuring this.

Further, the studies discussed in this volume – as with most evaluations of employment and training programs – did not attempt to measure
the programs' general equilibrium or macroeconomic effects. Implicitly,
these studies assumed that the increased employment of welfare recipients would not change the labor market opportunities available to
people not on welfare (e.g., that there would be little or no displacement
or replacement of other low-wage workers). Some of the studies used
sensitivity tests to examine the importance of this assumption to the
conclusions reached in the benefit-cost analysis.[23]

* * * * *

This chapter has argued that studies of welfare-to-work programs
are shaped by two things: the nature of the program (including its
context) and the methodological choices made by the evaluators. They
influence both the results of an evaluation and its policy relevance.
Using the ideas presented in this chapter, the remainder of this synthesis discusses the completed and ongoing studies that are relevant to
the JOBS program.

---

[23]See, in particular, Kemper, Long, and Thornton, 1984; and also Goldman, Friedlander,
and Long, 1986.

Chapter 3

The Studies of
Welfare-to-Work Programs

This chapter describes the data base for this synthesis: primarily field experiments used to evaluate welfare-to-work and other programs directly relevant to JOBS. Despite the challenge of mounting such studies of complex social programs, a substantial number have been completed, and more are under way.

Practical considerations limited the scope of this synthesis. Among the more notable and important bodies of research that were excluded are evaluations of school dropout-recovery programs, teen pregnancy prevention programs, and summer work programs for youth. These studies are not discussed here because they usually do not focus specifically on AFDC recipients and because few have used experimental research designs. Their exclusion from this review does not imply that they are not valuable sources of information for designers of state JOBS programs.

Ideally, this chapter would present results separately for each element in the framework in Figure 2.1 in Chapter 2. However, most evaluations assess multi-dimensional programs, each of which combines into a single treatment its choice, for example, between emphasizing immediate job placement versus up-front education and training, its resources, its degree of mandatoriness, its support services, and its target populations. Evaluations reflect these "packages" of activities and attributes, and researchers have rarely structured studies to estimate with any rigor the impact of particular aspects of a program.

Reflecting this reality, this review groups studies into two basic categories that share important design dimensions, rather than presenting evidence on each individual program feature. The studies are of "broad-coverage" programs, which include all the elements of a complete service delivery system, and "selective-voluntary" programs, each of which is the equivalent of a program component within a broader system. The categories, which were introduced in Chapter 2, can be described as follows:

- **Studies of service delivery systems.** One group of program evaluations includes not only individual service components but also administrative activities (such as intake, orientation, assessment, case management, and monitoring) that affect the allocation of services, and which together make up a service delivery system. Because the systems studied are intended to reach a wide range of AFDC eligibles, with no screening, they are called **broad-coverage programs.** Almost all of the completed studies in this category were of mandatory programs that, to varying degrees, required participation from people who were not likely to seek services on their own.[1]

- **Studies of program components.** Another group of program evaluations does not encompass full systems but, in most cases, looks at small-scale demonstrations of a component (or potential component) of a much larger broad-coverage program. All of the completed studies are of programs that encouraged but did not require participation by a subset of the AFDC population. These programs are "selective" in one or two ways: Eligible people can select whether or not to enroll, and program operators can select among eligible applicants. Because of these recruitment practices, these are called **selective-voluntary programs or demonstrations.** This category also includes the Job Training Partnership Act (JTPA) system, which provides components of many JOBS programs.[2]

In addition, this chapter discusses three groups of studies that are relevant to particular policy issues raised by new provisions of JOBS:

- **Studies of education services** in broad-coverage or selective-voluntary programs.

- **Studies of youth-oriented services** in broad-coverage or selective-voluntary programs.

---

[1] This category also includes two studies in progress of broad-coverage voluntary programs: Massachusetts' Employment and Training (ET) Choices program and Washington's Family Independence Program (FIP). As discussed below, the two Louisville demonstrations had both voluntary and mandatory aspects.

[2] JTPA is itself a service delivery system. However, in the context of the JOBS program, JTPA usually provides particular training components or assessment functions to selected participants.

- **Studies of support services** in broad-coverage or selective-voluntary programs.

As a result, this chapter consolidates a number of the dimensions discussed in Chapter 2, on the basis of the available results.

In understanding the relevance of these studies for JOBS, the most fundamental distinction is that between the broad-coverage and selective-voluntary programs. Broad-coverage programs are total service delivery systems that include linked decisions on program components, management strategies, support services, and caseload targeting. Usually, they try to involve a large group or cross section of the eligible caseload. On a demonstration or ongoing basis, they in effect replace or are the WIN or JOBS system. Their evaluations thus assess the impact not only of the individual service components, but of the accompanying administrative activities and degree of mandatoriness. Selective-voluntary programs, in contrast, usually target a more narrow population with a particular program approach; their evaluations assess the effectiveness of the particular employment-directed service. (See Figures 2.2 and 2.3 and the discussion in Chapter 2 on "Estimating Impacts for Broad-Coverage and Selective-Voluntary Programs.")

Broad-coverage programs can be mandatory or voluntary, although the studies completed to date are almost all of nominally mandatory programs. While individual program components could also be implemented as mandatory or voluntary options within a broad-coverage system, all of the experimental tests to date have been of selective and voluntary programs, prompting the nomenclature used in this synthesis.

Table 3.1 summarizes the broad-coverage programs and studies. Some of them reflect WIN or JOBS programs implemented at full scale; others were smaller-scale demonstrations of WIN programs. With the exceptions noted in the table, all of these studies estimate the impact of a welfare-to-work delivery system on a cross section of the then-mandatory single-parent (mostly female) AFDC caseload with school-age children. These studies thus cover a wide range of welfare applicants and recipients, including those not likely to seek services on their own.

The other tables contain information on evaluations that illuminate particular aspects of the welfare-to-work system. These studies provide information about elements inside the "black box" of state JOBS programs, but they were and are sometimes conducted under conditions that may not be directly relevant to the scale of the JOBS program. Table

3.2 lists evaluations of selective-voluntary welfare-to-work programs, which test particular employment services for groups of AFDC recipients who volunteer to participate and are screened by the programs (to meet specific eligibility or other requirements). These programs provide some of the components that are part of the broad-coverage system, but they are always voluntary and designed to target a caseload that is less broad than the full JOBS-mandatory population.

Table 3.3 shows evaluations of educational programs. Table 3.4 lists evaluations of related programs for youth (often not limited to young people on AFDC). Table 3.5 shows tests of support services (e.g., testing the effectiveness of different child care services in increasing maternal employment). Within each table, the studies that have been completed are described first, followed by the studies that are still in progress.

A great deal of program diversity is contained within each of the five clusters listed above. For example, the broad-coverage programs vary in their philosophy and message, their service model, their scale, and the intentions and goals of the state policymakers who designed them. This category includes programs that are mandatory and some that are voluntary; even the nominally mandatory programs vary in the extent of enforcement activities and aggressive outreach that they use to raise participation levels. The coherence of the category is empirical: All of the programs that are included involve a broad slice of the AFDC caseload, and thus represent an approximation of the operational issues that will confront the states' JOBS programs. Programs were assigned to all five clusters based on their observed target groups and program design features.

The outcome measures used were a key attribute of the studies included in this synthesis. Because of funding limitations, the studies often estimated direct impacts for no more than three years after program enrollment on a series of outcomes that could be measured relatively cheaply using computerized administrative records: earnings, employment rates, AFDC receipt, and AFDC grants. Important impacts that were either less frequently or never measured included impacts on wage rates, the nature of jobs held by welfare recipients, family formation, total household income, poverty rates, longer-term self-sufficiency, educational attainment and achievement, health status, and the well-being of children in AFDC families. Some of these impacts will be measured in several of the current studies, described below.

In addition to material on outcome measures, the tables in this chapter contain the following information:

- The date the impact evaluation began (which was not necessarily the same as the date the program began).

- The evaluation's focus (the treatment received by the experimental group but not by the control group), identifying programs that assigned participants to a fixed sequence of activities.

- The net cost per experimental (not the gross operating cost, but the difference between the total cost of the program per experimental and the program cost per control, with all sample members included in the calculations), in nominal (not constant) dollars.[3]

- Whether participation in the program was by design mandatory or voluntary (mandatory programs may also have allowed non-targeted persons to volunteer).

- The target groups included in the evaluation.

- The type of research design used, and whether a net impact or differential impact analysis was conducted.

- The scale of the study, in terms of the operational and administrative units covered by the evaluation (the number of counties, welfare offices within counties, or demonstration service providers studied) – e.g., the study may have been statewide, or it may have covered six counties or two welfare offices in one county or a fixed number of slots.

- The length of the follow-up period from the time of enrollment in the program (these are generally the longest follow-up data reported and may not cover the full sample or all outcome measures).

- A summary of the impact findings (for completed studies) or the date impact findings are expected.

---

[3] Because some controls participated in these services, average net cost is less than the average cost of operating the program per person in the experimental group. See Appendix A for further explanation.

For each of the studies described in this chapter's tables, references are provided in a list at the end of the chapter.

Broad-Coverage Programs

Table 3.1 shows that there are 19 studies in progress or completed on welfare-to-work programs that are targeted broadly to include a wide range of AFDC recipients.[4] These programs are usually mandatory (e.g., Arkansas' WORK or New Jersey's Realizing Economic Achievement [REACH]), but they may be voluntary (e.g., Massachusetts' ET Choices); they may be relatively small-scale (Baltimore Options, also referred to in this synthesis simply as Baltimore) or statewide for all eligibles (Virginia and West Virginia).[5] They are distinguished from the selective-voluntary demonstrations and programs listed in Table 3.2 in that, for the relevant scale and population, they are highly inclusive programs. That is, instead of serving small numbers of self-selected, often highly motivated volunteers, they attempt to serve everyone who is targeted (or, in some cases, recruited) in a large population defined by specified eligibility criteria. Thus, usually through a participation requirement, but sometimes through persistent recruitment, they seek to enroll and serve as many people in the targeted AFDC caseload as feasible or affordable.

Two of the nine completed studies – the Louisville, Kentucky, experiments – were implemented prior to OBRA and are therefore not discussed at length in this chapter. (They are, however, included in Table 3.1 because they represent a rare use of an experimental design during this earlier period.) These two studies assessed the effect of providing services designed to help individuals search for jobs. At the time, they were unusual in offering this assistance to new AFDC applicants – immediately, before they had been approved for welfare – as well as to

---

[4] Two earlier studies are particularly noteworthy, although their results are less directly relevant because they reflected programs implemented prior to the passage of the Omnibus Budget Reconciliation Act (OBRA) of 1981, which substantially changed the calculation of AFDC work incentives. The large-scale evaluation of the WIN program used a quasi-experimental design to study the effects of WIN (and different WIN components) on a sample of 1974 and 1975 WIN enrollees (see Ketron, 1980). The evaluation of the Employment Opportunity Pilot Project (EOPP), a large-scale, ten-site demonstration fielded between 1979 and 1981, used a quasi-experimental design to test a saturation program providing a sequence of intensive job search assistance followed by subsidized employment or training to those who did not obtain a regular job (see Brown et al., 1983). (EOPP was mandatory for AFDC recipients with children over 5 years old and voluntary for other single mothers.)

[5] These state programs may have been modified since their evaluations.

TABLE 3.1 EVALUATION STUDIES RELATED TO JOBS: BROAD-COVERAGE PROGRAMS

	Arkansas WORK Program	Baltimore Options	Cook County WIN Demonstration
Start Date[a]	1983	1982	1985
Major Program Activities	Sequence of group job search (followed by individual job search) and (for a few) unpaid work experience	Choice of individual or group job search, unpaid work experience, education, job skills training, on-the-job training	Test of 2 programs: (1) individual job search; (2) sequence of IJS and unpaid work experience
Net Cost[b]	$118	$953 for AFDC	$127 for IJS; $157 for IJS/WE
Mandatory or Voluntary	Mandatory	Mandatory	Mandatory
Target Groups	AFDC applicants and recipients with children 3 or older	Applicants and recipients: AFDCs with children 6 or older; AFDC-UPs with children of any age	AFDC applicants and recipients with children 6 or older
Research Design	Random assignment, net impact	Random assignment, net impact	Random assignment, net and differential impacts
Study Scale	2 of 75 counties	10 of 18 income maintenance centers	Countywide
Length of Follow-Up[c]	36 months	36 months	18 months
Outcomes Measured	Employment, earnings, welfare receipt and payments	Employment, earnings, welfare receipt and payments	Employment, earnings, welfare receipt and payments
Impact Findings[d] (or Date Expected)	Increased employment and earnings; reduced welfare receipt and payments	For AFDC: short-term increase in employment; increased earnings; no impact on welfare receipt and payments	For IJS and IJS/WE: no impact on employment and earnings; small reductions in welfare receipt and payments; no effect of WE component over and above the effect of IJS

(continued)

TABLE 3.1 *(continued)*

	Louisville WIN Laboratory Experiments		San Diego I (EPP/EWEP)
	Individual Job Search	Group Job Search	
Start Date[a]	1978	1980	1982
Major Program Activities	Individual job search	Group job search	Test of 2 programs: (1) group job search; (2) sequence of group job search and unpaid work experience
Net Cost[b]	$136 (1985 $)	$230 (1985 $)	For AFDC: $562 for JS; $636 for JS/WE. For AFDC-UP: $586 for JS; $727 for JS/WE
Mandatory or Voluntary	Mandatory and voluntary	Mandatory and voluntary	Mandatory
Target Groups	AFDC applicants and recipients with children of any age	AFDC applicants and recipients with children of any age	AFDC applicants with children 6 or older; AFDC-UP applicants with children of any age
Research Design	Random assignment, net impact	Random assignment, net impact	Random assignment, net and differential impacts
Study Scale	1 office	1 office	Countywide
Length of Follow-Up[c]	33 months	12 months	18 months
Outcomes Measured	Employment, earnings, welfare receipt and payments	Employment, earnings, welfare receipt and payments	Employment, earnings, welfare receipt and payments
Impact Findings[d] (or Date Expected)	Increased employment and earnings; reduced welfare receipt and payments	Increased employment and earnings; no impact on welfare receipt and payments	For AFDC — JS only: inconsistent impact on employment and earnings; short-term reduction in welfare payments. JS/WE: increased employment and earnings; reduced welfare payments. For AFDC-UP — JS only and JS/WE: no impact on employment and earnings; reduced welfare receipt and payments

(continued)

TABLE 3.1 *(continued)*

	San Diego SWIM	Virginia ESP	West Virginia CWEP
Start Date[a]	1985	1983	1983
Major Program Activities	Sequence of group job search, unpaid work experience, and education and job skills training; ongoing participation requirement	Sequence of individual or group job search, unpaid work experience, and some education or job skills training (but only slightly more than controls received on their own)[e]	Open-ended unpaid work experience
Net Cost[b]	$919 for AFDC; $817 for AFDC-UP	$430	$260 for AFDC
Mandatory or Voluntary	Mandatory	Mandatory	Mandatory
Target Groups	Applicants and recipients: AFDCs with children 6 or older; AFDC-UPs with children of any age	AFDC applicants and recipients with children 6 or older	Applicants and recipients: AFDCs with children 6 or older; AFDC-UPs with children of any age
Research Design	Random assignment, net impact	Random assignment, net and differential impacts	AFDC: random assignment, net impact; AFDC-UP: matched-county comparison design, net impact
Study Scale	2 of 7 welfare offices	11 of 124 welfare agencies[f]	AFDC: 9 of 27 administrative areas;[f] AFDC-UP: 8 of 27[f]
Length of Follow-Up[c]	27 months	33 months	21 months
Outcomes Measured	Employment, earnings, welfare receipt and payments	Employment, earnings, welfare receipt and payments	Employment, earnings, welfare receipt and payments
Impact Findings[d] (or Date Expected)	For AFDC: increased employment and earnings; reduced welfare receipt and payments. For AFDC-UP: increased employment and short-term impact on earnings; short-term impact on welfare receipt and reduced welfare payments	Increased employment and earnings; reduced welfare payments	For AFDC: no impact on employment and earnings; reduced welfare receipt and payments in final follow-up quarter

(continued)

TABLE 3.1 *(continued)*

	California GAIN	Florida Project Independence	Food Stamp Employment and Training Program
Start Date[a]	1988	1990	1988
Major Program Activities	Education and job search followed by assessment and further education, unpaid work experience, job skills training, or on-the-job training	Job search for "job-ready" enrollees; assessment followed by education, training, or unpaid work experience for others and completers of job search without a job	Job search, job club, education, job skills training, unpaid work experience
Net Cost[b]	N/A	N/A	N/A
Mandatory or Voluntary	Mandatory	Mandatory	Mandatory
Target Groups	Applicants and recipients: AFDCs with children 6 or older; AFDC-UPs with children of any age	AFDC applicants and recipients with children 3 or older	Food Stamp recipients
Research Design	Random assignment, net impact	Random assignment, net impact	Random assignment, net impact
Study Scale	6 of 58 counties[f]	9 of 67 counties[f]	55 sites in 23 states
Length of Follow-Up[c]	24 months	24 months	12 months
Outcomes Measured	Employment, earnings, job characteristics, welfare receipt and payments, household income, educational achievement and attainment, attitudes	Employment, earnings, job characteristics, welfare receipt and payments, family composition, educational attainment	Employment, earnings, job characteristics, household income, Food Stamp and welfare receipt and payments
Impact Findings[d] (or Date Expected)	Interim, 1991; final, 1993	Interim, 1992; final, 1994	1990

(continued)

TABLE 3.1 *(continued)*

	Illinois Early Access Program	Massachusetts ET Choices	New Jersey REACH
Start Date[a]	1989	1986	1987
Major Program Activities	For most recipients, job search followed by assessment, job club, pre-employment training, education, job skills training, work experience; for a few recipients, education followed by other services	Assessment followed by choice of job search, job club, education, job skills training, and/or supported work; transitional child care, health care	Assessment, education, job skills training, job placement, support services
Net Cost[b]	N/A	N/A	N/A
Mandatory or Voluntary	Mandatory	Voluntary	Mandatory
Target Groups	AFDC recipients with children 3-5	AFDC and AFDC-UP recipients with children of any age	AFDC recipients with children 2 or older
Research Design	Random assignment, net impact	Comparison group	Matched comparison group
Study Scale	1 county	Statewide[f]	Statewide[f]
Length of Follow-Up[c]	18-60 months	36 months	24 months
Outcomes Measured	Employment, welfare receipt and payments, Medicaid receipt	Employment, earnings, wage rates, job retention; welfare receipt, payments, and recidivism; post-program day care use	Employment, earnings, welfare receipt and recidivism, household composition, child support collection
Impact Findings[d] (or Date Expected)	N/A	1990	Interim, 1991; final, 1994

(continued)

TABLE 3.1 *(continued)*

	Ohio Transitions to Independence Evaluation	Pennsylvania Saturation Work Program	Riverside, California, Case Management Study
Start Date[a]	1989	1986	1988
Major Program Activities	Assessment, job club, unpaid work experience, subsidized employment, education, job skills training	Ongoing participation requirement, enhanced case management, day care	Test of GAIN activities with case management provided with registrant-to-staff ratios of approximately (1) 50:1 or (2) 100:1
Net Cost[b]	N/A	N/A	N/A
Mandatory or Voluntary	Mandatory	Mandatory	Mandatory
Target Groups	AFDC recipients with children 6 or older and AFDC-UP recipients	Applicants and recipients: AFDCs with children 6 or older; AFDC-UPs with children of any age	Applicants and recipients: AFDCs with children 6 or older; AFDC-UPs with children of any age
Research Design	Random assignment, net impact	Random assignment, net impact	Random assignment, net and differential impacts
Study Scale	15 counties	6 welfare districts in Philadelphia	Countywide
Length of Follow-Up[c]	48 months	24 months	24 months
Outcomes Measured	Employment, earnings, job characteristics; welfare receipt, payments, duration, and recidivism; child support payments, family formation	Employment, earnings, welfare receipt and payments	Employment, earnings, job characteristics, welfare receipt and payments, household income, educational attainment, attitudes
Impact Findings[d] (or Date Expected)	Interim, 1990, 1991, 1992; final, 1993	1990	1992

(continued)

TABLE 3.1 *(continued)*

	Washington FIP
Start Date[a]	1988
Major Program Activities	Financial incentives for participation, education, job skills training, increased subsidies for in-program child care, extended transitional benefits, cashing out Food Stamps
Net Cost[b]	N/A
Mandatory or Voluntary	Voluntary
Target Groups	AFDC and AFDC-UP recipients with children of any age
Research Design	2 matched groups of 5 counties each were created; 1 group was randomly selected to operate FIP, while the other group does not operate FIP
Study Scale	10 counties, 5 operating FIP and 5 in a comparison group
Length of Follow-Up[c]	36 months
Outcomes Measured	Employment, earnings, welfare receipt, duration, and recidivism
Impact Findings[d] (or Date Expected)	Interim, 1992; final, 1993

(continued)

TABLE 3.1 *(continued)*

NOTES: The programs are organized alphabetically within two categories: completed evaluations, beginning with the Arkansas WORK Program, and those still in progress, beginning with California GAIN.

[a]The start date refers to the start of intake for the research sample.

[b]The costs reported are per experimental unless otherwise noted. All net costs are in nominal dollars except for the costs of the Louisville WIN Laboratory Experiments, which are in 1985 dollars. These net cost estimates include all expenditures by the operating agency specifically for the programs under study, as well as any expenditures by other organizations for services that were considered an essential part of the program treatment (in most of the programs included in this table, participation in these services was mandatory once an individual was assigned to them). However, the costs to operating agencies and to other organizations of serving members of the control groups have been subtracted in order to arrive at the *net* cost estimates. See Appendix A for further discussion.

[c]The follow-up period refers to the longest amount of follow-up available, although it may not apply to all groups or all measures in the study.

[d]For the most part, only statistically significant impacts are reported. In a few cases, however, findings may reflect impacts that are consistent through the follow-up period, but not statistically significant in the final months of follow-up. In multi-year studies, impacts are based on the final year of follow-up.

[e]The Virginia research design called for testing two program models: one providing a sequence of job search and unpaid work experience and the other adding education or job skills training. In practice, the two experimental groups received fairly similar program services and there were not statistically significant differences between them in welfare and employment outcomes. Thus, the results are combined for the two experimental groups. (See Riccio et al., 1986.)

[f]The program operated statewide.

recipients. The first program provided three days of intensive instruction in job search techniques followed by up to six weeks of counselor-directed, structured individual job search, where people followed up and reported back on job leads provided by WIN workers. The second program used group job clubs, where participants were offered one week of classroom instruction in job search skills, followed by up to five weeks of making at least 50 daily calls to prospective employers from a telephone room at the WIN office.[6] Both programs provided incentive payments and reimbursement for job search-related expenses and both were technically voluntary, but had voluntary and mandatory aspects.[7]

The other seven studies of WIN and WIN Demonstration programs of the 1980s – Arkansas; Baltimore; Cook County (Chicago), Illinois;[8] Virginia;[9] West Virginia; San Diego I;[10] and San Diego's Saturation Work Initiative Model (SWIM) – are most relevant to JOBS. These programs

---

[6] The job club process contains a number of elements. "Participants were told to treat job search as a full-time job and were encouraged to use friends and relatives to obtain leads. They were trained in interviewing and social skills and used standardized scripts on the telephone to uncover job openings and get interviews. The basic philosophy is that there are many jobs that become vacant and subsequently filled without going through an elaborate job referral network. Frequent telephone calls will locate these vacancies and provide participants with opportunities they would not have had had they relied on job developers or want ads. As part of the program, they were also given regular staff supervision and assistance and were involved in a peer support network" (Goldman, 1989, p. 393).

[7] For mothers with children under age 6 (i.e., those outside the traditional WIN-mandatory category), participation was voluntary. Mothers with no children under age 6 could choose either to remain in the regular WIN program or to be randomly assigned for the special demonstration program. After they made their choice, however, compliance was nominally mandatory, although monetary sanctions were not imposed. For this reason, the two Louisville programs are described as "mandatory and voluntary" in Table 3.1.

[8] In the Cook County WIN Demonstration, two program models were tested: one providing individual job search and the other a sequence of individual job search and unpaid work experience. Throughout this book, Cook County participation, impact, and cost findings are reported for the job search/work experience sequence.

[9] In the Virginia evaluation, the research design called for testing two program models: one providing a sequence of job search and unpaid work experience and the other a sequence of job search, unpaid work experience, and education or job skills training. In practice, the two experimental groups received fairly similar program services, and there were no statistically significant differences between them in welfare and employment outcomes. Thus, the participation, impact, and cost findings reported in this volume, as in the evaluation report, combine the results for the two experimental groups. (See Riccio et al., 1986.)

[10] In the San Diego I evaluation, two program models were tested: the Employment Preparation Program (EPP) and the Employment Preparation Program/Experimental Work Experience Program (EPP/EWEP). Throughout this book, San Diego I participation, impact, and cost findings are reported for the EPP/EWEP sequence of job search and unpaid work experience.

were operated in states with diverse AFDC benefit levels and administrative structures and under different local conditions. In addition, the programs themselves were quite varied along a number of dimensions, reflecting differences in resources, objectives, scale, and program design.

Program Goals. The programs in Arkansas, Cook County, and Virginia and the first San Diego program sought to get people into jobs and off welfare. The goal was job placement. The second San Diego program (SWIM) shared this goal but also had an explicit process objective: maximizing participation and imposing an ongoing obligation. In contrast, the Baltimore program sought to improve the long-term economic security of participants by improving their skills and placing them in better jobs with higher job retention, even at the cost of an initial longer stay on welfare. Finally, the West Virginia program stressed the value of work per se; this recognized the difficulty of any unsubsidized placements, given the extremely high unemployment rate in the state during the study period.

Targeted Population. Five of the programs targeted the typical WIN-mandatory caseload (applicants and recipients with children age 6 or over, plus AFDC-UPs, where applicable);[11] Arkansas extended this to women with children age 3 or older; the first San Diego program limited this to AFDC applicants. There were also some differences in the coverage of the samples across the different studies, which should be considered in comparing participation rates and impacts.[12]

Scale. The programs differed widely in scale. West Virginia, Virginia, Arkansas, Cook County, and San Diego I (for applicants only) sought to

---

[11] Since some of the programs were already operating before the start of random assignment, the study samples usually were composed of applicants and new mandatories (e.g., people whose youngest child turned 6 years of age during the study period).

[12] For example, the Arkansas, Baltimore, and Cook County samples included all WIN-mandatory applicants and those recipients who were newly determined to be WIN-mandatory following the start of random assignment (generally because their youngest child had turned 6 years old). The San Diego I study contained all WIN-mandatory applicants *except* those who, at the time of application, were employed part- or full-time, were refugees, or were monolingual in a language other than English or Spanish. The San Diego SWIM study consisted of all WIN-mandatory applicants, recipients who were newly determined to be WIN-mandatory following the start of random assignment, and recipients who were currently mandatory and renewing their registration. The Virginia sample also consisted of all WIN-mandatory applicants and recipients (including those currently mandatory) except those who, at the time of random assignment, were active or already scheduled to be active in the ESP program, had previously been in the ESP program, or were in full-time non-ESP education or training. The West Virginia sample contained all WIN-mandatory applicants and recipients (including those not newly mandatory) except

include everyone in the targeted population who resided in the areas where the program operated, with the exception of members of the control group.[13] As a result, in contrast to earlier studies, these were evaluations of full-scale WIN programs that were implemented under normal operating procedures. San Diego's SWIM program was also implemented at full scale in two of the largest offices in the county (while the other five offices continued to operate the San Diego I approach). Baltimore was the most constrained, with a program that could serve about 1,000 new enrollees per year, drawn at random from eligibles in about half of the city.

In addition, San Diego SWIM for AFDCs and AFDC-UPs, and the AFDC-UP component of the West Virginia project, were specially funded to test the feasibility of imposing an open-ended participation requirement on as many people as possible. While the other sites also sought to reach everyone in the targeted population, they often did not have the funds or the active mandate to maximize participation rates.

In all of these studies, because random assignment occurred at either the welfare or welfare employment program office, the programs' impacts were estimated across everyone in the targeted population – i.e., the full WIN-mandatory caseload, all applicants (in San Diego I), or a cross section of 1,000 applicants and recipients (in Baltimore) – rather than for the smaller number who actually received services.

Average Cost. The programs differed widely in average net cost (the operating agency's average cost per enrolled experimental minus its cost

---

those who, at the time of random assignment, were employed part- or full-time or in full-time school or training.

The two Louisville experiments involved females newly registering with WIN during the study periods (those who were new mandatories and those who volunteered), including both applicants and recipients. The Louisville Immediate (Individual) Job Search Assistance Experiment sample contained all people in this group except for the 24 percent who, at the time of random assignment, were employed or in school or training and not interested in looking for a job or the very small number who refused to participate in the study. The Louisville Group Job Search study had less broad coverage, since it screened out women who were unlikely to participate. Overall, about 56 percent of all new female WIN registrants were excluded from the sample because they refused to participate in the program and the study, had personal or family medical problems, were in school or training full-time, or were employed full-time. In other studies, many of these people would have been included in the sample and possibly deferred from participation. (See Wolfhagen, 1983, Appendix D.)

[13] That is, within the study counties, and in West Virginia and Virginia also throughout the state, all WIN-mandatories were required to participate, with the exception of members of the control group.

for the average control) from a low of less than $200 per targeted eligible person in Arkansas and Cook County – which used only their regular WIN funds and could provide only minimal services[14] – to a high of more than $900 per eligible in SWIM and Baltimore. Gross costs (the cost of all services provided to members of the experimental group, including program operating costs, support services and allowance costs, and the costs of registrant-initiated education and training not provided directly by the program) were somewhat higher, ranging from $162 and $421 in Arkansas and Cook County, respectively, to $1,545 per targeted AFDC eligible in SWIM.[15] Many state JOBS budgets are likely to have resources per targeted case that fall within this range.

The studies of the seven programs also differed in the requirements imposed upon and services offered to members of the control groups. In Arkansas, Cook County, San Diego SWIM, and Virginia, controls were excused from WIN participation requirements and services except, depending on the program, registration, orientation, assessment, or allowances and support services. In San Diego I, Baltimore, and West Virginia, controls were treated as mandatory registrants in the "regular" WIN program that had been operating at the site before the introduction of the more enriched programs (Options in Baltimore and EPP/EWEP in San Diego) or CWEP (in West Virginia). Because of these differences, the study results should be interpreted somewhat differently. The first four studies show the net impact of the new WIN or WIN Demonstration program, compared to controls who were not offered any particular services. In contrast, the San Diego I, Baltimore, and West Virginia studies, in effect, estimated the incremental impact of the new program over and above the relatively inactive WIN program then operating in those sites.[16]

Program Model: Duration. While all seven programs were mandatory – i.e., people could be sanctioned and lose some benefits if

---

[14] While Table 3.1 shows the Cook County and Arkansas programs as having similar nominal costs, the research team involved in both studies concluded that lower staff salaries in Arkansas probably suggested that greater real program resources were available there.

[15] See Appendix A for further details. In particular, because of data limitations, the Arkansas gross cost estimates may not capture all the indirect program expenditures.

[16] In the two other completed broad-coverage studies – the Louisville Individual Job Search study and the Louisville Group Job Search study – controls received regular WIN services.

they refused to meet program requirements – five imposed obligations that usually lasted no more than four or five months. Only two – West Virginia and San Diego SWIM – actually mandated participation for as long as someone remained on welfare.

Program Model: Activities and Sequencing. West Virginia required recipients, in exchange for their benefits, to do unpaid work as part of the state's Community Work Experience Program (CWEP). (The requirement to work in exchange for welfare benefits is commonly referred to as "workfare.") The other programs imposed a participation rather than a work requirement. All of the programs except Baltimore used a fixed sequence starting with two to four weeks of job search, an activity in which a person is required to look for a job. This component of the programs reflected the general job search approach:

> Rather than training welfare recipients or developing specific jobs for them, such programs presume that with instruction, modest financial assistance, and some structure within which to operate, many welfare recipients will be able to find jobs and begin to support themselves through their own efforts. Individual job search programs supply job leads; participants assume much of the burden of job hunting and report back to their counselors on their efforts. Group job search programs generally begin with classes on job search techniques and then place participants in group settings where they make "cold calls" to prospective employers.[17]

Some of the programs (e.g., San Diego I and San Diego SWIM) used the group job search/job club technique and provided considerable assistance; in other cases (e.g., Cook County), aid was extremely minimal. If they did not find employment, program registrants might next be required to work for up to three months in an unpaid work experience position in a public or private nonprofit agency, where the monthly work hours usually equaled the grant divided by the minimum wage. (This requirement was strictly enforced in the two programs in San Diego, and much less so in Arkansas, Chicago, and Virginia. As a result, as shown in Table 4.1, only a minority of participants moved from job search into

---

[17] Goldman, 1989, p. 390.

work experience.) After this, in Arkansas, Chicago, Virginia, and San Diego I, the participation requirement ended.[18]

With the variations noted, the Arkansas, Chicago, San Diego I, Virginia, and West Virginia programs represented an Option 1 choice of low-cost services, using the categories presented in Chapter 2's section on "Funding for the Program." The other two broad-coverage programs reflected an Option 3 mixed strategy, and thus came closer to meeting the vision in the JOBS legislation. While job search remained the largest single activity, these two programs included some more intensive services. These programs also reflected the main JOBS alternatives for deciding how to allocate and target intensive services. In San Diego SWIM, services were provided in a fixed sequence, with assessment and referral to education and training required and reserved for those who did not find employment as a result of initial job search followed by work experience. In contrast, Baltimore used a process of assessment, case manager guidance, and client choice to determine how people were assigned to a variety of employment-directed services provided by the CETA/JTPA program: job search, unpaid work experience, or a range of short- or longer-term education and training activities.[19]

In Baltimore, as a result, as distinct from the other six programs except SWIM, a substantial share (one-fifth) of enrollees received education and training, which included classes designed to introduce them to the world of work, tutoring, adult basic education, preparation for the GED (General Educational Development) test, and classroom-based job skills training (see Table 4.1). These activities varied in length, from one or two weeks in the world-of-work sessions to 18 months in some training programs, with average participation of about 19 weeks for the 14 percent of

---

[18] Some of these programs called for "recycling" through the components for those who did not find jobs. In Virginia, for example, registrants were to be reassessed after each component or at least every 90 days; however, persons who were employed part-time or were enrolled in long-term training activities were to be reassessed every six months. In one version of Virginia's program (see Table 3.1), people were supposed to go into education and training after unpaid work experience. However, the study found that the program caused little increase in participation in these activities. Thus, in practice, the Virginia model was also a job search/work experience program.

[19] The Baltimore program was managed by the Office of Manpower Resources – the local CETA prime sponsor (which subsequently became the JTPA Service Delivery Area).

registrants who were in activities other than world-of-work or tutoring (Friedlander et al., 1985a).[20]

Ten studies of broad-coverage welfare-to-work programs are in progress. These should prove particularly relevant to JOBS administrators, since they include programs that are multi-component, serve women with younger children, or operate under JOBS regulations. Most studies test mandatory programs, but two of them examine broad-coverage voluntary initiatives.

For example, California's GAIN program requires people to participate in a range of services, starting with education for those who score poorly on a test, lack a high school diploma or GED, or are not proficient in English. Others receive job search training and other services. Florida's Project Independence provides up-front job search for more job-ready enrollees, and assessment followed by a range of services for others. The Pennsylvania Saturation Work Program (PSWP) shares some of the features of San Diego's SWIM program, since it was also funded as a special demonstration to test the maximum feasible participation in program services. The evaluations of Massachusetts' ET, Ohio's Transitions to Independence, and New Jersey's REACH programs focus on multi-component initiatives that allocate services based on a more comprehensive assessment. Washington's FIP program goes beyond the usual welfare-to-work services and restructures work incentives and transitional services. The California, Pennsylvania, and Ohio evaluations include only AFDC applicants and recipients with school-age children (and AFDC-UPs), but the Florida, Massachusetts, New Jersey, and Washington studies also include welfare recipients with younger children.

Three other broad-coverage studies are listed. The Riverside Case Management study tests the impact and cost-effectiveness of GAIN services offered through regular or enriched case management. (Enriched case management is defined in this study as an increased staff-to-client ratio.) The goal of this differential impact study is to determine both the program's overall impact, and whether enhanced case management

---

[20] The substantial nature of the education program in Baltimore is reflected in the high average costs: $2,360 per experimental assigned to education or job skills training (Friedlander et al., 1985a). Further, the Baltimore program – as with SWIM and West Virginia – was designed to require continuous participation as long as someone remained on welfare; however, this was not, in fact, implemented.

improves program results. The Food Stamp Employment and Training Program requires participation in a range of services by Food Stamp recipients who are not required to participate in WIN or JOBS programs. The Illinois Early Access program focuses on AFDC recipients with children age 3 to 5 in one county, and evaluates mandatory welfare-to-work services for this new JOBS population.

Selective-Voluntary Programs

This category includes selective-voluntary programs that do not seek to serve as broad a group in the AFDC caseload, including large-scale programs such as the JTPA system and smaller demonstration programs such as the Minority Female Single Parent (MFSP) program and the National Supported Work Demonstration. By nature, these programs serve a group of people who are motivated to seek out services and, sometimes, screened to meet program eligibility and other standards. Such programs are usually substantially more expensive[21] and tend to be operated on a smaller scale than broad-coverage programs. They have thus been able to offer more complex, comprehensive services.

Selective-voluntary programs are components within welfare-to-work systems, and the studies provide valuable information on the pay-off of providing particular services to groups within the welfare caseload who are interested in and seek to receive the services. They also provide lessons relevant to JOBS' new emphasis on targeting and intensive services. In some cases, these studies are directly relevant to the likely scale of these components in state JOBS programs; in others, they were special, multi-site, small-scale demonstrations of programs that could be expanded as specifically targeted components of broader JOBS initiatives.[22] In addition, the findings are relevant to JOBS programs that recruit welfare recipients to participate in various voluntary components; this "brokering" approach to JOBS may resemble the recruitment processes used in the evaluations of voluntary welfare-to-work programs.

---

[21] The average unit cost of selective-voluntary programs may exceed the average unit cost of broad-coverage programs for two reasons: First, the selective-voluntary programs may provide more expensive services; second, since they serve only volunteers, they may have very high rates of service utilization. Thus, if the services in these programs were provided in JOBS, the cost per targeted person would be lower than in the demonstrations.

[22] If these test programs are substantially expanded or retargeted under JOBS, it would be important to determine whether the results from the small-scale demonstrations could be replicated.

**TABLE 3.2   EVALUATION STUDIES RELATED TO JOBS:
SELECTIVE-VOLUNTARY PROGRAMS**

	AFDC Homemaker-Home Health Aide Demonstrations	Maine OJT	National Supported Work Demonstration
Start Date[a]	1983	1983	1976
Major Program Activities	Home health aide training and subsidized employment	Sequence of employability training, unpaid work experience, and subsidized on-the-job training	Structured, paid work experience
Net Cost[b]	$9,505 ($5,957-$12,457 across states) [$5,684][c]	$2,019 [$1,635][c]	$17,981 [$9,447][c,d] (1985 $)
Mandatory or Voluntary	Voluntary	Voluntary	Voluntary
Target Groups	AFDC recipients for at least 90 days and not employed as home health aide during that time, with children of any age	Unemployed AFDC recipients on welfare for at least prior 6 months, with children of any age	AFDC recipients on welfare for 30 of prior 36 months with children 6 or older, unemployed with limited recent work experience
Research Design	Random assignment, net impact	Random assignment, net impact	Random assignment, net impact
Study Scale	70 sites in 7 states	Statewide	7 sites
Length of Follow-Up[e]	33 months after the end of program participation	33 months	27 months (plus supplemental follow-up averaging 33 months)
Outcomes Measured	Employment, earnings, job characteristics, welfare receipt and payments	Employment, earnings, welfare receipt and payments	Employment, earnings, hours worked, wage rates, welfare receipt and payments, total income, child care use
Impact Findings[f] (or Date Expected)	Increased employment in 4 states; increased earnings in 5; increased wage rates in 4; increased hours of work in 4; reduced AFDC and Food Stamp payments in 4; no effect on Medicaid	Increased employment and earnings; no reductions in welfare receipt and payments	Increased earnings, hours worked, wage rates; decreased welfare receipt and payments; no impact on total income; increased use of child care[g]

(continued)

101

TABLE 3.2 *(continued)*

	New Jersey OJT	Minority Female Single Parent Demonstration	National JTPA Study
Start Date[a]	1984	1984	1987
Major Program Activities	Subsidized on-the-job training	Education, job skills training, employability training, counseling, child care, other support services	JTPA services, including job search, job skills training, on-the-job training
Net Cost[b]	$787 [$439][c]	$2,679-$4,824 (gross cost) across sites	N/A
Mandatory or Voluntary	Voluntary	Voluntary	Voluntary
Target Groups	AFDC recipients over 18 with children of any age	Minority single mothers with children of any age; 72% on AFDC or other public assistance at baseline	Economically disadvantaged adults and out-of-school youths
Research Design	Random assignment, net impact	Random assignment, net impact	Random assignment, net impact
Study Scale	9 of 21 counties	4 sites[h]	16 service delivery areas
Length of Follow-Up[e]	24 months	60 months	30 months
Outcomes Measured	Employment, earnings, welfare receipt and payments	Employment, earnings, job characteristics, welfare receipt and payments, family formation, home environment, educational attainment, child care use	Employment, earnings, household income, welfare receipt, family composition, educational attainment, criminal behavior
Impact Findings[f] (or Date Expected)	No effect on employment; increased earnings; reduced welfare payments	At 12 months: increased employment, earnings, hours worked, wage rates at 1 site;[h] increased welfare receipt and payments at 1; increased GED attainment at all sites. Interim, 1990, 1991; final, 1993	Interim, 1991; final, 1992

(continued)

TABLE 3.2 *(continued)*

	New York State Comprehensive Employment Opportunity Support Centers (CEOSC)
Start Date[a]	1988
Major Program Activities	Assessment followed by pre-employment training, job skills training, education, job search assistance, support services including on-site child care
Net Cost[b]	N/A
Mandatory or Voluntary	Voluntary
Target Groups	AFDC recipients with children under 6
Research Design	Random assignment, net impact at 1 site; comparison group design at 2 sites
Study Scale	3 sites
Length of Follow-Up[e]	24 months
Outcomes Measured	Employment, earnings, welfare receipt and payments
Impact Findings[f] (or Date Expected)	1991 (comparison group); 1992 (random assignment)

(continued)

TABLE 3.2 *(continued)*

NOTES: The programs are organized alphabetically within two categories: completed evaluations beginning with the AFDC Homemaker-Home Health Aide Demonstrations, and those still in progress, beginning with the Minority Female Single Parent Demonstration.

[a]The start date refers to the start of intake for the research sample.

[b]The costs reported are per experimental unless otherwise noted. All net costs are in nominal dollars except for the costs of the National Supported Work Demonstration, which are in 1985 dollars These net cost estimates include all expenditures by the operating agency specifically for the programs under study, as well as any expenditures by other organizations for services that were considered an essential part of the program treatment. However, the costs to operating agencies and to other organizations of serving members of the control groups have been subtracted in order to arrive at the *net* cost estimates. See Appendix A for further discussion.

[c]The bracketed figure excludes wage subsidy payments for participants, whereas the other figure includes them.

[d]Supported Work projects generated revenues of $4,352 per experimental (in 1985 dollars), which offset part of the cost reported here.

[e]The follow-up period refers to the longest amount of follow-up available, although it may not apply to all groups or all measures in the study.

[f]For the most part, only statistically significant impacts are reported. In a few cases, however findings may reflect impacts that are consistent through the follow-up period, but not statistically significant in the final months of follow-up. In multi-year studies, impacts are based on the final year of follow-up. In programs that tested the effects of subsidized employment, the impacts are for the post-demonstration period.

[g]Because the Supported Work impact sample is not consistent for all years of follow-up, the findings reflect estimates from different samples and follow-up periods.

[h]Each of the four Minority Female Single Parent (MFSP) Demonstration sites is a community-based organization. One of the four, the Center for Employment Training (CET), operated MFSP in several northern California locations, but is referred to here as a single site. CET is the MFSP operator that was found to produce statistically significant 12-month impacts on employment, earnings, hours worked, and wage rates.

104

The section on "Estimating Impacts for Broad-Coverage and Selective-Voluntary Programs" in Chapter 2 discussed some of the methodological reasons for caution in comparing results across selective-voluntary and broad-coverage studies. These relate to the different research designs (even when both use random assignment) that follow from the fact that one group of studies is of voluntary programs, while the other is of programs that are usually mandatory. In particular, participants in selective-voluntary programs may differ from the caseload in broad-coverage studies in a variety of ways that affect measured program impacts. For example, they may be more motivated, more likely to use program services, and less burdened by barriers to participation such as child care or family problems.[23] However, some selective-voluntary programs have explicitly targeted highly disadvantaged populations. For example, AFDC participants in Supported Work averaged 8.5 years on welfare at enrollment, suggesting that voluntary programs can succeed in reaching very hard-to-serve groups.

This group of studies provides important information to JOBS administrators, which can complement the lessons from the broad-coverage studies. Some of these evaluations, for example, provide findings for subgroups of AFDC recipients who were not assigned to broad-coverage, mandatory participation programs under the WIN regulations (women on AFDC whose youngest child was between 1 and 6 years old) or who may not benefit from lower-cost services (e.g., people who have received welfare for many years). Others offer reliable estimates of the impact of more expensive services that will always be provided on a relatively limited scale. Finally, these studies also provide useful information on program operations, costs, and outcomes.

Two of the evaluations of selective-voluntary programs provide information on the impact of subsidized on-the-job training (OJT) programs for welfare recipients and were implemented as full-scale components of state WIN Demonstration programs: the studies in Maine and New Jersey.[24] In New Jersey, job developers identified and screened

---

[23] These factors also mean, however, that members of the control group in selective-voluntary programs may be more likely to receive alternative services in the community, which would make the estimates of program impacts more conservative.

[24] While a number of other studies of OJT programs funded through the diversion of AFDC grants were conducted during the 1980s, they did not include rigorous evaluations or large study samples.

active WIN registrants and sought to place them in OJT positions with local employers, primarily in the private sector. Enrollees were hired on a trial basis for up to six months, with the understanding that individuals who performed satisfactorily would be retained as regular full-time employees. The state reimbursed employers for half the wages paid to OJT employees during the trial period. In Maine, carefully screened enrollees were offered a prescribed sequence of activities that included: first, two to five weeks of pre-vocational training that stressed personal growth as well as job-seeking and job-holding skills; second, for those not judged ready for OJT, up to 12 weeks of 20-hour-per-week unpaid work experience in the public or nonprofit sector; and, finally, placement in jobs, primarily in the private sector, where employers were subsidized for 50 percent of the wages for up to six months. The three-phase program sought to help single mothers obtain jobs that paid more than the minimum wage and offered opportunities for advancement.[25]

The National Supported Work Demonstration provided very disadvantaged AFDC recipients with subsidized employment and related monitoring and support designed to improve basic work habits and skills. Supported Work offered highly structured, full-time work experience positions (paying approximately the minimum wage) for up to a year or 18 months (depending on the site) under conditions of gradually increasing demands, close supervision, and peer group support. Supported Work was operated by nonprofit corporations, which established small factories or work crews structured to provide worksites for crews of AFDC recipients, ex-addicts, ex-offenders, and young high school dropouts. Supported Work crews produced goods and services the sales of which generated revenues that partly offset project costs. Examples included the manufacture and sale of office furniture, house painting, operation of a gas station, and janitorial services. Supported Work wages, as was the case with earnings from OJT positions in Maine and New Jersey, were treated similarly to any unsubsidized income in terms of their effect on reducing AFDC and Medicaid benefits received by the participants.

---

[25] Because the New Jersey and Maine programs were components within the states' WIN systems and because of the nature of program recruitment, controls received substantial WIN services, costing between $410 and $660 per control. These control costs included the regular WIN administrative expenses for processing mandatory cases, which are not included in the costs of the specific selective-voluntary programs that are components within those systems. (See Appendix A.)

The AFDC Homemaker-Home Health Aide Demonstrations tested the feasibility of training AFDC recipients to assist functionally impaired people in their own homes. Implemented in seven states, the model called for trainees to receive four to eight weeks of formal training followed by up to a year of subsidized employment, generally with established public and private nonprofit home care agencies such as those certified under Medicare. During the period of subsidized employment, trainees remained covered by Medicaid and received work-related support services; their wages were comparable to those paid to other such workers. The Health Care Financing Administration of HHS was the lead agency charged with implementing the demonstrations.

The National JTPA Study will evaluate the varied approaches to job preparation that are offered by JTPA contractors. Two other selective-voluntary demonstrations, the Minority Female Single Parent (MFSP) Demonstration and New York's Comprehensive Employment Opportunity Support Centers (CEOSC) program, test approaches that provide comprehensive services, including education, job skills training, employability training, and support services. Among the participants in the MFSP Demonstration are some women with children under age 6, while the CEOSC program exclusively targets AFDC recipients with preschool children. Because women with preschool children are not included in most of the evaluations of broad-coverage, mandatory welfare-to-work programs, these studies are of particular interest. State JOBS programs will cover welfare recipients whose youngest child is age 3 (or, at state option, age 1) and may provide education and training services similar to those provided in MFSP and CEOSC.

Education Services

Several welfare-to-work programs have included significant education activities in the package of services they provide to participants. GAIN emphasizes up-front education for those who lack a high school diploma or GED, are not proficient in English, or fail a basic skills test. SWIM provided education for some participants after they completed a work experience component. Virginia's Employment Services Program (ESP) referred some participants to education providers. The MFSP Demonstration provided a mixture of education and job skills training to participants. Florida's Project Independence assigns to education some

TABLE 3.3 EVALUATION STUDIES RELATED TO JOBS: EDUCATION SERVICES

	Job Corps Computer-Assisted Instruction Evaluation	SIME/DIME Manpower Experiment
Start Date[a]	1987	1970
Major Program Activities	Substitution of some computer-assisted instruction for regular classroom instruction	Test of 50% and 100% subsidies of education, job skills training, and related child care; vocational counseling
Net Cost	N/A	N/A
Mandatory or Voluntary	Voluntary	Voluntary
Target Groups	Job Corps members; 31% female, 7% parents, 31% from families on public assistance	Low-income persons 16-58 in families with at least 1 child, who were capable of employment, and who were in the Negative Income Tax Experiment
Research Design	Random assignment, net impact	Random assignment, net and differential impacts
Study Scale	10 Job Corps Centers	Research samples in Seattle and Denver
Length of Follow-Up[b]	4 months (average) from pre-test to post-test	6 years
Outcomes Measured	GED test scores, TABE subtest scores, GED attainment, attendance, length of stay in Job Corps	Employment, earnings, participation in education and training
Impact Findings[c] (or Date Expected)	No impacts, except for a small increase in GED class attendance	No consistent impacts on employment or earnings; for single female heads of families, impact on community college attendance of up to 1 college quarter

NOTES: [a]The start date refers to the start of intake for the research sample.

[b]The follow-up period refers to the longest amount of follow-up available, although it may not apply to all groups or all measures in the study.

[c]Only statistically significant impacts are reported.

108

participants who, it is determined, are not job-ready. These programs demonstrate the feasibility of including education in a welfare-to-work program, and provide information on participation in education activities. The evaluations of these programs use net impact designs, which compare the employment, earnings, and welfare receipt outcomes for those targeted for the treatment services – including services other than education – to the outcomes for those in the control groups. This net impact design does not provide a specific test of the effectiveness of education services because the effects of education are not separated from the effects of other services. Therefore, these studies and their findings are discussed elsewhere (see the sections on "Broad-Coverage Programs" and "Selective-Voluntary Programs" in this chapter). Learnfare programs and programs using education and other services to serve young welfare recipients are discussed in the next section, "Youth-Oriented Services."

The GAIN evaluation will include a study of the program's literacy impacts. It will focus on experimentals and controls who met GAIN criteria for being "in need of education" at the time of random assignment (see above). A literacy test will be administered to a sample of these persons two years after they were randomly assigned. This study will measure the effect of GAIN on educational achievement. In addition, the impact of GAIN on registrants' attainment of educational credentials (the GED or a high school diploma) will be measured for this sample. This research will begin the process of understanding how the educational impacts of broad-coverage programs are related to their economic impacts. However, the complexity of this issue calls for considerable additional research, including differential impact studies that directly compare the economic effects of programs that emphasize education to those that do not.

Two studies have used a differential impact design specifically to measure the effectiveness of education services. They are described in Table 3.3. In the Job Corps Computer-Assisted Instruction Evaluation, Job Corps members were randomly assigned to receive instruction in basic academic skills and GED preparation either in traditional classroom settings or in settings that used a significant amount of computer-assisted instruction. In the Seattle-Denver Income Maintenance Experiment's (SIME/DIME) Manpower Experiment, the volunteer participants were randomly assigned to groups that were offered a 100 percent subsidy of their education and training expenditures, a 50 percent subsidy of those expenditures, or no subsidy. These evaluations provide the only experimental studies of related programs that are specifically focused on education services. However, the synthesis of research presented in Chapter 5 also draws on the evaluations of broad-coverage and selective-voluntary adult- and youth-oriented programs whose findings are relevant to understanding the role of education in welfare-to-work programs.

Youth-Oriented Services

Programs that serve young people who are welfare recipients are not, properly speaking, welfare-to-work programs. Their goals include preventing dropping out of school, returning teens to school, and providing additional education and/or training to dropouts. Education plays a larger role in these programs than in the broad-coverage welfare-to-work programs discussed earlier, and job search has less prominence. Some of these programs also provide instruction in parenting skills because many young welfare recipients are the mothers of infants. Given these diverse goals, the outcomes measured in evaluations of youth-oriented programs often include educational attainment as well as employment and earnings.

The studies summarized in Table 3.4 include evaluations of broad-coverage, mandatory programs that include aspects of "learnfare" (Ohio's Learning, Earning, and Parenting [LEAP] Program and the Teenage Parent Demonstration) for young AFDC mothers, and selective-voluntary, comprehensive service models for males and females (Job Corps and JOBSTART) as well as teen mothers (Project Redirection and New Chance). With their focus on mandatory education and other services for teenage parents on AFDC, the ongoing Ohio LEAP and Teenage Parent Demonstration evaluations are directly relevant to JOBS, since school attendance is likely to be the sole JOBS activity for most custodial parents under age 20 who have not completed high school. The Teenage Parent Demonstration will also provide information on the effects of job skills training and job search for older teens. Its education activities include a life skills instruction component. Project Redirection, which has been completed, provides evidence about the effects of a voluntary program model that coordinated an array of services – education, parenting instruction, and employability training – to teen mothers age 17 or younger. The ongoing New Chance Demonstration is targeted to older teens and is more comprehensive in scope, including more emphasis on counseling, case management, and occupational

**TABLE 3.4 EVALUATION STUDIES RELATED TO JOBS:
YOUTH-ORIENTED SERVICES**

	Job Corps	Project Redirection	JOBSTART
Start Date[a]	1977	1980	1985
Major Program Activities	Education, job skills training, job placement, support services, health care, in a residential setting	Education, health and parenting education, family planning, other services	Education, job skills training, job placement, support services
Net Cost[b]	$5,735 per enrollee	$3,540 per participant	N/A
Mandatory or Voluntary	Voluntary	Voluntary	Voluntary
Target Groups	Economically disadvantaged youths 16-21; 42% of females were in families receiving cash welfare prior to enrollment	Teen mothers or pregnant teens, 17 or younger, on AFDC, without high school diploma or GED	Dropouts 17-21, reading below eighth-grade level, JTPA eligible; 50% of females on AFDC at baseline
Research Design	Comparison group, net impact	Matched-sites comparison group, net impact	Random assignment, net impact
Study Scale	One-third of residential Job Corps enrollees	4 sites	13 sites
Length of Follow-Up[c]	54 months	60 months	Approximately 48 months
Outcomes Measured	Employment, earnings, welfare receipt, enrollment in further education or training, military service, criminal behavior, health	Employment, earnings, welfare receipt, educational attainment, household income, parenting skills, child outcomes, fertility	Employment, earnings, educational attainment, welfare receipt, family formation, criminal behavior
Impact Findings[d] (or Date Expected)	Increased employment and earnings; reduced welfare receipt; increased educational attainment; a shift from more to less serious crimes; improved health	Increased employment and earnings; decreased welfare receipt; no effect on educational attainment or household income; positive parenting and child impacts; increase in live births	At 12 months: decreased employment and earnings; increased educational attainment; no impact on welfare receipt. Final, 1993

(continued)

TABLE 3.4 *(continued)*

	New Chance	Ohio LEAP	Teenage Parent Demonstration
Start Date[a]	1989	1989	1987
Major Program Activities	Education, employability training, job skills training, work internship, family planning and health education, health services, parenting education, life skills training, counseling, job placement, on-site child care in most sites	Required school attendance, financial incentives and penalties, case management, child care, transportation, guaranteed summer job	Education, job skills training, job search, life skills instruction, support services, child support enforcement
Net Cost[b]	N/A	N/A	N/A
Mandatory or Voluntary	Voluntary; in some states will meet JOBS participation requirement	Mandatory	Mandatory
Target Groups	AFDC recipients 17-21 who gave birth as teens and are dropouts, with children of any age	Custodial parents on AFDC, under 19, without high school diploma or GED, with children of any age	Teenage AFDC recipients who have 1 child of any age or are pregnant with first child
Research Design	Random assignment, net impact	Random assignment, net impact	Random assignment, net impact
Study Scale	16 sites	12 of 88 counties[e]	2 sites in New Jersey; 1 in Illinois
Length of Follow-Up[c]	36 months	24-48 months	24 months
Outcomes Measured	Employment, earnings, educational attainment and achievement, welfare receipt, fertility, parenting skills, child outcomes	Employment, earnings, welfare receipt, educational attainment, health, family formation, attitudes	Employment, earnings, welfare receipt, educational attainment and achievement, family formation, establishment of paternity and child support, parenting skills
Impact Findings[d] (or Date Expected)	Interim, 1993; final, 1995	Interim, 1992; final, 1995	Interim, 1990; final, 1992

(continued)

112

TABLE 3.4 *(continued)*

NOTES: The programs are organized alphabetically within two categories: completed evaluations, beginning with Job Corps, and those still in progress, beginning with JOBSTART.

[a]The start date refers to the start of intake for the research sample.

[b]The costs reported are per experimental unless otherwise noted. These net cost estimates exclude the cost of any services that were also provided to members of the control group by the operating agency. The estimates are not strictly equivalent across studies, primarily due to differences in calculating the cost of services to controls.

[c]The follow-up period refers to the longest amount of follow-up available, although it may not apply to all groups or all measures in the study.

[d]For the most part, only statistically significant impacts are reported. In a few cases, however, findings may reflect impacts that are consistent through the follow-up period, but not statistically significant in the final months of follow-up. In multi-year studies, impacts are based on the final year of follow-up. In programs that tested the effects of subsidized employment, the impacts are for the post-demonstration period.

[e]The program operated statewide.

training. The evaluations of these last two programs measure outcomes for children as well as mothers. The Job Corps evaluation studied the effects of a model combining education and training with support services and job placement assistance at residential sites; the JOBSTART Demonstration – for which data are still being analyzed – provided similar services to a target population of young dropouts in nonresidential settings. All of these evaluations provide important information on the success of treatments intended to prevent long-term welfare receipt, a key goal of JOBS.

Support Services Tests

Welfare-to-work programs often provide support services that are intended to enable welfare recipients to participate in activities such as education, job search, and employment. These support services may include child care, medical benefits, transportation, information on family planning and life skills, counseling, and transitional benefits for a limited period after the welfare recipient becomes employed. Several rigorous evaluations have examined programs that randomly assigned participants to groups receiving different amounts of support services. Such studies are the only source of experimental research on the effects of support services on welfare recipients' subsequent employment, earnings, and welfare receipt.

In some of these studies, researchers measured the impacts of support services on both the mothers and their children. Research findings on child impacts have been carefully reviewed elsewhere (Polit and O'Hara, 1989; Brooks-Gunn, 1989). For this reason, and because this report is focused on the employment-related impacts of welfare-to-work programs, the impacts of support services on children are not discussed here.

The studies described in Table 3.5 examine three kinds of support services: child care, child-care-related instruction for new mothers, and transitional benefits. One study, the Expanded Child Care Options (ECCO) Demonstration, uses a differential impact design to compare the effects of child care available under New Jersey's JOBS program – REACH, plus up to one year of post-REACH transitional benefits – to two alternatives. To do this, participants will be randomly assigned to child care as it is normally available through REACH (and its transitional benefits) or to one of two alternatives: (1) child care paid for at REACH rates but available on a continuing basis, even after the participant leaves REACH, until the participant's youngest child enters first grade; or (2)

TABLE 3.5 EVALUATION STUDIES RELATED TO JOBS: SUPPORT SERVICES TESTS

	Abecedarian Project	Johns Hopkins Center for School-Aged Mothers	Nurse Home Visitation Program: Pregnancy/ Early Infancy
Start Date[a]	1972	N/A	1978
Major Program Activities	Free educational day care for children from birth to kindergarten entry	Comprehensive hospital-based program including education, social services, outreach	Nurse visits from child's birth until age 2, referrals to services, encouragement to resume school or work
Net Cost	N/A	N/A	N/A
Mandatory or Voluntary	Voluntary	Voluntary	Voluntary
Target Groups	Teenage mothers with risk factors: poverty, low education, mental retardation, psycho-social problems, etc.	Black teenage mothers with infants	First-time mothers under 19 or single or low SES, plus some other volunteers
Research Design	Random assignment, net impact	Hospital comparison group, net impact	Random assignment, net and differential impacts
Study Scale	29 families in 1 site	100 mothers in 1 site	400 mothers in 1 site
Length of Follow-Up[b]	54 months	24 months	46 months postpartum
Outcomes Measured	Maternal welfare receipt, maternal education, fertility	Maternal educational progress, fertility	Maternal school return, welfare receipt, employment, fertility
Impact Findings[c] (or Date Expected)	Less maternal welfare receipt; increased maternal school completion by experimentals; fewer subsequent births	Increased school persistence and gradu-ation; fewer repeat pregnancies	For poor single mothers: smaller or no impacts on schooling and welfare; 82% more months worked; 43% fewer pregnancies

(continued)

TABLE 3.5 *(continued)*

	Teenage Pregnancy Intervention Program	Expanded Child Care Options (ECCO) Demonstration	Illinois Career Advancement Demonstration
Start Date[a]	1979	1990	1989
Major Program Activities	Home visits providing child care instruction, training as nursery aides	Test of 3 programs: (1) high-quality developmental child care and parenting support until youngest child enters first grade; (2) regular-quality, welfare agency-subsidized child care until youngest child enters first grade; (3) regular-quality, welfare agency-subsidized child care while parent is in JOBS plus up to 1 transitional year	Payment for training-related expenses (transportation, child care, fees other than tuition), materials paid to $300
Net Cost	N/A	N/A	N/A
Mandatory or Voluntary	Voluntary	Mandatory (but child care is offered, not required)	Voluntary
Target Groups	Black teenage mothers with infants	AFDC recipients with a child under 3	Former welfare recipients earning less than 185% of standard of need
Research Design	Random assignment, net and differential impacts	Random assignment, net and differential impacts	Random assignment, net impact
Study Scale	120 mothers in 1 site	1,800 families in urban New Jersey	Statewide
Length of Follow-Up[b]	24 months	15 years or more	60 months
Outcomes Measured	Repeat pregnancies, return to school or work	Maternal employment, earnings, welfare receipt and payments, use of education and training, use of child care	Employment, earnings, welfare receipt and payments, Medicaid receipt, Food Stamps
Impact Findings[c] (or Date Expected)	Training reduced repeat pregnancies and speeded return to school or work; home visits had similar, but smaller, impacts	N/A	N/A

(continued)

TABLE 3.5 *(continued)*

	Memphis Nurse Home Visitation Program	Montgomery County, Ohio, Demonstration	North Carolina Guaranteed Child Care Demonstration
Start Date[a]	1990	1989	1988
Major Program Activities	Test of 2 programs: nurse visits for group 1 during pregnancy, for group 2 until child is 2; referrals to services; encouragement to resume school or work	Transitional Medicaid and child care (effective 4/1/90, controls also could receive these services); mandatory assessment; access to employment-related activities	Offer of a guarantee of transitional child care, compared to transitional child care on a space-available basis
Net Cost	N/A	N/A	N/A
Mandatory or Voluntary	Voluntary	Mandatory	Voluntary
Target Groups	Disadvantaged first-time mothers; oversampling women under 18	AFDC recipients with children under 6	AFDC recipients with children 1-5
Research Design	Random assignment, net and differential impacts	Random assignment, net impact	Random assignment, net impact
Study Scale	Over 1,400 mothers in Memphis	1 county	1 county
Length of Follow-Up[b]	24 months postpartum	48 months	12 months
Outcomes Measured	Maternal education, employment, welfare receipt, Medicaid, Food Stamps, fertility, health habits, infant care, service use	Employment, earnings, job characteristics; welfare receipt, duration, and recidivism; Medicaid and child support payments, family formation	Employment, welfare receipt and payments
Impact Findings[c] (or Date Expected)	Reports: 1995, 1997, 1998	Interim, 1990, 1991, 1992; final, 1993	1990

(continued)

TABLE 3.5 *(continued)*

	Texas Transitional Child Care and Medicaid Study	Wisconsin Income Disregard and Transitional Medical Benefits Study
Start Date[a]	1989	N/A
Major Program Activities	Offer of extended transitional child care and Medicaid benefits for those who become employed (effective 4/1/90, controls also could receive these services)	Test of incentives for leaving welfare: 1 year of extended Medicaid eligibility for those who become employed vs. a revised income disregard for those who become employed while on welfare vs. status quo (effective 4/1/90, FSA transitional benefits were made available to all persons affected by the research)
Net Cost	N/A	N/A
Mandatory or Voluntary	Mandatory	Mandatory
Target Groups	AFDC applicants and recipients (age of youngest child not specified)	Current and new AFDC recipients with children 3 months or older
Research Design	Random assignment, net impact	Random assignment, differential impact
Study Scale	Statewide; 90,000 applicants and recipients offered 12 months of transitional benefits; 10,000 applicants and recipients offered 4 months of transitional benefits; both groups offered 12 months of transitional benefits effective 4/1/90	N/A
Length of Follow-Up[b]	36 months	N/A
Outcomes Measured	Employment, earnings, child care use and cost, welfare receipt, payments, and recidivism	Employment, earnings, welfare receipt and payments, Medicaid receipt, job retention
Impact Findings[c] (or Date Expected)	1993	N/A

(continued)

TABLE 3.5 *(continued)*

NOTES: The programs are organized alphabetically within two categories: completed evaluations, beginning with the Abecedarian Project, and those still in progress, beginning with the Expanded Child Care Options (ECCO) Demonstration.

[a]The start date refers to the start of intake for the research sample.

[b]The follow-up period refers to the longest amount of follow-up available, although it may not apply to all groups or all measures in the study.

[c]Only statistically significant impacts are reported.

high-quality, developmental child care and parenting support, also until the youngest child enters first grade. Another study, the Abece-darian Project, measured the net impact of high-quality educational day care compared to the child care arrangements made by control group members.

Four studies examine the effects on mothers' employment of providing instruction to new mothers on child care and related issues. These studies use visiting nurses and hospital staff to help women learn how to gain access to child care and other resources that they need in order to return to school or work. These are net impact studies; members of the control group or comparison group do not have access to the child care instruction program.

Five states are currently completing random assignment studies of pre-FSA transitional support services for former AFDC recipients. In Illinois, a study is analyzing the effects of reimbursing some training-related expenses incurred by former welfare recipients who seek to upgrade their vocational skills. North Carolina offered a guaran-tee of access to transitional child care to persons leaving AFDC; the members of the control group received no guarantee, but were eligible to receive child care if slots were available. Studies in Texas and Ohio examine the effects of extending transitional child care and Medicaid. Wisconsin is conducting a comparison of two incentives to leave wel-fare: a change in the earned income disregard (permitting welfare recipients to remain on welfare and receive part of their welfare benefits for up to one year when they accept employment) and the provision of one year of extended Medicaid coverage for those who become em-ployed. When the FSA transitional benefits took effect on April 1, 1990, they were extended to cover all members of the experimental and control groups in these states.

References for Evaluation Studies Discussed in Chapter 3

Abecedarian Project
Campbell, Frances A.; Breitmayer, Bonnie; and Ramey, Craig T. 1986. "Disadvantaged Single Teenage Mothers and Their Children: Consequences of Free Educational Day Care." *Family Relations*, 35(1): 63-68.

AFDC Homemaker-Home Health Aide Demonstrations
Bell, Stephen H.; Burstein, Nancy R.; and Orr, Larry L. 1987. *Overview of Evaluation Results: Evaluation of the AFDC Homemaker-Home Health Aide Demonstrations*. Cambridge, Mass.: Abt Associates Inc.
Bell, Stephen H.; Enns, John H.; and Orr, Larry L. 1986. "The Effects of Job Training and Employment on the Earnings and Public Benefits of AFDC Recipients: The AFDC Homemaker-Home Health Aide Demonstrations." Draft. Paper presented at the Annual Research Conference of the Association for Public Policy Analysis and Management, Austin, Texas.
Bell, Stephen H.; and Orr, Larry L. 1988. "Screening (and Creaming?) Applicants to Job Training Programs: The AFDC Homemaker-Home Health Aide Demonstrations." Paper presented at the Annual Research Conference of the Association for Public Policy Analysis and Management, Seattle, Washington.
Cella, Margot. 1987. *Operational Costs of Demonstration Activities: Evaluation of the AFDC Homemaker-Home Health Aide Demonstrations*. Cambridge, Mass.: Abt Associates Inc.

Arkansas WORK Program
Friedlander, Daniel; Hoerz, Gregory; Quint, Janet; and Riccio, James. 1985b. *Arkansas: Final Report on the WORK Program in Two Counties*. New York: MDRC.

Baltimore Options
Friedlander, Daniel. 1987. *Maryland: Supplemental Report on the Baltimore Options Program*. New York: MDRC.
Friedlander, Daniel; Hoerz, Gregory; Long, David; and Quint, Janet. 1985a. *Maryland: Final Report on the Employment Initiatives Evaluation*. New York: MDRC.

California GAIN
Riccio, James; Goldman, Barbara; Hamilton, Gayle; Martinson, Karin; and Orenstein, Alan. 1989. *GAIN: Early Implementation Experiences and Lessons*. New York: MDRC.

Cook County WIN Demonstration
Friedlander, Daniel; Freedman, Stephen; Hamilton, Gayle; and Quint, Janet. 1987. *Illinois: Final Report on Job Search and Work Experience in Cook County*. New York: MDRC.

Expanded Child Care Options (ECCO) Demonstration
New Jersey Department of Human Services. 1989. *Child Care Plus: A Demonstration of Enhanced Child Care Options for Low-Income Families*. Draft Report. Trenton: New Jersey Department of Human Services. (ECCO was previously known as Child Care Plus.)

Florida Project Independence
Manpower Demonstration Research Corporation. 1989. Unpublished internal documents.

Food Stamp Employment and Training Program
Puma, Michael; Werner, Alan; and Hojnacki, Marjorie. 1988. *Evaluation of the Food Stamp Employment and Training Program: Report to Congress on Program Implementation.* Cambridge, Mass.: Abt Associates Inc.

Illinois Career Advancement Demonstration
Interagency Low Income Opportunity Advisory Board, Executive Office of the President. (no date). *Special Terms and Conditions.* Unpublished internal document.

Illinois Early Access Program
Interagency Low Income Opportunity Advisory Board, Executive Office of the President. (no date). *Special Terms and Conditions.* Unpublished internal document.

Job Corps
Mallar, Charles; Kerachsky, Stuart; Thornton, Craig; and Long, David. 1982. *Project Report: Evaluation of the Economic Impact of the Job Corps Program, Third Follow-Up Report.* Princeton, N.J.: Mathematica Policy Research, Inc.

Job Corps Computer-Assisted Instruction Evaluation
Shugoll Research; Battelle Human Affairs Research Centers; and Kearney/Centaur Division, A. T. Kearney, Inc. 1989. *Job Corps Computer-Assisted Instruction Pilot Project Evaluation.* Report prepared for the U.S. Department of Labor. Bethesda, Md.: Shugoll Research.

JOBSTART
Auspos, Patricia; Cave, George; Doolittle, Fred; and Hoerz, Gregory. 1989. *Implementing JOBSTART: A Demonstration for School Dropouts in the JTPA System.* New York: MDRC.

Johns Hopkins Center for School-Aged Mothers
Hardy, J. B.; King, T. M.; Shipp, D. A.; and Welcher, D. W. 1981. "A Comprehensive Approach to Adolescent Pregnancy." In K. G. Scott, T. Field, and E. Robertson, eds., *Teenage Parents and Their Offspring.* New York: Grune & Stratton.

Louisville WIN Laboratory Experiment: Group Job Search
Gould-Stuart, Joanna. 1982. *Welfare Women in a Group Job Search Program: Their Experiences in the Louisville WIN Research Laboratory Project.* New York: MDRC.
Wolfhagen, Carl. 1983. *Job Search Strategies: Lessons from the Louisville WIN Laboratory.* New York: MDRC.

Louisville WIN Laboratory Experiment: Individual Job Search
Goldman, Barbara. 1981. *Impacts of the Immediate Job Search Assistance Experiment.* New York: MDRC.
Wolfhagen, Carl. 1983. *Job Search Strategies: Lessons from the Louisville WIN Laboratory.* New York: MDRC.

Maine OJT
Auspos, Patricia; Cave, George; and Long, David. 1988. *Maine: Final Report on the Training Opportunities in the Private Sector Program.* New York: MDRC.

Massachusetts ET Choices
Nightingale, Demetra Smith; Burbridge, Lynn C.; Wissoker, Douglas; Bawden, Lee; Sonenstein, Freya L.; and Jeffries, Neal. 1989. *Experiences of Massachusetts ET Job Finders: Preliminary Findings.* Washington, D.C.: Urban Institute.

Memphis Nurse Home Visitation Program
Olds, David L.; Belton, Jann; Cole, Robert; Foye, Howard; Helberg, June; Henderson, Charles R., Jr.; James, David; Kitzman, Harriet; Phelps, Charles; Sweeney, Patrick; and Tatelbaum, Robert. (no date). *Nurse Home-Visitation for Mothers and Children: A Research Proposal.* Unpublished document. Rochester, N.Y.: New Mothers Study, Department of Pediatrics, University of Rochester.

Minority Female Single Parent Demonstration
Gordon, Anne; and Burghardt, John. 1990. *The Minority Female Single Parent Demonstration: Short-Term Economic Impacts.* New York: Rockefeller Foundation.

Montgomery County, Ohio, Demonstration
Bell, Stephen H.; and Fein, David J. Forthcoming. *Ohio Transitions to Independence Demonstration: Program Impacts in the First Fiscal Year.* Cambridge, Mass.: Abt Associates Inc.
Hollenbeck, Kevin; Hufnagle, John; and Kurth, Paula. 1990a. *Implementation of the JOBS Program in Ohio: A Process Study.* Second Annual Report. Columbus: Ohio State University, Center on Education and Training for Employment.
Hollenbeck, Kevin; Hufnagle, John; and Kurth, Paula. 1990b. *Implementation of the JOBS Program in Ohio: A Process Study.* First Annual Report. Columbus: Ohio State University, Center on Education and Training for Employment.

National JTPA Study
Bloom, Howard; Orr, Larry; Doolittle, Fred; Hotz, Joseph; and Barnow, Burt. 1990. *Design of the National JTPA Study.* Washington, D.C.: Abt Associates Inc. and MDRC.
Doolittle, Fred; and Traeger, Linda. 1990. *Implementing the National JTPA Study.* New York: MDRC.

National Supported Work Demonstration
Board of Directors, Manpower Demonstration Research Corporation. 1980. *Summary and Findings of the National Supported Work Demonstration.* New York: MDRC.

New Chance
Quint, Janet C.; and Guy, Cynthia A. 1989. *New Chance: Lessons from the Pilot Phase.* New York: MDRC.

New Jersey OJT
Freedman, Stephen; Bryant, Jan; and Cave, George. 1988. *New Jersey: Final Report on the Grant Diversion Project.* New York: MDRC.

New Jersey REACH
Mathematica Policy Research, Inc. 1988. *REACH Welfare Initiative Program Evaluation: Technical Proposal.* Princeton, N.J.: Mathematica Policy Research, Inc.

New York State Comprehensive Employment Opportunity Support Centers (CEOSC)
Werner, Alan; and Nutt-Powell, Bonnie. 1988. *Evaluation of the Comprehensive Employment Opportunity Support Centers, Vol. 1: Synthesis of Findings.* Cambridge, Mass.: Abt Associates Inc.

North Carolina Guaranteed Child Care Demonstration
North Carolina Department of Human Resources. (no date). *Child Care Recycling Fund Demonstration Project: Pretest and Evaluation.* Unpublished internal document.

Nurse Home Visitation Program: Pregnancy/Early Infancy
Olds, David L.; Henderson, Charles R., Jr.; Tatelbaum, Robert; and Chamberlin, Robert. 1988. "Improving the Life-Course Development of Socially Disadvantaged Mothers: A Randomized Trial of Nurse Home Visitation." *American Journal of Public Health*, 78(11): 1436-1445.

Ohio LEAP
Long, David; and Bloom, Dan. 1989. *Design of the Project Learn Evaluation*. Unpublished document prepared for the Ohio Department of Human Services. New York: MDRC. (LEAP was previously known as Project Learn.)

Ohio Transitions to Independence Evaluation
Bell, Stephen H.; Hamilton, William L.; and Burstein, Nancy R. 1989. *Ohio Transitions to Independence Evaluation: Design of the Cost-Benefit Analysis*. Cambridge, Mass.: Abt Associates Inc.

Pennsylvania Saturation Work Program
Hogarth, Suzanne; Martin, Roger; and Nazar, Kathleen. 1989. *Pennsylvania Saturation Work Program Impact Evaluation*. Draft Report. Harrisburg, Pa.: Department of Public Welfare.

Project Redirection
Polit, Denise; Quint, Janet; and Riccio, James. 1988. *The Challenge of Serving Teenage Mothers: Lessons from Project Redirection*. New York: MDRC.

Riverside, California, Case Management Study
Manpower Demonstration Research Corporation. 1988. *Research Design for a Special Study of Case Management in the Riverside County GAIN Program*. Unpublished internal document.

San Diego I (EPP/EWEP)
Goldman, Barbara; Friedlander, Daniel; and Long, David. 1986. *California: Final Report on the San Diego Job Search and Work Experience Demonstration*. New York: MDRC.

San Diego SWIM
Hamilton, Gayle; and Friedlander, Daniel. 1989. *Final Report on the Saturation Work Initiative Model in San Diego*. New York: MDRC.

SIME/DIME Manpower Experiment
Hall, Arden R. 1980. "Education and Training." In Philip K. Robins, Robert G. Spiegelman, Samuel Weiner, and Joseph G. Bell, eds., *A Guaranteed Annual Income: Evidence from a Social Experiment*. New York: Academic Press.
SRI International. 1983. *Final Report on the Seattle-Denver Income Maintenance Experiment, Volume 1: Design and Results*. Menlo Park, Ca.: SRI International.

Teenage Parent Demonstration
Hershey, A.; and Nagatoshi, C. 1989. *Implementing Services for Welfare Dependent Teenage Parents: Experiences in the DHHS/OFA Teenage Parent Demonstration*. Prepared for the Department of Health and Human Services. Princeton, N.J.: Mathematica Policy Research, Inc.

Teenage Pregnancy Intervention Program

Field, T.; Widmayer, S.; Greenberg, R.; and Stoller, S. 1982. "Effects of Parent Training on Teenage Mothers and Their Infants." *Pediatrics*, 69: 703-707.

Texas Transitional Child Care and Medicaid Study

Interagency Low Income Opportunity Advisory Board, Executive Office of the President. (no date). *Special Terms and Conditions*. Unpublished internal document.

Virginia ESP

Friedlander, Daniel. 1988a. "An Analysis of Extended Follow-Up for the Virginia Employment Services Program." Unpublished internal document. New York: MDRC.

Riccio, James; Cave, George; Freedman, Stephen; and Price, Marilyn. 1986. *Virginia: Final Report on the Employment Services Program*. New York: MDRC.

Washington FIP

Urban Institute. 1989. *Evaluation Design for the Family Independence Program: Third Draft.* Prepared for the Legislative Budget Committee, State of Washington. Washington, D.C.: Urban Institute.

West Virginia CWEP

Friedlander, Daniel; Erickson, Marjorie; Hamilton, Gayle; and Knox, Virginia. 1986. *West Virginia: Final Report on the Community Work Experience Demonstrations.* New York: MDRC.

Wisconsin Income Disregard and Transitional Medical Benefits Study

Interagency Low Income Opportunity Advisory Board, Executive Office of the President. (no date). *Special Terms and Conditions*. Unpublished internal document.

Chapter 4
The Knowledge Base: Broad-Coverage Programs

Chapter 2 presented a conceptual structure for understanding how JOBS programs can affect behavior and for organizing this synthesis. Chapter 3 identified the relevant completed and current studies, pointed to the outcomes that they address, and summarized the research designs. This chapter and the next discuss what we do and do not know about the effectiveness of different welfare employment program designs and components for different populations[1] and the information likely to emerge from current research. These two chapters basically follow the organization of Chapter 3 and discuss the following topics:

- Broad-Coverage Programs

- Selective-Voluntary Programs

- Subgroups and Targeting

- Education Services

- Youth-Oriented Services

- Support Services Tests

- Program Model Combinations

This chapter presents the findings on broad-coverage welfare-to-work programs.

As indicated in Table 3.1, there are a substantial number of studies of broad-coverage, mostly mandatory WIN (and now JOBS) programs, some of which were implemented on a relatively small scale, while others

---

[1] For other summaries of the recent research on the effectiveness of welfare-to-work programs, see Barnow, 1987; Burtless, 1989; U.S. Congressional Budget Office, 1987; Grossman, Maynard, and Roberts, 1985; Friedlander and Gueron, forthcoming; Gueron, 1987, 1990; Gueron and Long, 1990; Interagency Low Income Opportunity Advisory Board, Executive Office of the President, 1988; Porter, 1990.

targeted all eligibles and were statewide. At this time, impact and cost-effectiveness results are available only from seven studies of a range of low- and moderate-cost programs in Arkansas, Baltimore, Cook County (Illinois), San Diego (San Diego I[2] and SWIM), Virginia, and West Virginia.[3] These findings are of particular relevance. They provide information on impacts for a cross section of the then-mandatory caseload and assess total WIN systems (either at full or smaller scale) that, to varying degrees, imposed a participation requirement. The programs reflect the range of average resources per eligible person likely to be available in most states implementing JOBS, and they represented different approaches and philosophies, from the very modest Arkansas and Cook County programs to the more complex (and JOBS-like) Baltimore Options and San Diego SWIM demonstrations, both of which included some form of education and training, case management, and assessment. They were clearly pre-JOBS, however, in requiring participation only of single parents with children over age 5,[4] in usually emphasizing immediate job placement over human capital development, and in the work incentives and support services they provided.

The studies show that these programs were usually successfully implemented and imposed obligations on a significant share of the targeted welfare caseload. Most of the programs led to a substitution of earnings for welfare, had durable impacts, and were cost-effective within in a relatively short period of time.

The next five sections discuss the lessons from the seven studies about program participation, impacts, and costs versus benefits. They are followed by four sections that summarize what is known about the relationship between the dimensions noted in Chapter 2 – e.g., particular employment-directed services, program cost (and cost-effectiveness), service sequencing, administrative practices, and contextual factors – and a program's impacts on employment and welfare receipt.

---

[2] As noted in Chapter 3, San Diego I participation and impact findings are reported for the job search/work experience sequence.

[3] Results are also available from the Louisville job search experiments, but they are discussed more briefly since they are from an earlier period and thus less relevant than some of the later, similar programs.

[4] As indicated in Chapter 3, Arkansas mandated participation for women with children age 3 or older.

Findings on Participation and Implementation

As noted in Chapter 2, some level of program participation (or behavior to avoid participation) is a precondition for mandatory programs to have an impact. Mandated participation can result in employment and welfare effects through three mechanisms. First, public assistance recipients who take part in such programs may be helped to find jobs and exit the welfare rolls. Second, if participation requirements are enforced, individuals who fail to comply with them may have their grants reduced or terminated, resulting in direct welfare savings. Third, imposition of a *quid pro quo* for welfare receipt may deter some individuals from remaining on welfare or from filing or completing an initial application for assistance.

This section briefly summarizes findings on participation and sanctioning as a basis for understanding the comparability of the findings on broad-coverage and selective-voluntary programs and for identifying the remaining open questions.

Most of the findings on participation come from the seven evaluations noted above. These studies presented two different concepts of participation: longitudinal measures (which showed the proportion of program registrants who ever reached a given activity milestone within a specified period of time)[5] and monthly participation rates (which showed the percentage of those eligible for the program in any given month who were actually active during that month). Longitudinal measures describe the "careers" that individual registrants have in a program. Thus, they help characterize the nature of the treatment being evaluated. Monthly participation rates reflect the aggregate level of activity, but do not indicate whether the same or different people are active. Both rates are influenced by the characteristics of the participants, the obstacles to participation, AFDC grant levels (and thus the extent to which people combine work and welfare), program policies on deferral and exemption, and the extent of outreach and enforcement.

Both of these participation measures differ fundamentally from the concept of countable participation introduced in the JOBS regulations, since they include as participants anyone who was active for at least a

---

[5] Longitudinal measures thus focus on the same cohort of registrants over a specified period of time.

day or hour (although usually substantially more) in a major program component (not counting registration, orientation, assessment, or counseling) in the designated period. In contrast, for purposes of receiving an enhanced federal match, JOBS includes as participants only those people who are active at least 75 percent of scheduled hours; in addition, the group of individuals counting toward the state's participation rate must, on average, be scheduled for 20 hours of participation a week. As noted below, the JOBS participation rate also differs in the people and activities included or excluded in the numerator or denominator.

Table 4.1 shows the longitudinal indicators for AFDC case heads targeted by the seven programs. (Rates for AFDC-UP case heads are quite similar.) The numerators and denominators in these rates are, respectively, those participating and the total number of people targeted by the program. In some cases, this latter number included all WIN-mandatory cases newly referred to the program; in others, it was only applicants or a subset of the caseload (e.g., 1,000 people in Baltimore [see Chapter 3]). This is an important distinction, because it costs money to monitor participation and provide services, and participation rates would have been lower if the same funds had been spread over a larger caseload.

The broadest indicator (row 1) shows that, within nine or twelve months after registration, between 38 and 64 percent of all targeted cases took part in a specific activity scheduled by the program.[6] Participation was lowest in Arkansas and Cook County, and highest in SWIM.[7] The other rows show the actual activities in which individuals participated.

---

[6] Row 1 includes all individuals who participated for at least one hour in a specific approved program component (e.g., job search, work experience, education, or training). (The minimum measure varied by state from one hour in SWIM and one day in Arkansas, Cook County, San Diego, Virginia, and West Virginia to three days in Baltimore. But people usually participated much longer.) Assessment, orientation, job placement, and counseling are not counted as "participation" in this table.

[7] Participation rates are not always directly comparable because of differences in the location of random assignment, which was either at the income maintenance or program office (see the notes to Table 4.1). The SWIM study differed in having random assignment at the program office, which was not co-located with the income maintenance office. Thus, measured rates would have been lower in SWIM if random assignment had been at the same point as in the other studies. Further, in Arkansas, the composition of the sample provided one reason for the low participation rate. Sixty percent of the sample members were new applicants for AFDC and almost 40 percent of them did not ultimately get on welfare (i.e., have their grants approved). Thus, they became deregistered from the program relatively rapidly and had little opportunity to participate. (See Friedlander et al., 1985b.)

TABLE 4.1 PERCENT OF AFDC ELIGIBLES EVER INVOLVED IN SPECIFIED ACTIVITIES WITHIN NINE OR TWELVE MONTHS AFTER RANDOM ASSIGNMENT, FOR SEVEN WELFARE-TO-WORK PROGRAMS

Activity Measure	Arkansas	Baltimore	Cook County	San Diego I	San Diego SWIM	Virginia	West Virginia
	Job Search, Work Experience	Multi-Component	Job Search, Work Experience	Job Search, Work Experience	Job Search, Work Experience, Education, Training	Job Search, Work Experience	Work Experience
Participated in Any Activity (%)	38.0	45.0	38.8	46.4	64.4	58.3	N/A[a]
Participated in:[b]							
Job Search Activities (%)	27.3[c]	24.7	36.1	44.1	50.6	51.0	N/A[a]
Work Experience (%)	2.9	17.5	7.3	13.0	19.5	9.5	23.9
Other Services, including Education and Training (%)[d]	N/A	17.3	4.1	N/A	24.3	11.6	N/A[a]
Deregistered (%)	57.5	37.6	56.9	60.6	61.5	42.3	42.3
Due to Request for Sanctioning (%)	N/A[e]	low[e]	12.4	8.0	10.6	3.8	1.8
Follow-Up Period in Months	9	12	9	9	12	9	9

SOURCES: Data from Friedlander et al., 1985b; Friedlander, 1987; Friedlander et al., 1987; Goldman, Friedlander, and Long, 1986; Hamilton, 1988; Riccio et al., 1986; Friedlander et al., 1986.

NOTES: Estimates are for AFDC applicants and recipients in all locations except San Diego I, which included only applicants. In SWIM, percentages were calculated using a base of all eligibles who registered in the program; in Baltimore, Cook County, San Diego I, and Virginia, the base includes nonregistrants. In Arkansas and West Virginia, the base includes all registrants; however, since the program office and income maintenance office were co-located in both these states, there is probably little difference between the number of people registered and the number eligible but not registered.

[a]West Virginia's program consisted almost exclusively of work experience.

[b]N/A under participation components indicates that such components were not available in the program.

[c]Participation in the individual job search component of the Arkansas demonstration is not included here.

[d]Includes only education and job skills training that were either provided or approved by the programs. Individuals in all seven programs also undertook other education and job skills training. Available data suggest that the experimental-control difference in participation in these services is substantially smaller than the experimental participation rates shown.

[e]While the percent of sample members deregistered owing to a request for sanction is not available in Arkansas or Baltimore, other data suggest that sanctioning was limited. In Baltimore, a special case file study was done of 70 enrollees initially assigned to a program component (or assigned after being in a short-term holding status) who did not attend activities for which they were scheduled. The review indicated that only three of the 70 enrollees were deregistered for noncompliance and that none of the 70 had a financial penalty imposed on them. Administrative records maintained by the Arkansas Department of Social Services indicate that in the two counties studied, 3 and 5 percent of persons in the full caseload (not just the sample) participating in an assessment were sanctioned or deregistered due to noncompliance.

As described in Chapter 3, in all of the programs except West Virginia and Baltimore, job search was usually the first in a fixed sequence of activities, followed by work experience. The table shows that the majority of participants were typically not active in subsequent components.[8] For example, while half of all eligibles in San Diego's SWIM initiative participated in job search, about a fifth were active in work experience. In Baltimore and SWIM, a substantial share of eligibles (17 and 24 percent, respectively) were active in education and training, two services of particular relevance to JOBS. (The SWIM study, which had more detailed data, also showed that the program increased experimentals' participation – when compared to that of the control group – in both education and training. It also found that about half of the SWIM education and training participation was in self-initiated education that was usually an alternative to, rather than sequenced after, job search.)[9]

---

[8] These rates are comparable to those found in the earlier study of the Employment Opportunity Pilot Project (EOPP), which provided a sequence of intensive job search assistance followed by a subsidized public service job or training to AFDC applicants and recipients with children age 6 or older. About two-thirds of those who enrolled in EOPP actually participated in the program. About 15 percent of enrollees (one-quarter of those who participated in the job search component) left job search assistance and went into EOPP-subsidized work positions. (See Brown et al., 1983; Zimmerman et al., 1983.)

[9] Table 4.1 shows average longitudinal activity rates in program-provided or program-approved services for AFDC applicants and recipients randomly assigned to the experimental group. (Experimentals also took part in activities not provided or approved by the welfare-to-work program.) While members of the control group did not participate in the programs being evaluated, a substantial number did participate on their own in activities provided through other programs and, in some cases, were also sanctioned. (In San Diego I, West Virginia, and Baltimore, controls were in the "regular" WIN program, which continued to operate during the study period but provided substantially less service than the broad-coverage programs being evaluated.) In sites with substantial control participation, the experimental-control difference in service receipt was smaller than suggested by the table.

The level of services received by controls is particularly important in interpreting row 4 of Table 4.1, since, in the cases where data are available, almost no controls participated in job search or work experience. While data on controls' receipt of education and training are not available for Baltimore, they are for SWIM (although over a different follow-up and using different data sources from those used in Table 4.1). During a two- to three-year period after random assignment, 34 percent of experimentals participated in program-approved or other community college programs, but so did 28 percent of controls. There were also significant differences in participation in JTPA-funded activities. Thus, while at a lesser rate than suggested by Table 4.1, SWIM did lead to a significant increase in enrollment in both education and training programs (Hamilton and Friedlander, 1989). In contrast, the Virginia and Cook County studies found almost equivalent levels of participation in education and training for experimentals and controls. Thus, the Virginia and Cook County studies compared two groups that differed primarily in their receipt of job search and work experience, not education and training (Riccio et al., 1986; Friedlander et al., 1987).

The discussion of welfare dynamics in Chapter 2 helps explain why no program can achieve a participation rate even close to 100 percent and why a significantly smaller proportion of eligibles will be involved at each succeeding program stage. It also suggests why a 40 or 65 percent "ever active" longitudinal rate does not mean that the remaining 35 to 60 percent of the caseload was untouched or overlooked by the program. Quite the contrary: The evaluations cited concluded that, to get these levels of participation, program staff had to contact, pursue, and thus spend resources on a much larger number of people.[10] The explanation for these statements comes from the several different reasons for nonparticipation.

First, many cases were temporarily deferred from participation requirements because of part-time employment,[11] illness, or other circumstances recognized by the program; these situations could easily have lasted throughout the nine- or twelve-month follow-up period. Second, welfare turnover and other behavior meant that as time passed 38 to 62 percent of people in the program became ineligible for and were thus deregistered from the program (row 5 of Table 4.1). They were deregistered because they left welfare (as part of normal turnover or to avoid program requirements) or for other reasons, such as having a child or getting a full-time job but remaining on the rolls. (Some of those deregistered were sanctioned, as indicated in the last row of Table 4.1. This would have directly resulted in welfare savings even if the person never participated in the program.) Finally, there will always be some cases that are "lost" and not reached by a program's mandate owing to lack of staff follow-up or inadequate case management and monitoring.

In order to isolate the last factor and determine the extent to which the programs reached those who were actually eligible, these studies included a second longitudinal measure. It showed that within nine or twelve months of registration, between 75 and 97 percent of the eligibles in the seven programs had, in some sense and at some time, satisfied the program mandate (if not through participation, then by getting a job or

---

[10] In the SWIM Demonstration, the evaluators concluded that program staff worked with almost the entire caseload to achieve a 64 percent longitudinal participation rate.

[11] For example, in SWIM, 12-month activity rates increased from the 64.4 percent shown in Table 4.1 to 77.3 percent if part-time work (15 to 30 hours per week) is also counted (Hamilton, 1988).

leaving welfare) or had their welfare grant reduced. Only 3 to 25 percent of eligibles remained completely "uncovered" by the program mandate.[12]

Two of the studies were of programs specifically funded to test ongoing participation requirements and the maximum feasible rates of monthly participation: San Diego's SWIM Demonstration (for AFDCs and AFDC-UPs) and West Virginia's workfare program for fathers in AFDC-UP cases.[13] The more exhaustive SWIM study measured the percent of people active in program-approved components during any month and also the percent of cases participating in other activities (e.g., part-time employment) that satisfied the program objectives. As illustrated in Figure 4.1, during a typical month in its second year, SWIM involved 52 percent of AFDC and AFDC-UP registrants either in the program (22 percent in program-arranged activities and another 11 percent in self-initiated education or training activities) or in part-time work (19 percent). (See Hamilton, 1988.) The West Virginia AFDC-UP program achieved monthly participation rates averaging over 60 percent (Friedlander et al., 1986). Both studies included a careful examination of nonparticipants and determined that most of the people who did not participate were only temporarily inactive or "frictional nonparticipants" (i.e., deferred or waiting for services to begin). For example, in SWIM, only about 10 percent of eligibles in any month failed to participate without a program-approved reason. The majority of these individuals were inactive as a result of staff failure to assign them to an activity or to follow up on an assignment; the remaining clients were inactive owing to noncooperation, and sanctioning began for most of these cases.

In both studies, the authors stressed the unusual circumstances for program administrators – in particular, the full funding of program services through special demonstration grants. San Diego's administrators also benefited from a strong labor market, a high-grant state (allowing many people to combine work and welfare), extensive local education and training services, and years of staff experience. West Virginia's administrators operated in a very rural state, with extremely high

---

[12] The advantage of this measure is that it includes the range of outcomes that meet program objectives or requirements. However, because it defines activities by whether they "ever" occurred, it is generous. The several studies in which MDRC examined the extent to which program participation was continuous suggest that the percent who participate continuously is substantially lower than the percent who ever participate. (See, e.g., Hamilton, 1988.)

[13] See Hamilton, 1988; Hamilton and Friedlander, 1989; Ball, 1984; Friedlander et al., 1986. Forthcoming findings from the Pennsylvania Saturation Work Program evaluation will provide additional information on participation rates in a program with an ongoing participation requirement.

**FIGURE 4.1   PERCENT OF AFDC AND AFDC-UP INDIVIDUALS ELIGIBLE
FOR SWIM DURING EACH MONTH WHO PARTICIPATED
IN PROGRAM-ARRANGED ACTIVITIES, SELF-INITIATED
ACTIVITIES, OR EMPLOYMENT, BY TYPE OF ACTIVITY**

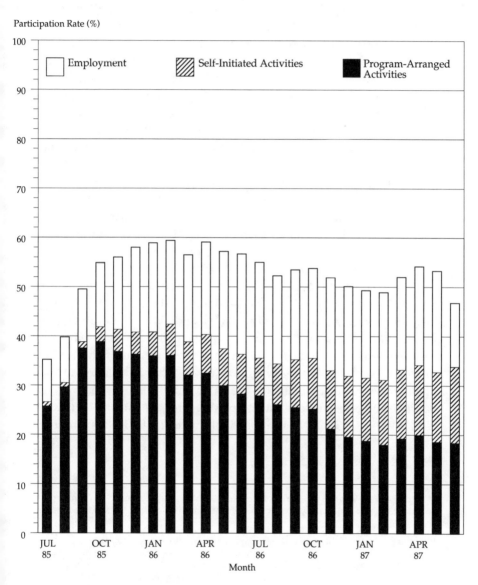

Participation Rate (%)

SOURCE: Adapted from Hamilton, 1988.

135

unemployment, a strong demand for subsidized labor, and a lengthy history of running other work programs.[14] Finally, and critically important in considering the relevance of these findings for state JOBS programs, neither the SWIM nor the West Virginia program or study set any specific minimum on weekly hours of participation.

If participation and sanctioning are seen as intermediate steps toward impacts, the seven studies reflect varied degrees of mandatoriness.[15] The evaluators concluded, however, that San Diego's SWIM program and the West Virginia AFDC-UP workfare initiative probably achieved the maximum possible monthly participation rates for those programs in those locations. While it is possible that rates could be higher under different conditions – e.g., in a program that places more restrictions on deferrals or part-time employment than did SWIM, or in a state with lower AFDC grant levels (and thus less opportunity to combine work and welfare) than in California – this does not seem very likely. Measured participation would have been higher, however, if other activities had been counted, e.g., orientation, assessment, job placement, or ongoing informal individual job search.

The SWIM and West Virginia studies provide information of clear relevance to states considering the feasibility and challenge of meeting the JOBS participation targets. The SWIM study is most useful, since it was an explicit test of a continuous participation requirement in a multi-component program targeted at a cross section of the AFDC caseload. However, the many differences in what is included in the numerator and denominator of the SWIM and JOBS calculations of participation rates make it hard to predict what the rates would have been had the JOBS rules been applied during the SWIM Demonstration.

---

[14] Also, the West Virginia rates are only for men. The program had much lower monthly participation rates (generally under 20 percent) for women on AFDC (Friedlander et al., 1986).

[15] The sixth line on Table 4.1 shows the percent of experimentals deregistered from the program because of a request for sanction (i.e., the percent of experimentals whose caseworkers sent notice to the eligibility worker requesting that a sanction be imposed; these experimentals were effectively deregistered from the program's mandate during the period of the sanction). The sanction rates for experimentals were highest in San Diego I, SWIM, and Cook County. In evaluating the relationship of sanctioning to impacts, however, it is important to consider the difference in sanctioning rates between experimentals and controls. In San Diego I and SWIM, few controls were sanctioned. In contrast, in Cook County, 7.6 percent of controls were sanctioned, for a net difference of 4.8 percentage points.

Some elements of the JOBS participation calculation are clearly more demanding. For example, if the JOBS standard – an average of 20 hours per week of activity – had been applied to SWIM as it operated, measured participation rates would have been substantially lower.[16] Also, JOBS expands the non-exempt population to include women with younger children. Other elements of the JOBS calculation are more generous than what was applied in SWIM: For example, under limited circumstances, counting in the numerator people who go to work if they recently participated in JOBS; hours spent in assessment and employability plan development meetings; and school enrollment of young custodial mothers. The JOBS calculation is more generous, too, in excluding from the denominator people excused from the JOBS participation requirement for good cause, and those without access to needed child care. On balance, however, measured monthly participation rates in SWIM would have been lower under the JOBS regulations, and probably substantially lower, principally because most SWIM activities would not have met the 20-hour requirement.

Other factors in many state JOBS programs may affect participation. The findings in Table 4.1 were mainly for the relatively simple, usually fixed-sequence programs of the early and mid-1980s. It will be very important to see whether the more complex programs initiated prior to and under JOBS achieve similar rates. There has been only one study of a broad-coverage program that used flexible assessments to assign participants to a range of components; Baltimore Options involved 45 percent of targeted persons in at least one activity. As indicated in Table 3.1, several studies are under way on broad-coverage programs that contain some of the more innovative aspects of JOBS, particularly the greater use of education, assessment, and case management, and the involvement of women with younger children. While no impact or cost-effectiveness results are available, there are extensive implementation and participation findings from the early start-up period of the implementation of California's GAIN program.

---

[16] For example, in SWIM, the two-week job search workshop consisted of three hours of classroom activity per day for the first week, followed by two to three hours of supervised telephone room activity per day during the second week. (Interviews with employers were usually held outside these hours.) Assigned hours for SWIM work experience generally ranged from 20 to 30 hours per week. The schedule for other SWIM components varied, from one or two days per month (e.g., for a follow-up job search activity) or eight half-days per month for English as a Second Language (ESL) classes, to 30 hours per week for some vocational training.

Initial findings on GAIN suggest that the more enriched – and complex – JOBS programs will not necessarily achieve higher longitudinal participation rates than those shown in Table 4.1. During the first 16 to 24 months of GAIN operations in 8 of the first 10 counties to begin implementation, and using a shorter period to measure longitudinal participation, GAIN rates varied substantially across counties and, on average, fell on the low end of rates shown in Table 4.1 (Riccio et al., 1989). Thus, 34 percent of people participated in some program activity within six months, or a shorter period than that shown in Table 4.1, although this rate varied from 26 to 56 percent across the eight counties.

Figure 4.2 shows the detail behind this rate by illustrating the movement of 100 typical AFDC single parents who were mandatory registrants in GAIN during this early period: Of the 100 registrants, 71 attended orientation and 34 of them participated in an initial component of the program. (Few reached a second activity in this very short, six-month follow-up period.) The data suggest that one of the greatest challenges in GAIN was getting people to show up for orientation.[17] Of those who did show up, almost half participated in GAIN, while more than 80 percent of those who did not participate were deferred or, to a lesser extent, deregistered.

The bottom part of Figure 4.2 shows the reasons for nonparticipation in GAIN components by all program registrants – including those who did not reach orientation – and suggests that many in fact met the program's mandates. Thus, two-thirds of them (or 44 of the 66 nonparticipants) were deregistered (many because of full-time employment) or deferred (mostly because of part-time work, illness, or family emergencies). Figure 4.2 also shows that GAIN is placing 41 percent of participants (14 out of the 34 entering an initial activity) in mandatory education, substantially more than have earlier initiatives.

In Massachusetts' Employment and Training (ET) Choices program, participation data are available, but were not collected in a form that is directly comparable to the participation measures in Table 4.1. Of all the adults who were on AFDC in Massachusetts during fiscal year 1987 (July 1, 1986, through June 30, 1987) – i.e., not just people who were normally

---

[17] This suggests that mandatory programs, even those offering many more opportunities than were typical in the 1980s programs, will still need to adopt aggressive outreach and follow-up procedures in order to match the Table 4.1 participation rates.

FIGURE 4.2   PARTICIPATION PATTERNS AND REASONS FOR NONPARTICIPATION FOR 100 TYPICAL MANDATORY SINGLE-PARENT REGISTRANTS WITHIN SIX MONTHS OF GAIN REGISTRATION

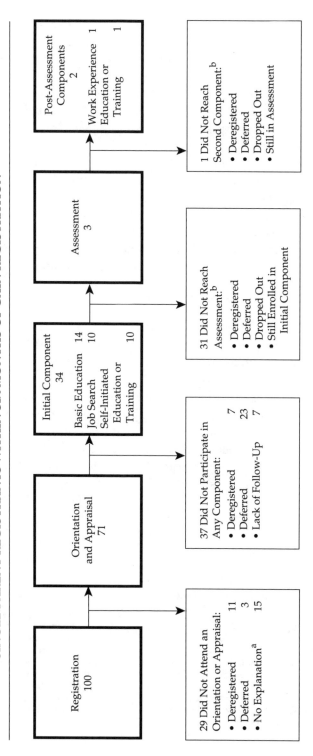

SOURCE: Adapted from Riccio et al., 1989.

NOTES: The 100 typical registrants represent the experiences of a 966-person random sample of single-parent (AFDC) GAIN-mandatory registrants from seven study counties.

Findings for heads of two-parent households (AFDC-UP registrants) were similar to those presented above for single parents.

[a] GAIN case files included no information explaining why these registrants did not attend orientation.

[b] The listed reasons are possible explanations for nonparticipation. Data showing the actual importance of each reason were not collected for this study.

139

required to register for WIN – 33 percent participated in training or another substantive activity other than orientation and assessment during the fiscal year. An additional 17 percent of those on welfare in FY 1987 had previously participated in a substantive ET activity, but were not active in FY 1987. Among those who participated in substantive ET activities, 44 percent became employed. Using a very broad definition of participation, a total of 67 percent of those on the AFDC rolls in FY 1987 had ever participated in ET orientation, assessment, or a substantive activity (Nightingale et al., 1989).

Findings from the evaluations of GAIN, New Jersey REACH, Florida Project Independence, the Pennsylvania Saturation Work Program (PSWP), and Ohio Transitions to Independence should provide additional information on participation in more complex JOBS programs.

Findings on Impacts for AFDCs

This section discusses whether the participation levels, services, and mandates in the seven programs produced impacts for AFDC eligibles.[18] Overall, the studies provide grounds both for optimism and caution. They show that these programs were generally successful in getting more people to work and in assuring that a greater share of their total income came from their own earnings, rather than public transfers. With two exceptions, these low- to moderate-cost programs led to 10 to 30 percent increases in employment rates and earnings (calculated as averages across all members of the targeted population in the caseload).[19] They also usually reduced welfare costs, although the welfare reductions were smaller and less consistent than the earnings gains. In general, this was true for both the very low-cost job search/work experience programs in

---

[18] No final results are currently available from the other studies of broad-coverage programs listed in Chapter 3, except for the Louisville studies.

[19] As indicated in Chapter 2, because random assignment occurred at the income maintenance or welfare employment program office, these studies included in the experimental groups all people targeted by the program, and not only those who actually participated. In four of the seven studies, random assignment took place at the income maintenance office, and the estimated impacts are averages for the full targeted caseload. In SWIM, Arkansas, and West Virginia, only those in the mandatory population who showed up at the program were randomly assigned. However, since the program office and income maintenance office were co-located in both Arkansas and West Virginia, the difference between the number of people eligible and number eligible but not registered was probably greatest in SWIM.

Arkansas and Virginia and the more enriched, multi-component programs in Baltimore and San Diego (SWIM). These impacts varied substantially for different subgroups of the caseload. The study of San Diego's SWIM also showed employment gains and welfare savings for AFDC-UP eligibles. When one looks behind the averages, the findings further suggest that the impacts probably resulted from substantial changes for some people and minimal changes for others. Finally, the combination of earnings increases and welfare reductions suggests that total income increased, but usually not by enough to move families out of poverty.

Table 4.2 summarizes the results for AFDC eligibles in the seven studies, showing data for three years following random assignment in Arkansas, Baltimore, and Virginia, and one or two years in the other locations.[20] (See Appendix Tables B.1 through B.7 for more detail on the quarterly trends behind these annual data.) The first column shows the outcomes for experimentals; the second, for controls, some of whom participated in alternative education or training programs;[21] the third column, the difference or net impact; and the final column, the percentage increase or decrease over the outcome for the control group. Several features of the table are important to interpreting the results. First, the data shown in the table are for *all* people in the experimental or control groups of the research sample. Thus, the earnings numbers average zero values for people who did not work during the year with positive amounts for people who did; the AFDC payments average the zero values for people who did not receive welfare during the year with the

---

[20] Appendix B contains impacts for up to 18 months for the Cook County (Illinois), San Diego I, and West Virginia studies. Those more detailed findings are consistent with the short-term impacts summarized in Table 4.2. Another document (Maxfield, 1990) also presents the impacts on annual earnings for the studies contained in Table 4.2, but gives different numbers. For the Arkansas and Virginia studies, Maxfield cites the first published impact data, which cover only 2 to 4 quarters of follow-up. Table 4.2 uses later results, which include about three years of follow-up. For some of the other studies, Maxfield's annual earnings impacts differ because they appear to be calculated by averaging impacts over different time periods, ranging from quarters 2 to 6 in San Diego I to quarters 6 to 9 in Baltimore and quarters 2 to 11 in Maine.

[21] While the extent of control services was not measured in all seven of the studies, the available findings suggest little receipt of program services but some self-initiated education and training activities. For example, in San Diego SWIM, few controls received job search or work experience, but more than a quarter of the AFDCs and almost 20 percent of AFDC-UP controls received some education or training. As a result, as noted in Chapter 2, the net impacts in Table 4.2 are conservative estimates of the gains that follow receipt of the services provided by the welfare-to-work programs.

TABLE 4.2 IMPACTS OF SEVEN WELFARE-TO-WORK PROGRAMS ON AFDC ELIGIBLES

Location, Outcome, and Follow-Up Period		Experimental Group Mean	Control Group Mean	Difference	Percentage Change
Arkansas					
Average Earnings	Year 1	$ 674	$ 507	$167**	33%
	Year 2	1,180	957	223	23
	Year 3	1,422	1,085	337**	31
Employed at End of	Year 1	20.4%	16.7%	3.7*	22%
	Year 2	23.9	20.3	3.6	18
	Year 3	24.5	18.3	6.2***	34
Average AFDC Payments	Year 1	$998	$1,143	-$145***	-13%
	Year 2	793	982	- 190***	-19
	Year 3	742	910	- 168***	-18
On Welfare at End of	Year 1	51.0%	59.1%	-8.1***	-14%
	Year 2	38.1	46.0	-7.9***	-17
	Year 3	32.8	40.1	-7.3***	-18
Baltimore					
Average Earnings	Year 1	$1,612	$1,472	$140	10%
	Year 2	2,787	2,386	401***	17
	Year 3	3,499	2,989	511***	17
Employed at End of	Year 1	34.7%	31.2%	3.5**	11%
	Year 2	39.5	37.1	2.4	6
	Year 3	40.7	40.3	0.4	1
Average AFDC Payments	Year 1	$2,520	$2,517	$ 2	0%
	Year 2	2,058	2,092	- 34	-2
	Year 3	1,783	1,815	- 31	-2
On Welfare at End of	Year 1	72.0%	73.3%	-1.4	-2%
	Year 2	58.7	59.0	-0.3	-1
	Year 3	48.2	48.4	-0.2	0
Cook County					
Average Earnings	Year 1	$1,227	$1,217	$10	1%
Employed at End of	Year 1	22.6%	21.4%	1.3	6%
Average AFDC Payments	Year 1	$3,105	$3,146	-$40	-1%
On Welfare at End of	Year 1	78.9%	80.8%	-1.9**	-2%
San Diego I (Applicants Only)					
Average Earnings	Year 1	$2,379	$1,937	$443***	23%
Employed at End of	Year 1	42.4%	36.9%	5.5***	15%
Average AFDC Payments	Year 1	$2,524	$2,750	-$226***	-8%
On Welfare at End of	Year 1	45.8%	47.9%	-2.0	-4%

(continued)

TABLE 4.2 (*continued*)

Location, Outcome, and Follow-Up Period		Experimental Group Mean	Control Group Mean	Difference	Percentage Change
San Diego SWIM					
Average Earnings	Year 1	$2,029	$1,677	$352***	21%
	Year 2	2,903	2,246	658***	29
Employed at End of	Year 1	34.7%	26.9%	7.7***	29%
	Year 2	34.7	29.3	5.4***	18
Average AFDC Payments	Year 1	$4,424	$4,830	-$407***	-8%
	Year 2	3,408	3,961	- 553***	-14
On Welfare at End of	Year 1	66.0%	72.4%	-6.4***	-9%
	Year 2	51.3	58.7	-7.4***	-13
Virginia					
Average Earnings	Year 1	$1,352	$1,282	$ 69	5%
	Year 2	2,268	1,988	280**	14
	Year 3[a]	2,624	2,356	268*	11
Employed at End of	Year 1	34.7%	31.0%	3.8**	12%
	Year 2	39.3	33.3	6.0***	18
	Year 3[b]	38.7	34.1	4.6***	13
Average AFDC Payments	Year 1	$1,961	$2,029	-$ 69	-3%
	Year 2	1,480	1,516	- 36	-2
	Year 3[a]	1,184	1,295	- 111**	-9
On Welfare at End of	Year 1	59.8%	59.4%	0.4	1%
	Year 2	44.0	44.9	-0.9	-2
	Year 3[b]	36.6	39.3	-2.6	-7
West Virginia					
Average Earnings	Year 1	$451	$435	$16	4%
Employed at End of	Year 1	12.0%	13.1%	-1.0	-8%
Average AFDC Payments	Year 1	$1,692	$1,692	$0	0%
On Welfare at End of	Year 1	70.9%	72.5%	-1.5	-2%

SOURCES: Data from Friedlander and Goldman, 1988; Friedlander, 1987; Friedlander et al., 1987; Goldman, Friedlander, and Long, 1986; Hamilton and Friedlander, 1989; Friedlander, 1988a; Friedlander et al., 1986; and additional MDRC estimates of annual values.

NOTES: The earnings and AFDC payments data include zero values for sample members not employed and for sample members not receiving welfare. Estimates are regression-adjusted using ordinary least squares, controlling for pre-random assignment characteristics of sample members. There may be some discrepancies in experimental-control differences because of rounding.

In all programs except the San Diego SWIM program, year 1 begins with the quarter of random assignment. For employment and earnings, the quarter of random assignment refers to the calendar quarter in which random assignment occurred. As a result, "average earnings" in year 1 may include up to two months of earnings prior to random assignment. For AFDC payments, the quarter of random assignment refers to the three months beginning with the month in which an individual was randomly assigned. In the San Diego SWIM program, where all outcomes were calculated for calendar quarters, year 1 begins with the quarter following the quarter of random assignment.

(continued)

143

TABLE 4.2 *(continued)*

"Employed" or "on welfare" at the end of the year is defined as receiving earnings or welfare payments at some point during the last quarter of the year.

Earnings and AFDC payments are not adjusted for inflation.

[a]Annual earnings and AFDC payments impacts are based on two and three quarters of follow-up, respectively.

[b]Percent employed and on welfare at the end of 2 1/2 and 2 3/4 years, respectively.

*Denotes statistical significance at the 10 percent level; **at the 5 percent level; and ***at the 1 percent level.

positive amounts for people receiving benefits. This means that the earnings and welfare payments of the people who actually worked or received benefits can be substantially higher than the values shown in columns one and two. For example, Table 4.2 shows that, in the second year after random assignment to the San Diego SWIM study, the *average experimental* earned $2,903; however, since only 49.4 percent of experimentals worked at some point during that year (not shown in the table), the *average employed experimental* earned about twice that amount. Second, the striking variation across the studies in the outcomes for members of the control groups points to the substantial differences in characteristics of the welfare populations and labor markets in these locations. Finally, in Table 4.2, and throughout this chapter, earnings and welfare payments are reported in nominal dollars for the period of the study.

Five of the seven programs had statistically significant impacts on employment rates at the end of the first year after program enrollment. These gains ranged from 3.5 percentage points in Baltimore to 7.7 percentage points in the SWIM program. For example, in San Diego I, 36.9 percent of the controls were employed at the end of the first year of follow-up compared to 42.4 percent of the experimentals, for a gain of 5.5 percentage points. Further, during the full year, experimentals (including both those who were working and those who were not) earned an average of $443, or 23 percent, more than the $1,937 earned by controls. In the other four programs, first-year earnings by experimentals were 5 to 33 percent above those for controls.

The longer-term (two- or three-year) follow-up available for four programs indicates that these short-term earnings impacts persisted or grew over time, possibly reaching a peak around the end of the second or beginning of the third year. Despite increases in the employment and earnings of controls over the three years, experimentals continued to do better than controls. (Figures 4.3 and 4.4 show, for Arkansas and Baltimore, the quarterly trends over the full three years in the sample's average earnings and in the percent of the sample that was working.) In Arkansas, by the end of year 3, the experimentals' employment rate was 6.2 percentage points above that for controls and they earned, over the year, an average of $337, or 31 percent, more than controls. In Baltimore, while there was no significant long-term difference in employment rates, experimentals in year 3 earned $511, or 17 percent, more than controls. Overall, earnings per eligible person in the caseload averaged $270 to $650 above the control rate in the final year of the study.

FIGURE 4.3 TRENDS IN AVERAGE QUARTERLY EARNINGS IN ARKANSAS AND BALTIMORE

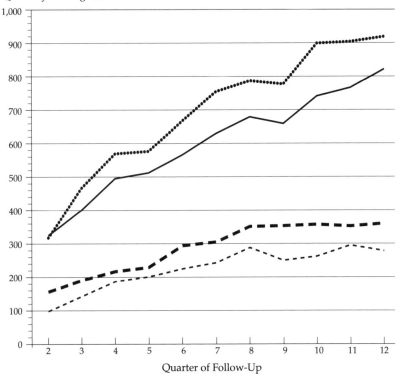

•••••••••• Baltimore Experimentals ▬ ▬ ▬ ▬ Arkansas Experimentals

───────── Baltimore Controls ─ ─ ─ ─ ─ Arkansas Controls

Quarterly Earnings ($)

Quarter of Follow-Up

SOURCES: Tables B.1 and B.2.

FIGURE 4.4   TRENDS IN AVERAGE QUARTERLY EMPLOYMENT RATES IN ARKANSAS AND BALTIMORE

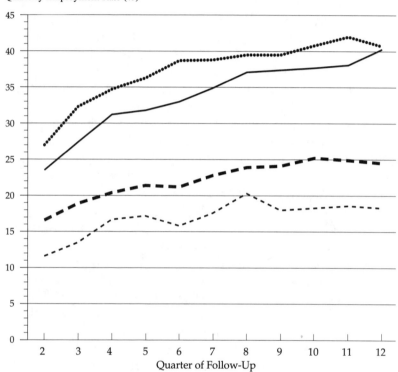

Quarterly Employment Rate (%)

SOURCES: Tables B.1 and B.2.

147

A more detailed examination of the earnings data in these studies suggests several further findings. First, in the programs that provided primarily job search assistance (e.g., Arkansas and Virginia), the earnings gains resulted principally from increases in the number of people who got jobs, not from higher earnings (wages or hours) for those working.[22] This was also the case in SWIM, where the relatively large impact on earnings resulted mostly from an increase in the number of people working (Hamilton and Friedlander, 1989). This was less true in Baltimore (a program providing some education and training), where some experimentals either were paid higher wages or worked longer weekly hours as a result of the program (Friedlander, 1987).[23] Second, in the SWIM and Baltimore programs, there was a statistically significant increase in the percent of people with somewhat higher earnings in the longer term: In Baltimore, there was a 3.8 percentage point gain in the share of people earning more than $6,000 a year; in SWIM, a 4.6 percentage point increase in the share of applicants and recipients earning $5,000 or more a year and a 3.2 percentage point gain in the share of recipients earning $10,000 or more a year. However, these increases resulted from two very different patterns of impacts on the earnings distribution of people who got jobs: SWIM increased the number of people with relatively low as well as relatively higher earnings and did not change the overall earnings distribution, whereas the employment increase in Baltimore was concentrated in the higher earnings category (Friedlander, 1987; Hamilton and Friedlander, 1989). Third, the Baltimore results suggest that the impacts of adding education and training in a mixed strategy may not show up quickly. Thus, while earnings impacts were a statistically insignificant $140 in the first year, they increased sharply to $401 in the second year and $511 in the third (see Table 4.2).

---

[22] The two Louisville studies found a similar pattern of employment gains. There were consistent and statistically significant increases in quarterly employment rates and earnings, and little evidence of any improvement in job quality. The studies found that the two programs had differing effects on welfare payments. The Louisville Individual Job Search Experiment found a statistically significant reduction in the percentage of people receiving welfare during most of the 11 quarters of follow-up and reduced AFDC payments in most quarters. The Louisville Group Job Search Experiment found no significant reductions in the percentage on welfare or on AFDC payments (see Wolfhagen, 1983).

[23] Since Unemployment Insurance earnings records were the source of follow-up data, it is not possible to determine whether earnings gains resulted from changes in work hours or wages.

Impacts on AFDC receipt were smaller and less consistent than those on employment and earnings. As Table 4.2 shows, only two of the five programs with employment effects – Arkansas and SWIM – resulted in statistically significant reductions in rate of receipt of AFDC benefits in the first and subsequent years of follow-up. In both cases, welfare receipt among the targeted WIN-mandatories was reduced 6 to 8 percentage points at the end of each year of the study, leading to welfare savings of 14 to 18 percent in the last year of follow-up. While it is not surprising that employment increases led to case closures in Arkansas (a state with very low welfare benefits), it is impressive that SWIM led to similar reductions in AFDC receipt, despite the relatively high grants in California.[24] The longer-term results for the four programs with two- to three-year follow-up show that impacts on average annual welfare payments ranged from close to zero in Baltimore to $553, or a 14 percent saving, in the second year of the SWIM program.[25] (Figures 4.5 and 4.6 indicate, for Arkansas and Baltimore, the quarterly trends over three years in average AFDC payments to the sample and the percent of the sample receiving AFDC benefits.)

Table 4.2 also shows a surprising lack of relationship between the size of the earnings and welfare impacts. For example, on average, Baltimore and SWIM had the highest earnings gains, but very different

---

[24] During the period of the study, the AFDC grant for a family of three was $164 per month in Arkansas and $663 per month in California.

[25] Earlier studies, conducted prior to the passage of the Omnibus Budget Reconciliation Act of 1981 (which increased the rate at which AFDC benefits were reduced when someone went to work) had found that earnings increases were not linked to reduced welfare payments. The WIN study (Ketron, 1980) found that the program increased the average earnings of female AFDC participants by $570 in the first post-program year, $520 in the second, and $340 in the third, with gains mainly for women with no previous employment. The study also concluded that the earnings impacts were not accompanied by any reduction in welfare payments. (See Burtless, 1989, for a useful summary of the findings and methodology in this study.)

The EOPP evaluation found that the program increased the employment of low-income, unmarried mothers in the program sites by 3 to 4 percentage points and the earnings by almost $300 per year. (The impacts on single mothers who actually enrolled in the program are less certain, but were estimated to be substantially larger.) The study concluded that there was no discernible reduction in welfare dependence and even a possible increase in average welfare benefits. The study attributes this to the low wages received by those who obtained employment, which allowed many to remain eligible for welfare, and to the possibility that earnings gains occurred for women who would have left the rolls even without the program. (See Brown et al., 1983; Burtless, 1989.)

FIGURE 4.5   TRENDS IN AVERAGE QUARTERLY AFDC PAYMENTS IN ARKANSAS AND BALTIMORE

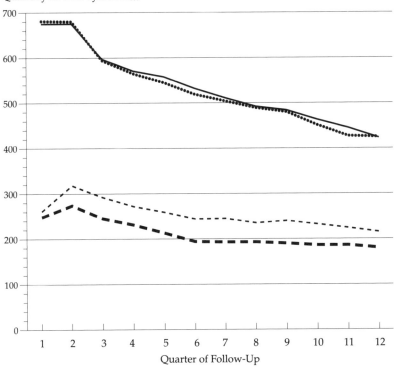

Quarterly AFDC Payments ($)

SOURCES: Tables B.1 and B.2.

FIGURE 4.6 TRENDS IN AVERAGE QUARTERLY AFDC RECEIPT IN ARKANSAS AND BALTIMORE

•••••••••••• Baltimore Experimentals   ▬ ▬ ▬ ▬ Arkansas Experimentals

━━━━━━━ Baltimore Controls   ‑ ‑ ‑ ‑ ‑ ‑ Arkansas Controls

Receiving AFDC (%)

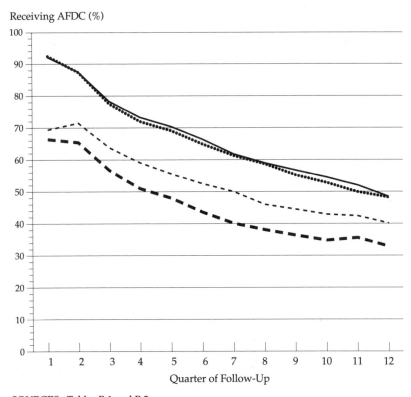

Quarter of Follow-Up

SOURCES: Tables B.1 and B.2.

welfare impacts. Friedlander (1987) offered several reasons why the Baltimore earnings gains were not accompanied by welfare savings. First, he confirmed that welfare grants were reduced as earnings increased, but that the reductions were limited.[26] Second, he noted that some of the people who got jobs through the program would probably have moved off welfare anyway, although to jobs in which they earned less. Finally, he suggested that there may have been welfare savings for those who found employment that were offset by increases in the time on welfare for others (e.g., for people in lengthy program activities).

A comparison of the earnings and welfare impacts in Table 4.2 suggests that the programs differed in their impact on average total income from the two sources. In some locations (e.g., Arkansas), the program caused people to rely more on employment and less on welfare, but did not result in much increase in average combined income from the two sources. In others, there was a clear increase in average total income and in the number of people in higher income brackets: For example, in Baltimore there was a 4.5 percentage point increase in the share of people with combined incomes of more than $6,000 a year (Friedlander, 1987).

These studies also provide useful information on how a welfare-to-work program can affect the rate at which people move in and out of four different combinations of work and welfare: not employed and on welfare, employed and on welfare, employed and not on welfare, and not employed and not on welfare. Appendix Table B.8 shows that in SWIM fewer experimentals than controls remained jobless and on welfare, that over time the percent combining work and welfare at first grew and then declined, and that by the end of the study more people were working and off welfare completely. The last panel in Appendix Table B.8 also shows that a substantial number (about a quarter) of women in the sample were both off AFDC and not working by the end of the two-year follow-up. Moreover, the SWIM program significantly increased the size of this group. Similar results were found in other studies (e.g., in Arkansas).[27]

---

[26] A study using case file data to examine the rate at which welfare grants were reduced as people in the samples in Baltimore, San Diego, Virginia, and West Virginia went to work indicated that the reductions were less than specified in the regulations. On average, the study showed that, among people in Baltimore simultaneously on welfare and working, an additional dollar of earnings reduced the monthly AFDC grant by 44 cents, the lowest reduction rate for the four areas studied. (See Goldman et al., 1985a.)

[27] These studies (because of their reliance on administrative records) could not examine the alternative sources of income for this group or whether there were any changes in household structure, suggesting the importance of further research in this area.

The findings from the two areas without statistically significant employment and earnings impacts constitute important exceptions. In West Virginia, a rural labor market with very high unemployment strongly conditioned program planners' expectations. They had little hope that the poor local labor market could provide jobs, and as a result did not incorporate a job search component. Thus, while the program reinforced community preferences for work, kept job skills from deteriorating, and provided useful public services, it did not translate these gains into unsubsidized employment. The program in Cook County, Illinois, also resulted in no significant increases in employment and earnings, although there were small welfare savings. Here, the explanation may lie in the program design. The Cook County program, one of the two least expensive of those studied (with net costs averaging less than $200 per experimental), mainly monitored people and sanctioned those who did not participate, providing little direct assistance even in its job search component. These exceptions provide useful reminders of the influence of labor market conditions and, possibly, of the need to provide some real assistance to get employment results (if not welfare savings).

Taken together, the employment and welfare impacts for AFDCs point to both the potential and limits of these programs. The earnings gains take on greater significance because they were averages that included all persons eligible for the program, not just the approximately 50 percent who actually received services, the smaller percent who worked during any three-month period, or the even smaller percent who actually benefited from these programs through new jobs or higher earnings. For this last group, the actual gains were probably much larger.

This seeming contradiction is because Table 4.2, as in most such studies, reports average impacts, and such averages can conceal a very mixed pattern of effects. As noted by Friedlander and Gueron in a discussion of the same results:

> We ... deal with impacts that are averages across a large number of individuals. But such averages probably give a misleading impression of how these programs affect individual behavior. An impact of $300 in average annual earnings, for example, may seem to suggest that a program raised the earnings of most sample members by about $300. In fact, impacts on employment rates ... suggest that it is more likely that only a small proportion of program enrollees actually change their employment behavior. For example, an earnings increase of $300 per experimental

in a job search program is probably concentrated among 5 to 10 percent of experimentals.[28] The annual earnings gains for many of these individuals may be several thousand dollars, especially for those who would not have worked without the program but who secure stable employment with its assistance. A similar situation exists for welfare impacts: Reductions of several thousand dollars can occur for the small number of long-term recipients who are induced to leave the rolls, with only minimal effects for the other program enrollees.[29]

While the results thus indicate that some people may have substantial earnings gains as a result of these programs, the overall findings (where many also remain unaffected) clearly also suggest caution. Alone, these initiatives do not offer an immediate cure for poverty or welfare dependence. Even with these programs, many people continue on welfare, and those who move off the rolls often remain poor.

Findings on AFDC Subgroup Impacts

A critical decision in the design of state JOBS initiatives will be whether programs should try to reach the entire mandatory caseload or target specific subgroups, e.g., potential long-term recipients. The programs summarized here shed light on this issue because they were not narrowly selective but, rather, tried to reach all welfare applicants and recipients meeting broad eligibility criteria.

An analysis of five programs – San Diego I, Baltimore, Virginia, Arkansas, and Cook County (but not San Diego SWIM) – addressed the targeting problem by examining program impacts for different AFDC subgroups within the overall samples (Friedlander, 1988b). The study investigated the possible connection between dependence and impact. The findings raised serious concerns about the "common sense" strategy of giving priority attention to the most job-ready candidates. They also suggested that the conclusion for targeting would depend on whether a program's major goal was reducing welfare costs or raising people's earnings.

Table 4.3, from the Friedlander study, shows the five programs' impacts on quarterly earnings and AFDC payments for different welfare

---

[28] Maximum quarterly impacts on employment rates fall within this range.

[29] Friedlander and Gueron, forthcoming.

TABLE 4.3   PROGRAM IMPACTS ON QUARTERLY EARNINGS AND AFDC PAYMENTS FOR MAJOR SUBGROUPS OF AFDC APPLICANTS AND RECIPIENTS

Subgroup and Outcome	San Diego I	Baltimore	Virginia	Arkansas	Cook County[a]
First Tier					
Applicants with No Prior AFDC:					
Earnings	$37	$121	-$13	$26	$ ---
AFDC Payments	-5	-9	-28	-31	---
Second Tier					
Applicant Returnees:					
Earnings	$158**	$188***	$114*	$211***	$ ---
AFDC Payments	-47	-15	-16	-19	---
Applicant Returnees with Less than $3,000 Prior Earnings:					
Earnings	151**	253***	20	202**	---
AFDC Payments	-63*	-19	-29	-22	---
Third Tier					
All Recipients:					
Earnings	$ ---	$37	$69*	$19	$46**
AFDC Payments	---	5	-24	-60***	-13
Recipients with More than 2 Years on AFDC:					
Earnings	---	0	110**	14	---
AFDC Payments	---	19	-48**	-44*	---
Recipients with No Prior Earnings:					
Earnings	---	104**	70	29	12
AFDC Payments	---	1	-26	-63***	-6
Recipients with No Prior Earnings and More than 2 Years on AFDC:					
Earnings	---	88	94*	28	---
AFDC Payments	---	-1	-48**	-48*	---
Full Sample					
Quarterly Impact:					
Earnings	$118**	$96***	$72**	$70**	$19
AFDC Payments	-33	-5	-23*	-40***	-13
Average for Control Group:					
Earnings	773	634	541	257	451
AFDC Payments	469	501	345	232	646

(continued)

TABLE 4.3 *(continued)*

SOURCE: Data from Friedlander, 1988b.

NOTES: Tiers are mutually exclusive; subgroups within tiers overlap. All values are quarterly averages for the fourth through the last quarter of follow-up. Estimates include zero values for sample members not employed and for sample members not receiving welfare.

A two-tailed t-test was applied to differences between experimental and control groups. Statistical significance levels are indicated as: * = 10 percent; ** = 5 percent; and *** = 1 percent.

[a]The definitions of "applicant" and "recipient" for Cook County are not strictly comparable to those of the other programs. See the text of Friedlander, 1988b, for discussion.

groups. In terms of earnings gains, the most employable people – women who were first-time welfare applicants, in the "first tier" of the table – usually had below-average or no earnings impacts. While this group showed high program outcomes (e.g., as measured by employment rates), high rates were also found for comparable people in the control group. That is, even without special assistance, many of these women stayed on welfare only for relatively brief periods. In contrast, more dependent groups – e.g., people applying for welfare who had previously received public assistance, including those who had limited prior earnings, the second tier of Table 4.3 – benefited more consistently from these programs, even though the programs (with the exception of Baltimore) offered only limited assistance and almost no intensive training. Despite the finding that more of these women remained on welfare after receiving services (i.e., their measured "outcomes" were lower), their performance relative to similar people in the control group was more impressive. However, the study also identified a third tier of current recipients – including long-term welfare recipients and those with no recent employment – who did not show as consistent or large earnings impacts.

Shifting the focus to welfare savings, the results suggest a different distribution of impacts. The finding for the most employable (i.e., those in the first tier) is the same: small and usually below-average welfare impacts. However, in contrast to the earnings gains, the largest and most consistent welfare savings usually occurred for the most disadvantaged groups.

This study thus provided strong evidence against "creaming" – i.e., serving only the most advantaged, who demonstrate high placement rates – but did not confirm narrow targeting of these low- to moderate-cost programs on the most disadvantaged.[30] It also suggested that groups whose level of disadvantage was greater than some threshold might require more than low-cost services in order to realize an earnings impact. Interestingly, the subsequent study of the SWIM program (completed after the five-program analysis), which provided a somewhat more intensive treatment than all of the five programs except Baltimore, did

---

[30] The link between these findings and program design is not clear. Since the findings are from programs that did not target specific groups, they do not address the operational challenge or possible stigma or isolating effect of actually running programs targeted to the groups with largest impacts. For example, a job search workshop that included *only* the more disadvantaged might not replicate the results indicated in Table 4.3.

show relatively large impacts on the more dependent half of the AFDC sample in the third tier. As shown in Table 4.4, people in the SWIM study who were already AFDC recipients at the time of random assignment showed surprisingly large impacts. At the end of the second year, the employment rate for recipients in the SWIM experimental group exceeded that for controls by 8 percentage points, and recipients were also 8 percentage points less likely to be on welfare. During that year, earnings were $889, or 50 percent, above those of controls, and welfare payments were $608, or 13 percent less. In contrast to other studies,[31] SWIM had less robust employment impacts for AFDC applicants.

Friedlander (1988b) also found that a small number of simple, objective characteristics collected at the point of program enrollment could distinguish groups with large differences in welfare receipt. For adults, prior earnings and welfare history were the most important characteristics; high school diploma status also contributed.[32] The study could not demonstrate which one of these three characteristics would be most closely linked with program impact. Thus, for example, the study could not conclude whether weak prior earnings would always be a better or worse targeting characteristic than long welfare history or the absence of a high school diploma. A variety of other variables – such as age, number of children, and ethnicity – increased the complexity of the model of long-term welfare receipt but did not dramatically improve predictive power. Appendix Table B.9 shows impact results for various subgroup characteristics.

The findings on the effectiveness of work programs for different subgroups of welfare recipients have implications for performance standards, i.e., for the extent to which the use of certain standards would encourage programs to maximize long-term earnings gains and reductions in welfare dependence. Specifically, the lack of correlation between simple outcomes and impacts confirms that unweighted placement rates or case closure rates do not provide valid performance standards for this population (Friedlander, 1988b).

Table 4.4 shows this distinction for applicants and recipients in the SWIM program. While annual earnings (outcomes) in the second year were higher for experimentals who were new applicants than for those

TABLE 4.4 IMPACTS OF THE SAN DIEGO SWIM PROGRAM ON AFDC APPLICANTS AND RECIPIENTS

Outcome and Follow-Up Period	AFDC Applicants				AFDC Recipients			
	Experimental Group Mean	Control Group Mean	Difference	Percentage Change	Experimental Group Mean	Control Group Mean	Difference	Percentage Change
Average Earnings								
Year 1	$2,607	$2,238	$369	16%	$1,652	$1,319	$333**	25%
Year 2	3,298	3,011	287	10	2,651	1,762	889***	50
Employed at End of								
Year 1	38.3%	33.2%	5.1**	15%	32.3%	22.9%	9.4***	41%
Year 2	34.2	33.8	0.4	1	34.9	26.5	8.4***	32
Average AFDC Payments								
Year 1	$3,381	$3,724	-$343**	-9%	$5,090	$5,546	-$456***	-8%
Year 2	2,354	2,821	-467***	-17	4,086	4,694	-608***	-13
On Welfare at End of								
Year 1	51.7%	58.0%	-6.4**	-11%	75.2%	81.8%	-6.5***	-8%
Year 2	37.4	43.4	-6.0**	-14	60.3	68.5	-8.1***	-12

SOURCE: Data from Hamilton and Friedlander, 1989.

NOTES: The earnings and AFDC payments data include zero values for sample members not employed and for sample members not receiving welfare. Estimates are regression-adjusted using ordinary least squares, controlling for pre-random assignment characteristics of sample members. There may be some discrepancies in experimental-control differences because of rounding. Year 1 begins with the quarter following the quarter of random assignment, and all outcomes were calculated for calendar quarters.

"Employed" or "on welfare" at the end of the year is defined as receiving earnings or welfare payments at some point during the last quarter of the year.

Earnings and AFDC payments are not adjusted for inflation.

** Denotes statistical significance at the 5 percent level; and *** at the 1 percent level.

who were already receiving welfare (on average, a more disadvantaged group), the program's net impacts were greater for recipients. Similarly, while AFDC receipt and average payments were substantially lower for experimentals who were new applicants, this did not reflect greater net impacts, but rather differences in characteristics that also had a powerful effect on the behavior of members of the applicant control group.

Findings on Impacts for AFDC-UPs

As indicated in Chapter 2, FSA requires all states to implement a public assistance program for two-parent families: the AFDC-UP (Unemployment Parent) program. It also calls on states to involve (with eventual very high participation rates) at least one parent in these families in JOBS activities that emphasize work. (For young parents who have not completed high school or its equivalent, education may be substituted.) In contrast to the strong record from numerous studies of pre-JOBS programs for single parents on AFDC (primarily women), there are only two comparably reliable studies – both from San Diego – for fathers, usually the adult involved in AFDC-UP work programs.

Table 4.5 presents the summary impact data from the San Diego I and SWIM studies. (Of the evaluations discussed in the preceding sections, three did not include AFDC-UPs, the Baltimore sample was too small to produce reliable findings, and the West Virginia study produced uncertain results.[33]) The first San Diego program, which served only applicants, resulted in no sustained employment and earnings impacts, but it did produce welfare savings that were somewhat larger than those for the AFDC women who were applicants in the same program.[34] Compared to the AFDCs, more of the mostly male experimentals were working and had higher earnings, but more of the controls were also working. A surprisingly high percent of the men were still receiving AFDC-UP benefits at the end of follow-up and, because of their larger case size, they had larger average grants than those of the AFDC women. The SWIM study, which included applicants and recipients, showed a more robust and consistent pattern of impacts for AFDC-UP eligibles than did the

---

[33] The West Virginia AFDC-UP study compared results across counties that implemented a saturation or more limited program. Because of differences in labor markets and the characteristics of welfare recipients, as well as data coverage, the evaluation did not reach a clear conclusion on the impact of saturation. (See Friedlander et al., 1986.)

[34] The study suggests that the explanation may be, in part, the different eligibility and sanctioning rules for AFDC-UPs that applied during the study period (Goldman, Friedlander, and Long, 1986).

TABLE 4.5 **IMPACTS OF TWO WELFARE-TO-WORK PROGRAMS ON AFDC-UP ELIGIBLES**

Location, Outcome, and Follow-Up Period		Experimental Group Mean	Control Group Mean	Difference	Percentage Change
San Diego I					
Average Earnings	Year 1	$4,563	$4,397	$166	4%
Employed at End of	Year 1	53.3%	53.7%	-0.4	-1%
Average AFDC Payments	Year 1	$2,289	$2,664	-$374***	-14%
On Welfare at End of	Year 1	36.0%	41.7%	-5.7***	-14%
San Diego SWIM					
Average Earnings	Year 1	$3,307	$2,806	$500*	18%
	Year 2	4,294	3,840	454	12
Employed at End of	Year 1	38.0%	33.7%	4.3*	13%
	Year 2	43.7	37.2	6.5**	17
Average AFDC Payments	Year 1	$4,883	$5,300	-$417**	-8%
	Year 2	3,897	4,448	-551***	-12
On Welfare at End of	Year 1	60.3%	62.8%	-2.6	-4%
	Year 2	49.3	50.5	-1.2	-2

SOURCES: Data from Goldman, Friedlander, and Long, 1986; Hamilton and Friedlander, 1989; and additional MDRC estimates of annual values.

NOTES: The earnings and AFDC payments data include zero values for sample members not employed and for sample members not receiving welfare. Estimates are regression-adjusted using ordinary least squares, controlling for pre-random assignment characteristics of sample members. There may be some discrepancies in experimental-control differences because of rounding.

In the San Diego I program, year 1 begins with the quarter of random assignment. For employment and earnings, the quarter of random assignment refers to the calendar quarter in which random assignment occurred. As a result, "average earnings" in year 1 may include up to two months of earnings prior to random assignment. For AFDC payments, the quarter of random assignment refers to the three months beginning with the month in which an individual was randomly assigned. In the San Diego SWIM program, where all outcomes were calculated for calendar quarters, year 1 begins with the quarter following the quarter of random assignment.

"Employed" or "on welfare" at the end of the year is defined as receiving earnings or welfare payments at some point during the last quarter of the year.

Earnings and AFDC payments are not adjusted for inflation.

*Denotes statistical significance at the 10 percent level; **at the 5 percent level; and ***at the 1 percent level.

earlier study. In SWIM, there were impacts on earnings, employment rates, and welfare payments, with impacts continuing throughout the two-year follow-up period. While the majority of the AFDC-UPs were applicants, most of the welfare savings were for recipients; there was no similar pattern for earnings gains.

The SWIM findings provide the first solid evidence of an AFDC-UP welfare-to-work program meeting the goals of producing both welfare savings and earnings gains. However, in terms of guiding JOBS administrators on program design, the knowledge base is approximately at the level it was for AFDC work programs in the late 1970s.

Benefit-Cost Findings

The preceding sections showed that most of the broad-coverage welfare-to-work programs evaluated to date produced sustained increases in employment and earnings and, to a lesser extent, welfare savings for single parents; the SWIM study showed a similar pattern for adults in two-parent families. These impacts were obtained for an average public investment of between $118 and $953 per experimental. (This is the net cost per experimental, not per person actually participating in particular program components. Net costs include all expenditures incurred specifically for the program under study by the operating agency, plus any expenditures by other organizations on services that were an essential part of the program treatment, minus the costs to the operating agency or other organizations of serving members of the control group.[35])

Researchers evaluating the seven programs also made a systematic effort to quantify a broader range of economic outcomes and compare them to their costs, using a benefit-cost framework. In doing this, they addressed several questions: From a government budget perspective, do savings exceed the initial investment? From the perspective of welfare families, do the gains exceed the losses? In overall economic terms (considering society as a whole, including both families on welfare and others), do the benefits justify the expenses? As with any benefit-cost analysis, these studies have limitations and rest on a number of assumptions. For example, certain benefits and costs were not measured (e.g., the value of society's preference for work over welfare or the various potential

---

[35] See Appendix A for a detailed discussion of net cost per experimental, using several alternative perspectives and definitions of costs.

effects on the children of women who participate in program services and, as a result, go to work). Estimates for others rest on assumptions about outcomes that were not directly measured (e.g., Medicaid savings) and the extrapolation of program impacts after the follow-up period (in this case, for a total of five years).

The estimates of these programs' effects on government budgets showed that, while the programs required an initial investment, budget outlays were usually more than offset by projected savings over two to five years. For example, the San Diego I program for AFDC single parents invested $636 per eligible person in the caseload and led to offsetting five-year savings from increased taxes and reduced AFDC, Medicaid, and other transfer payments of $1,586, or $2.50 for each dollar of costs. The San Diego SWIM program returned $3 for every dollar of initial costs, and Arkansas led to even higher benefits per dollar of costs.[36] Among the studies, the estimates from the Arkansas, Virginia, and Cook County programs for AFDCs also showed budget savings, as did the two San Diego programs for AFDC-UPs. The Baltimore and West Virginia AFDC programs incurred some small net costs. In four of the states, more than half the savings went to the federal government. This provides a strong rationale for substantial federal participation in the funding of such programs, particularly in low-grant states.

Benefits and costs can also be viewed from the perspective of the welfare recipients targeted for participation. For AFDC women, the projected earnings gains associated with the programs usually exceeded the estimated reductions in welfare benefits and losses in other transfer payments, such as Medicaid and Food Stamps. In some of the programs, however, gains in earnings approximately balanced reductions in transfers. AFDC-UP men broke even in SWIM (with their earnings gains about matching their losses from AFDC, other transfers, and tax payments). The men in the San Diego I study incurred net losses.

Since benefits usually exceeded costs from both the government budget perspective and the perspective of the welfare eligibles targeted by the programs, the studies found positive results from the perspective

---

[36] The following section uses a somewhat different measure to show the relative cost-effectiveness of low- or higher-cost approaches. Instead of estimating either the total benefit or net present value (benefits minus costs) per dollar of net investment, it compares the final years' earnings and welfare impacts per dollar of program costs.

of society as a whole – the measure economists often use to judge whether a program results in an economically efficient use of resources. (This perspective measures whether there is a net gain or loss in total social resources as a result of each person's involvement with the welfare-to-work program.)

The Effect of the Program Model and Funding

The preceding five sections have discussed what is known about broad-coverage programs in each of the three primary categories into which evaluation findings typically fall: participation (as part of the study of program implementation), impact, and benefit-cost analysis. It is also useful, however, to discuss these findings in the context of the framework for understanding the effects of state JOBS programs that was presented in Chapter 2. There it was suggested that particular features of a welfare-to-work program – such as its "mandatoriness" and target population – help define the program's nature and strength. The impact of these factors is examined in this and the next two sections, which are followed by a discussion of the research on the impact of the local economic and program context.

Broad-coverage welfare-to-work models can differ in the components, cost (and resulting cost-effectiveness), sequencing, and duration of services.

The Effect of Different Program Components. Unfortunately, the seven studies do not compare programs that differed on single dimensions, and only one – the first San Diego study – included a well-executed differential impact study.[37] The strongest consistent evidence is for job search approaches. Six of the seven studies were of sequenced programs, where job search was the initial and most frequent activity. These results, combined with the earlier Louisville experiments (Goldman, 1981;

---

[37] The research design in three evaluations (San Diego I, Virginia, and Cook County) included a differential impact study, in which sample members were randomly assigned to either of two different treatment streams or to a control group, which was not eligible for either set of services. In these studies, outcomes for the two service groups were to be compared to each other and to the control group to isolate the differential effect of adding a work experience component to job search, or to job search and other activities. However, in two of these programs (Cook County and Virginia), only a small percent of the sample received the alternative treatment, resulting in participation patterns that were not sufficiently distinct to test the differential impacts of the two approaches.

Wolfhagen, 1983), provide compelling evidence on the long-term effectiveness of different forms of job search.[38] The findings suggest that job search has almost always led to some increase in employment rates, but not to higher wages or longer hours (and thus higher earnings) for those working.[39] Job search has also usually resulted in some welfare savings.

There is much less evidence on unpaid work experience. San Diego I included an experimental test of the incremental return from adding three months of unpaid community work experience (CWEP) after an initial job search program.[40] The overall findings for AFDC applicants indicate that the addition of CWEP after job search did increase program effectiveness, but the lack of consistent results across cohorts enrolling during different labor market conditions suggests that, at most, the incremental impact was small. Thus, for AFDCs, there is some evidence of greater earnings (but not welfare) effects, but this evidence was driven by findings for the half of the sample that was enrolled during a period of economic recovery. For AFDC-UPs, there were inconsistent and contradictory impacts on employment versus earnings, and on receipt of welfare versus the amount of welfare received. This lack of consistent findings from San Diego, and the absence of impacts from West Virginia's

---

[38] These studies also provide extensive information on how job search was implemented and on participants' reactions. See Gould-Stuart, 1982; Goldman et al., 1985b; Quint and Guy, 1986.

[39] Employment and earnings information for the seven broad-coverage studies came from Unemployment Insurance earnings automated records (which contain quarterly earnings and employment rates), rather than from surveys. The nature of this data source does not allow researchers to determine how much of the gain in earnings came from increases in hours or weeks worked versus hourly wages, although the combined effect of these factors on earnings could be measured.

[40] The Cook County study included a similar test, in which people were randomly assigned to a program where work experience followed job search, or to a program without work experience, or to a control group. The authors of that study concluded that there was no evidence that adding work experience increased the 18-month employment, earnings, or welfare impacts over and above those of job search alone. They did find that the addition of work experience led to a small but statistically significant decrease in welfare savings in the last few quarters of follow-up: Savings were lower for the job search and work experience sequence than for job search alone. (See Friedlander et al., 1987.) However, the Cook County test addressed this differential impact issue less successfully than did San Diego I, since, as shown in Table 4.1, only 7.3 percent of the experimentals in the Cook County job search/work experience sequence actually participated in work experience, compared to 13 percent in the San Diego I sequence.

pure workfare program for AFDCs,[41] means that there is little evidence on whether unpaid work experience, following job search or alone, has an independent effect on program impacts (Goldman, Friedlander, and Long, 1986; Friedlander et al., 1986).

In addition to providing information on program impact and cost-effectiveness, the 1980s studies also looked at how unpaid work experience was implemented and how welfare recipients viewed mandatory work requirements. In-depth interviews with a random sample of workfare supervisors and participants in six of the seven studies examined whether the positions were "punitive" and "make-work" or produced useful goods and services, provided dignity, and developed work skills. In an earlier volume, Gueron summarized these results:

- The jobs were generally entry-level positions in maintenance, clerical work, park service, or human services.

- Although the positions did not primarily develop skills, they were not make-work either. Supervisors judged the work important and indicated that participants' productivity and attendance were similar to those of most entry-level workers.

- A large proportion of the participants responded positively to the work assignments. They were satisfied with the positions and with coming to work, and they believed they were making a useful contribution.

- Many participants nevertheless believed that the employer got the better end of the bargain, or that they were underpaid for their work. In brief, they would have preferred a paid job.

These findings suggest that most states did not design or implement workfare with a punitive intent. This may explain results from the worksite survey that indicated that the majority of the participants in most states shared the view that a work requirement was fair.[42]

---

[41] As noted earlier, the AFDC-UP study in West Virginia used a comparison group design and produced uncertain results.

[42] Gueron, 1987, p. 20. See Hoerz and Hanson, 1986, for a summary of results from studies in the six sites plus New York City. These results should not be used to draw conclusions about workfare programs lasting longer than the typical 13-week assignments that were studied or involving the creation of so many positions in a site that the quality of individual job assignments would be affected.

Because so few of the broad-coverage programs included education, training, or on-the-job training (OJT) services, and because of the relatively short follow-up periods, they provide limited evidence on whether these services are successful in getting people into better jobs than they would otherwise obtain. The Baltimore program did seem to lead to an improvement in the type of jobs obtained (i.e., in wages or hours worked), and not just increased job-holding, but surprisingly showed no overall welfare savings. (Chapter 5 continues this discussion, focusing on what is known about the effectiveness of providing particular services as selective-voluntary components of broad-coverage systems. It also presents separately what we know about three JOBS-relevant types of services: education, support services, and services targeted on young welfare recipients.)

The Effect of Low- Versus Higher-Cost Services. As indicated in a recent analysis by Friedlander and Gueron of these same seven broad-coverage studies, there are several alternative measures that can be used to assess the relative effectiveness of low- and higher-cost services: the average impact per enrollee, the impact per dollar outlay, the benefit net of program cost, the effect on income and poverty, and the impact on potential long-term recipients.[43]

Using the first measure (the one used in the second and third sections of this chapter), overall they find some support for the conclusion that programs that include some higher-cost, more intensive components (usually education and training) lead to larger absolute earnings gains per person in the study than those that provide only lower-cost job search and work experience.[44] (The evidence does not suggest that they produce larger welfare savings.) This can be seen in Table 4.6, which summarizes impacts for programs listed in ascending order of net cost (defined, in most cases, as the operating agency's average cost per enrolled experimental minus its costs for controls) and also includes

---

[43] See Friedlander and Gueron, forthcoming, for a detailed discussion of the evidence from welfare-to-work experiments on the relationship between cost and impact and the interpretation of these four measures.

[44] This is similar to the conclusion reached by Burtless, 1989, and Grossman, Maynard, and Roberts, 1985.

TABLE 4.6   AFDC WELFARE-TO-WORK PROGRAMS: CHARACTERISTICS, COSTS, AND IMPACTS

Program (Ordered by Increasing Net Cost)	Program Activities and Study Characteristics	Coverage/ Mandatoriness	Net Cost Per Experimental	Outcome	Annual Impacts for All Years of Follow-Up	
					Experimental-Control Difference	Percent Change Over Control Group Level
Broad-Coverage Programs						
Arkansas WORK Program	Sequence of group job search and (for a few) unpaid work experience; controls excused from all WIN requirements except assessment; low-grant state; highly disadvantaged population; evaluation began in 1983	Mandatory; targeted AFDC applicants and recipients with children 3 or older; few sanctions; 38% ever participated in job search or work experience during 9-month follow-up	$118	Earnings Year 1 Year 2 Year 3	$167** 223 337**	33% 23 31
				AFDC payments Year 1 Year 2 Year 3	-$145*** -190*** -168***	-13% -19 -18
Louisville WIN Lab–Individual Job Search	Individual job search; controls eligible for regular WIN services; low-grant state; evaluation began in 1978	Mandatory and voluntary; targeted AFDC applicants and recipients with children of any age; 55% ever participated in individual job search during 8-month follow-up	$136[a]	Earnings Year 1 Year 2 Year 3	$289**[b] 456**[b] 435**[b]	18% 20 18
				AFDC payments Year 1 Year 2 Year 3	-$75*[b] -164**[b] -184**[b]	-3% -8 -10

Program	Description		Measure		
Cook County WIN Demonstration	Sequence of individual job search and unpaid work experience; controls excused from all WIN requirements except orientation; program provided little direct assistance, mainly monitored and sanctioned those who did not participate; medium-grant state; highly disadvantaged population; evaluation began in 1985	$157	Earnings Year 1	$10	1%
			AFDC payments Year 1	-$40	-1%
Louisville WIN Lab-Group Job Search	Group job search; controls eligible for regular WIN services; low-grant state; evaluation began in 1980	$230[a]	Earnings Year 1	$464**[c]	43%
	Mandatory and voluntary; targeted AFDC applicants and recipients with children of any age; 65% ever participated in group job search during 6-month follow-up		AFDC payments Year 1	-$40[c]	-2%
West Virginia CWEP	Open-ended unpaid work experience; controls eligible for all other WIN services; rural labor market with very high unemployment; low-grant state; highly disadvantaged population; evaluation began in 1983	$260	Earnings Year 1	$16	4%
	Mandatory; targeted AFDC applicants and recipients with children 6 or older; few sanctions; 24% ever participated in work experience during 9-month follow-up		AFDC payments Year 1	$0	0%

(continued)

TABLE 4.6 *(continued)*

Program (Ordered by Increasing Net Cost)	Program Activities and Study Characteristics	Coverage/ Mandatoriness	Net Cost Per Experimental	Outcome	Annual Impacts for All Years of Follow-Up	
					Experimental-Control Difference	Percent Change Over Control Group Level
Virginia ESP	Sequence of individual or group job search, unpaid work experience, and some education or job skills training (but only slightly more than controls received on their own); controls excused from all WIN requirements; medium-grant state; disadvantaged population; evaluation began in 1983	Mandatory; targeted AFDC applicants and recipients with children 6 or older; few sanctions; 58% ever participated in any activity during 9-month follow-up	$430	Earnings Year 1 Year 2 Year 3 AFDC payments Year 1 Year 2 Year 3	$69 280** 268* -$69 -36 -111**	5% 14 11 -3% -2 -9
San Diego I (EPP/EWEP)	Sequence of group job search and unpaid work experience; controls eligible for other WIN services; substantial program assistance provided; high-grant state; less disadvantaged population; evaluation began in 1982	Mandatory; targeted AFDC applicants with children 6 or older; many sanctions; 46% ever participated in job search or work experience during 9-month follow-up	$636	Earnings Year 1 AFDC payments Year 1	$443*** -$226***	23% -8%

San Diego SWIM	Sequence of group job search, unpaid work experience, and education and job skills training; controls excused from all WIN requirements; high participation and ongoing participation requirement; high-grant state; less disadvantaged population; evaluation began in 1985	Mandatory; targeted AFDC applicants and recipients with children 6 or older; many sanctions; 64% ever participated in any activity during 12-month follow-up	$919	Earnings
				Year 1	$352***	21%
				Year 2	658***	29
				AFDC payments
				Year 1	-$407***	-8%
				Year 2	-553***	-14
Baltimore Options	Choice of services, including individual or group job search, education, job skills training, unpaid work experience, and on-the-job training; controls eligible for regular WIN services; program constrained to serve 1,000 enrollees per year; medium-grant state; less disadvantaged population; evaluation began in 1982	Mandatory; targeted AFDC applicants and recipients with children 6 or older; few sanctions; 45% ever participated in any activity during 12-month follow-up	$953	Earnings
				Year 1	$140	10%
				Year 2	401***	17
				Year 3	511***	17
				AFDC payments
				Year 1	$2	0%
				Year 2	-34	-2
				Year 3	-31	-2

(continued)

TABLE 4.6 (continued)

Program (Ordered by Increasing Net Cost)	Program Activities and Study Characteristics	Coverage/ Mandatoriness	Net Cost Per Experimental	Outcome	Annual Impacts for All Years of Follow-Up		
					Experimental-Control Difference	Percent Change Over Control Group Level	

Selective-Voluntary Programs

Program	Program Activities and Study Characteristics	Coverage/ Mandatoriness	Net Cost Per Experimental	Outcome	Experimental-Control Difference	Percent Change Over Control Group Level
New Jersey OJT	Subsidized on-the-job training; controls eligible for other WIN services; enrollees quite disadvantaged in terms of prior welfare receipt and recent work histories, but had relatively high levels of GED attainment; medium-grant state; evaluation began in 1984	Voluntary; targeted selected AFDC recipients over 18 with children of any age; 40% participated in employment with OJT (84% ever participated in any WIN or JTPA activity) during 12-month follow-up	$787 [$439][d]	Earnings Year 1 Year 2 AFDC payments Year 1 Year 2	N/A[e] $591*[e] -$190**[e] -238*	N/A 14% -6% -11
Maine OJT	Sequence of employability training, unpaid work experience, and subsidized on-the-job training; controls eligible for regular WIN services; enrollees quite disadvantaged in terms of prior welfare receipt and recent work histories, but had relatively high levels of GED attainment; medium-grant state; evaluation began in 1983	Voluntary; targeted selected unemployed AFDC recipients on rolls for at least prior 6 months, with children of any age; 90% ever participated in any activity during 12-month follow-up	$2,019 [$1,635][d]	Earnings Year 1 Year 2 Year 3 AFDC payments Year 1 Year 2 Year 3	$104 871** 941*[f] $64 29 80[f]	8% 38 34 2% 1 4

Program	Description	Treatment	Net cost	Outcome		
AFDC Homemaker-Home Health Aide Demonstrations	Job skills training and subsidized employment program; varied population; low-, medium-, and high-grant states; evaluation began in 1983	Voluntary; targeted selected AFDC recipients on rolls for at least 90 days who were not employed as home health aides during that time; 84% participated (i.e., entered training)	$9,505 ($5,957-$12,457 across states) [$5,684][d]	Earnings Year 1 Year 2 Year 3 AFDC and Food Stamp benefits Year 1 Year 2 Year 3	$2,026[g] 1,347[g] 1,121[g] -$696[g] -855[g] -343[g]	N/A N/A N/A N/A N/A N/A
National Supported Work Demonstration	Structured, paid work experience; targeted extremely disadvantaged AFDC recipients; low-, medium-, and high-grant states; evaluation began in 1976	Voluntary; targeted selected AFDC recipients on rolls for 30 of prior 36 months, with children 6 or older; 97% participated (i.e., showed up for their program jobs)	$17,981[a] [$9,447][d,h]	Earnings Year 1 Year 2 Year 3 AFDC payments Year 1 Year 2 Year 3	$6,402***[i] 1,368***[i] 1,076***[i] -$2,200**[i] -1,165***[i] -401**[i]	327% 36 23 -39% -26 -10

(continued)

SOURCES: Data from the reports listed at the end of Chapter 1 and additional MDRC estimates.

NOTES: The cost estimates reported in this table are the net costs of these programs. These include all expenditures incurred specifically for the programs under study by the operating agency, plus any expenditures by other organizations for services that were an essential part of the program treatment, minus costs to the operating agency or other organizations of serving members of the control groups. See Appendix A for further discussion.

Net costs and annual impacts are in nominal dollars except where noted.

[a]The net cost is adjusted to 1985 dollars.

TABLE 4.6 (continued)

[b]The impact is adjusted to 1985 dollars. Year 1 begins with the quarter of random assignment. The annual earnings impact for year 3 is based on one quarter of follow-up. The annual AFDC payments impact for year 3 is based on three quarters of follow-up. Statistical significance was not calculated for year 3. However, since the quarterly impacts are statistically significant, the annual impacts are assumed also to be significant.

[c]The impact is adjusted to 1985 dollars. The annual earnings impact is based on two quarters of follow-up. Statistical significance was not calculated. However, since the quarterly impacts are statistically significant, the annual impact is assumed also to be significant. The annual AFDC payments impact is based on four quarters of follow-up.

[d]The bracketed figure excludes wage subsidy payments for participants, whereas the other figure includes them.

[e]A year 1 earnings impact is not available in New Jersey for the same sample as the year 2 impact and is therefore not shown. The annual earnings impact for year 2 is based on three quarters of follow-up. Statistical significance was not calculated for year 2. However, since the earnings impact for quarters 5-7 is statistically significant, the annual impact is assumed also to be significant. Similarly, the quarterly AFDC payments impacts for quarters 2, 3, and 4 of year 1 are statistically significant, so the annual impact is assumed also to be significant.

[f]Annual earnings and AFDC payments impacts for year 3 are based on three quarters of follow-up. Statistical significance was not calculated for year 3. However, since the quarterly earnings impacts are statistically significant, the annual earnings impact is assumed also to be significant.

[g]Cross-state annual impacts are estimated from state-specific impacts presented in Table 5.2, so statistical significance and experimental and control group means are not available. Year 1 is defined by the original researchers as the number of months from random assignment until the typical experimental left subsidized employment. Year 2 is defined as the 12-month period following the time when the typical experimental left subsidized employment. Year 3 is based on all months in the follow-up period after year 2. Average annual impacts for each year were calculated by multiplying the average monthly impacts for that period by 12. Total earnings of the experimental group include both demonstration and non-demonstration earnings. Since the Homemaker-Home Health Aide Demonstrations offered up to a year of subsidized paid employment, earnings and consequently reduced AFDC and Food Stamp benefits during the first two years partly reflect wages earned in the program, and not post-program impacts. In year 2, there were statistically significant gains in monthly earnings in all seven states and welfare savings in four. In year 3, there were significant gains in monthly earnings in five of the seven states and welfare savings in four.

[h]Supported Work projects generated revenues of $4,352 per experimental (in 1985 dollars), which offset part of the cost reported here.

[i]The impact is adjusted to 1985 dollars. Since Supported Work offered up to 18 months of subsidized paid employment, earnings and consequently reduced AFDC payments during the first two years partly reflect wages earned in the program, and not post-program impacts. The annual earnings and AFDC payments impacts for year 3 are based on quarter 9, the last quarter for which there are common follow-up data for all recipients who responded to the final survey. AFDC payments impacts include impacts on General Assistance, Supplemental Security Income, and other unspecified cash welfare.

*Denotes statistical significance at the 10 percent level; ** at the 5 percent level; and *** at the 1 percent level.

information on four selective-voluntary programs, which are discussed in Chapter 5.[45] While the table shows that even the very low-cost Arkansas program had persistent effects, average earnings impacts in the final year of follow-up tended to increase with cost. Thus, impacts were larger for San Diego SWIM and Baltimore than for San Diego I and Virginia. In contrast, average welfare impacts showed no clear relationship to cost: There were no welfare savings in Baltimore and clear savings in Arkansas.

In interpreting the table, it is important to remember that differences in program impacts may be attributable to factors other than cost (i.e., to the other dimensions discussed in Chapter 2). For example, programs that serve more disadvantaged persons are likely to have different impacts than those serving less disadvantaged persons; low-cost programs may be more effective in low-grant than in high-grant states;[46] programs that make limited use of sanctioning may have different impacts than those that sanction frequently. (Table 4.6 includes some of the information relevant to interpreting this cost-impact relationship. It lists as program activities only those components in which experimentals' participation exceeded controls' and notes when this increase in service was small. For example, in Virginia, a substantial number of experimentals participated in education and training but, as indicated in the discussion of Table 4.1, so did controls; thus, the program led to an increase in services for only a few people.)

---

[45] In almost all cases, impacts are stated in nominal dollars, not adjusted for inflation, with the evaluation's starting date shown in the table. The exceptions are the two Louisville job search programs and Supported Work, which began before 1980 and where ignoring the effects of inflation would have been particularly distorting. Both the costs and impacts for these programs have been inflated to 1985 dollars. While the same principles were used in calculating costs in most of these studies, the varying availability of data and different structures of the programs make some of the estimates not directly comparable. For example, in Supported Work, values from the mid-1970s were inflated to 1985, which may overstate both the costs of operating the program and the wages earned by program graduates, given the limited increase in the minimum wage during these years. In addition, the costs of all of the selective-voluntary programs include the subsidized share of wages paid to program participants. These were a particularly high fraction of average costs in the Supported Work Demonstration and resulted in offsetting AFDC savings, which are shown separately in the table but not deducted from costs. Finally, for budgetary purposes, the cost of Supported Work should also be reduced because the programs generated partially offsetting revenue from the sale of goods and services the programs produced. (See the notes to Table 4.6.)

[46] The two low-cost job search programs that had impacts on employment and welfare receipt were both implemented in low-grant states – Kentucky and Arkansas – where even a low-wage job would result in a case closure. It is not clear whether a similar program would have been equally successful, for example, in California.

In particular, it is not clear whether the larger earnings gains in San Diego SWIM and Baltimore reflect the use of some more intensive services or other aspects of the program or environment: e.g., the scale and local conditions, the extensive experience and capability of the programs' administrators, or the strong enforcement of the ongoing participation requirement in the SWIM saturation demonstration.[47]

Turning to the second measure – impact per dollar invested in the welfare-to-work program – Friedlander and Gueron find that the addition of cost considerations changes the picture substantially. They note that as long as costs were above a threshold level (not met in Cook County),[48] there seems to have been an inverse relationship between a program's average cost and its earnings impact/cost ratio: i.e., the higher the program cost, the lower the earnings gain per dollar outlay.[49] Based on this, they conclude that cost-effectiveness – using this particular measure – appears to have decreased from low- to higher-cost systems, apparently because the higher-cost systems used a combination of low-cost job search and work experience enriched with more expensive components such as education, training, and OJT, and the latter components seemingly had lower impact per dollar outlay. The relationship for welfare impacts was less consistent, but also suggested diminishing returns in moving from programs that began with job search (either as the only service or followed by other activities

---

[47] In terms of scale – which could affect placements and thus program impacts – Virginia served the full mandatory caseload; Baltimore covered a cross section of the caseload, but only 1,000 people; San Diego I served only welfare applicants; and San Diego SWIM operated in only two of the seven offices of the county's social services department. In terms of administrative capacity, the San Diego social services department had a reputation for unusual expertise, and the Baltimore Office of Manpower Resources – which ran Options – was among the most experienced and highly regarded CETA/JTPA operators in the country.

[48] In dollar terms, Cook County did not have a lower net cost per experimental than the Arkansas and first Louisville programs. However, in these two low-grant areas, staff salaries were lower than in Chicago. Thus, the Cook County program may have spent the least in real terms. It also used resources differently, focusing on monitoring and processing people rather than providing direct services.

[49] The impact per dollar outlay is obtained by dividing the impact estimate for the last year of follow-up by the net cost (both from Table 4.6). Using this measure, the annual earnings impact per dollar invested was 50 to 75 cents in Virginia, San Diego I, SWIM, and Baltimore compared to $2 or more in Arkansas and the similarly low-cost Louisville job search programs. Note that this measure – the impact per dollar outlay – is not the same as the total benefit per dollar outlay used in the preceding section.

as part of a mixed strategy) to those that provided mainly higher-cost components.

Focusing only on this measure, Friedlander and Gueron note that, faced with a choice of using a fixed budget to provide either higher-cost services to a smaller number of enrollees or lower-cost (primarily job search) services to a much greater number, the latter strategy (as long as the services are above the threshold level) is more likely to maximize aggregate program impacts (i.e., the total sum of earnings impacts or welfare savings for all individuals exposed to the program).[50] (The findings for the third measure – net taxpayer benefits – are similar to those for this other cost measure.)

However, Friedlander and Gueron point out that many people are equally or even more interested in other measures of effectiveness, e.g., the ability of a program to reduce poverty or to prevent long-term welfare receipt. Because of the limited data collected in most studies, they note that there is very little evidence on whether higher-cost programs are more successful in increasing family income and reducing poverty, but there is evidence they are more likely to get people into jobs with higher wages or hours. There is an indication of this type of effect in Baltimore.[51] There is also very limited information on whether higher-cost components are more successful with people who are more likely to be long-term recipients. Only Baltimore and SWIM had some more intensive services. As indicated in Table 4.3, the Baltimore program was not particularly successful with recipients. Since SWIM's impacts for subgroups of recipients are not yet available, it is not clear whether the strongly positive average impacts for recipients found in that study (see Table 4.4) extended to the most disadvantaged subgroups. As discussed in Chapter 5, among the selective-voluntary programs, Supported Work had a strong record of effectiveness with very long-term AFDC recipients who had little or no prior employment.

---

[50] As indicated in Chapter 2, however, states usually do not face a fixed budget limit that is independent of their choice of program approach. Particular JOBS services are often funded out of different agency budgets. Certain ones (e.g., case management) may be paid for directly with JOBS funds, while others (e.g., skills training or education) may be provided by JTPA agencies or community colleges. Given the JOBS legislation's focus on interagency coordination, the welfare agency's real budget constraint will depend on the extent to which it can access services from these other agencies.

[51] See also the discussion of the higher-cost selective-voluntary programs in Chapter 5.

Friedlander and Gueron conclude their review by pointing to the operational implications of these findings and the major uncertainties that remain. In their view, the findings suggest that administrators may face a trade-off in meeting different program objectives: Programs with some higher-cost services may lead to greater impacts per person and get some people better jobs, but those with mainly lower-cost, job search services may get greater total impacts because more people are served. This may prompt administrators interested in achievements in both directions to favor a mixed mode (following the SWIM or Baltimore model), using a combination of lower-cost services to assure immediate welfare savings and carefully targeted, more expensive services with the hope of benefiting longer-term recipients.[52] This mixed strategy would allow states both to target the more disadvantaged and to serve a relatively large share of the welfare population, two explicit goals of JOBS. The logic for this would also follow from what the research suggests about the strengths and limits of past approaches. Job search has been demonstrated to have consistent employment and welfare impacts and to be cost-effective, but also to leave many without work and on welfare, especially among those who are more disadvantaged. A program like SWIM, which contains some higher-cost activities, and some of the selective-voluntary programs discussed in Chapter 5 have benefited the more disadvantaged in the JOBS population (on-board recipients), and SWIM and Baltimore suggest that including some higher-cost services (beyond job search assistance) can increase the percent of people with somewhat higher earnings. In addition, there is uncertainty about the point at which any trade-off among program objectives would be affected by program scale; it is possible (although there is no evidence on this) that diminishing returns may set in if particular welfare-to-work services are provided to an expanded share of the caseload.

While this analysis of past studies suggests a possible trade-off in meeting diverse program objectives, the nature of this trade-off and its

---

[52] SWIM was more successful than Baltimore in meeting these diverse goals, since it obtained both unusually large welfare savings and relatively large earnings gains. Baltimore achieved only the latter. This difference may have followed from SWIM's greater reliance on job search, or from its much more mandatory implementation and resulting higher participation (see Table 4.1), or from other differences in the program approaches.

relevance to JOBS remain highly uncertain. There are a number of reasons for this and hence for caution in using these results. The completed studies are of broad-coverage programs that differed substantially from those emerging under JOBS: i.e., they provided less education, skills training, and other intensive services; did not specifically target difficult-to-serve people or women with preschool children; and made less use of assessment and case management. The one program (Baltimore) that implemented the up-front assessment model emerging under JOBS was tested as a relatively small demonstration for 1,000 people, leaving unclear the feasibility of managing this process with similar results at a much expanded scale. Follow-up was limited to at most three years, not an adequate time to determine the long-term return to larger investments, or to see whether the impacts of low- or higher-cost services are more likely to increase or decrease over time. The number of completed studies is small and, as noted in Chapter 2, the programs differed on many other important dimensions in addition to cost, confounding an analysis of this relationship. In addition, the relative cost-effectiveness of low- and high-cost services may not be the same under FSA as it was in the pre-JOBS period, if the introduction of a year of transitional child care and Medicaid for people who leave welfare for a job reduces the total savings that occur when people take low-wage positions. Finally, administrators may structure state JOBS programs with other objectives in mind: e.g., a state may emphasize education in the hope that this will have a positive effect on the children in welfare families or that it will upgrade the state's human capital as part of a broader economic development strategy.

The critical importance of these issues to states deciding on the use of JOBS resources – in particular, those considering what services to provide to potential long-term recipients in the JOBS target groups who (where studied) were shown not to benefit consistently from low-cost services – points to the need for further evaluations of different program approaches.

The results from the current studies of more intensive programs – e.g., GAIN, REACH, and ET – will be of clear relevance. While those programs represent different strategies, each includes a greater emphasis on education and training than was typical in the mid-1980s. In addition, given the many competing explanations that inevitably arise when comparing results across locations and studies, it would also be particularly useful to try to address this issue directly, through well-designed differential impact studies, in which people in the same location are randomly assigned to different program approaches. As discussed further in Chapter 5, which extends the discussion by drawing on the added lessons from the selective-voluntary demonstrations, these types of studies could be designed to determine the relative effectiveness of alternative moderate- to high-cost models, or of models with different cost, intensity, and objectives. If these could be successfully implemented, they would help clarify the relationship between program cost and the diverse measures of effectiveness.

The Effect of Fixed Versus Open Sequence. The participation findings summarized in Table 4.1 point to the importance of how a program determines the first activity in which people are to participate, since a much smaller number reach subsequent services. There are two major options for structuring the flow of people through a program and allocating resources for more expensive services: (1) fixed-sequence models (starting with job search), or (2) reliance on an assessment process, which may be more or less elaborate but usually involves substantial choice and gives attention to welfare recipient and case manager preferences. Deciding between these two options is critical in the design of a welfare-to-work program since, given resource constraints, this is the mechanism for determining who receives the more intensive services.

Most broad-coverage models of the 1980s had a fixed sequence beginning with some form of job search followed by other activities for those who failed to locate jobs. This approach assumes that any type of employment will benefit recipients – regardless of their basic skills – because it moves them into the labor market, building a work history that can lead to long-term access to better jobs. From this perspective, low-income and welfare status are viewed, to a significant extent, as a result of limited work experience, job-seeking skills, references, and contacts, as well as a lack of self-esteem and motivation. Employment is seen as a way to provide the experience that will build confidence and open doors. Some job search assistance programs focus on structuring the search in ways that help clients take advantage of the normally high turnover in entry-level positions. While proponents of up-front job search recognize that a mix of factors affect income, they argue that it is not possible to determine a priori who is or is not "employable."

Based on these assumptions, fixed-sequence models that start with job search use the labor market as a screening device to determine which people can get a job with minimal assistance and which need further employment-enhancing services, i.e., education or training, thereby focusing more expensive services on the population most in need. Job search, in this case, is viewed as an alternative to a more comprehensive, initial assessment, although assessment may follow job search. Proponents of this view also argue that even if welfare recipients fail to become employed during the job search component, they gain valuable information on what they need to do to become employed.

The assessment/choice model is based on a different view of how clients should be matched to services and how more expensive services should be rationed: that there is no single cause of low income and no single "treatment" appropriate for all people. Instead, the particular barriers to employment and self-sufficiency and needs for service should be identified through testing, counseling, and other means, and an individualized plan developed, with both case managers and welfare recipients influencing the nature and sequence of services. Involving welfare recipients in the process is seen as a way to help them define their goals and to motivate them to take the steps needed to achieve those goals. Proponents of this approach argue that it will result in a more appropriate sequence of activities, lead to an increase not only in job-holding but also in the quality of the jobs, and reduce the extent to which people finding jobs subsequently return to welfare.

Unfortunately, while there is extensive information on up-front job search programs, there is only one completed impact study of a broad-coverage program – the Baltimore program – that used assessment and emphasized client choice. As a result, the relative effectiveness of these two approaches is not clear. The findings on job search, however, indicate that it is difficult to determine in advance who will find a job through a job club. (See the discussion of this issue in the section on "Findings on Subgroups and Targeting" in Chapter 5.) The New Jersey REACH, Washington FIP, Pennsylvania Saturation Work Program (PSWP), and Massachusetts ET studies should provide further information on participant flow and impacts of non-fixed-sequence programs. The GAIN evaluation is examining a fixed-sequence program in which many participants are assigned to education, thus broadening the knowledge base on the effects of sequenced services.

The Effect of Mandating Participation

As noted in Chapter 2, among broad-coverage programs, mandatory ones may have greater impacts than voluntary ones because they (1) reach more – and more disadvantaged – people, (2) deter people from applying for or remaining on welfare, or (3) sanction people. On the other hand, it is also possible that voluntary programs may have larger impacts because they serve more motivated people, who will take greater advantage of program services. Unfortunately, we have only limited evidence on these issues.

People Served. The field experiments summarized in this synthesis do not provide clear evidence on whether more mandatory programs are able to reach more or different people. Programs that include a participation mandate vary in their enforcement of that requirement. Among the seven broad-coverage programs evaluated, three were more likely to threaten or invoke sanctions for nonparticipation – San Diego I, SWIM, and Cook County – while the others rarely used sanctions, and saw the mandate primarily as a means to get in the door people whom they would not normally reach. As indicated in Table 4.1, while SWIM had the highest longitudinal participation rate, the other two more mandatory sites did not have particularly high participation rates. Further, Table 4.6 suggests no evident relationship between either sanctioning or participation – both possible proxies for the extent to which a program was mandatory – and program impacts.[53] However, SWIM's atypically strong impacts, overall and for the more disadvantaged two-thirds of the caseload, may at least in part reflect that program's unusually strict enforcement of a continuous participation mandate.

Comparisons between mandatory and voluntary programs are even more difficult. Since state WIN programs have been more or less mandatory since the early 1970s, there is no information on broad-coverage, totally voluntary programs. The evaluation of the most

---

[53] For a contrasting opinion, see Mead, 1986 and 1990. Mead argues that welfare-to-work programs must be mandatory if they are to succeed. His conclusion derives from his different view of how to measure program success: not by impact on employment, welfare, or self-sufficiency, but by the extent to which the program increases "work effort" (which he defines in terms of activity in program components). Measured against this goal of maximizing participation, mandatory programs, he concludes, are more successful. Mead also states that higher participation raises job entries and, because it causes programs to reach more disadvantaged people, increases net impacts.

visible large-scale program that is primarily voluntary – Massachusetts' ET program – has not yet been completed.[54] An interim report from this study, however, provides important information on the population reached. Initial findings show that as of mid-1987, approximately one-third of all Massachusetts' FY 1987 adult AFDC recipients had participated in activities such as training within the previous year. ET participation levels are clearly substantial for a voluntary, statewide program, and reflect an emphasis on recruitment (Nightingale et al., 1989).

Some of the selective-voluntary programs discussed in Chapter 5 (e.g., Supported Work and Project Redirection) suggest that – at least at the relatively small scale at which they were implemented – they were able to reach very disadvantaged welfare recipients (Board of Directors, MDRC, 1980; Polit, Quint, and Riccio, 1988). Others (e.g., Maine's Training Opportunities in the Private Sector – TOPS – program) targeted disadvantaged groups but served a more job-ready subset within that group (Auspos, Cave, and Long, 1988). Finally, programs such as JTPA reach a more motivated or advantaged group within the AFDC caseload. Evidence from several of these studies suggests that only a small share of potential eligibles volunteered for services.

Deterrence. Advocates of mandatory programs argue that, in addition to reaching different people, the persistent follow-up and threat and reality of sanctions will deter some people from going on welfare, cause some people not to complete a welfare application, and prompt others to leave the rolls to avoid the "hassle" of participation or because they were "smoked out" of unreported jobs. The field experiments of the 1980s provide only limited evidence. As discussed in the section on "Estimating Entry and Macroeconomic Effects" in Chapter 2, these studies were not

---

[54] In ET, participation in individual activities is voluntary, but registration for the program is required. A recent non-experimental study of ET (O'Neill, 1990) used a time series analysis to estimate the effect of the program on the size of the welfare caseload in Massachusetts. The author concluded that little if any of the reduction in the AFDC caseload during the 1980s appeared to have been caused by ET. She also compared Massachusetts to other states in regard to the participation of single mothers in welfare or in work. She found that single women in Massachusetts had a higher probability of receiving welfare than single women in other states in all but two of the eight years from 1980 through 1987, and she argued that ET did not reduce this effect, except possibly in 1984 (ET's first full year of operation). She also found that ET had no apparent effect on the likelihood of employment among single mothers. The methods used in this work, and the research questions posed, are very different from those of the ongoing evaluation of ET or the field experiments discussed in this document.

designed to measure whether these initiatives deterred people from applying for welfare. On the other issues, the lack of any clear relationship between sanctioning rates and impacts argues against any consistent interpretation. For example, the San Diego I demonstration, with its relatively high participation and sanctioning rates, did not appear to deter new applicants from eventually getting on welfare. While the tough enforcement of participation requirements and relatively high sanctioning in SWIM may have led to some caseload reductions, the study did not distinguish these from other sources of higher program impacts.

Sanctioning. In WIN and WIN Demonstration programs, staff could impose sanctions – reductions in the welfare grant for AFDC case heads, or case closure for AFDC-UPs – on targeted persons who refused to participate without good cause.[55] Research findings, particularly for the Cook County program for single mothers, suggest that sanctioning can translate directly into some modest welfare savings.[56] For the other six completed studies, it is uncertain what role sanctioning played in increasing participation and producing program impacts (see Tables 4.1 and 4.2). For example, as noted above, it is not clear whether the relatively large impacts for AFDCs and AFDC-UPs in the SWIM Demonstration came from the relatively high sanctioning, the saturation mandate (with the resulting high and ongoing participation), the use of education and training services, or other conditions particular to San Diego (notably, the experience of the program staff).

The Impact of Administrative Practices

It has proven difficult to quantify the returns to different case management, assessment, and monitoring approaches.

Case Management. The study of early GAIN implementation shows that counties organized case management in different ways and had registrant-to-staff ratios that ranged from 50:1 to 200:1. While the authors

---

[55] Sanctioning rules differ under JOBS.

[56] Cook County sanctioned a relatively high number (12 percent) of experimentals but, as noted in the discussion of Table 4.1, a substantial number of controls were also sanctioned. The program's impact on net sanctioning probably does account for some of the very small welfare savings that occurred, even in the absence of any earnings gains. But it is not the only explanation, since some of the savings also came from an increase in case closures, as additional people either left the rolls or had their cases closed for administrative reasons as a result of the program.

report that the higher rates did not seem to hinder reporting on attendance, they note that they did delay follow-up on nonparticipation and
affected the nature of staff procedures for dealing with noncompliance.
GAIN participation rates do not seem to be clearly related to registrant/
staff ratios, but GAIN staff indicated that these ratios did affect attendance for those participating (Riccio et al., 1989). While cross-county
information in later GAIN reports should provide further insight on this
question, the most important results are likely to come from the Riverside, California, case management experiment. In this differential impact
study, welfare-to-work outcomes will be measured for welfare recipients
whose case managers have a caseload one-half the normal size and for
welfare recipients whose case managers have a normal-size caseload.
This experiment will be the first formal test of the impacts of intensive
case management.

Assessment. Assessments can be conducted in a wide variety of
ways including case managers' use of objective and subjective
characteristics, such as prior work experience, to make assignments to
particular activities; participants' self-assessment and choice of program
activity; and formal testing and recommendations by professional
employment counselors. There is currently no reliable information on the
effect of different assessment approaches (or the location of assessment
in the sequence of activities) on program participation, impact, or
cost-effectiveness. Moreover, none of the planned evaluations directly
address this issue.

Some early anecdotal evidence identifies issues that may arise in
states implementing JOBS programs that rely on complex cross-referral
and coordination among many agencies and that emphasize assessment
and caseworker discretion. This evidence suggests that, unless there are
clear procedures and, especially where there are large caseloads, a
well-designed management information system (MIS), people can fail to
show up at some point in the assessment process, and possibly be lost
to the program. In programs with many stops, steps, and cross-referrals,
participation may thereby be reduced. The evaluations of REACH,
FIP, PSWP, ET, and Ohio Transitions to Independence should
provide further information on caseload flow in more complex and
discretionary programs.

Caseload Monitoring Strategies. Some of the relatively simple
WIN and WIN Demonstration projects of the early and mid-1980s
achieved relatively high participation rates with quite primitive management information systems support. Even in the more complex SWIM

Demonstration, staff relied partially on manual management systems. The early reports from the GAIN evaluation, however, suggest that the efficient managing of this complex program will require effective automated tracking systems in all but the smallest counties (Wallace and Long, 1987; Riccio et al., 1989).

The Importance of Labor Market Conditions and Area Characteristics

Chapter 2 pointed to several ways in which the local economic and program context can affect JOBS' impacts.

Labor Market Conditions. Labor market conditions influence the characteristics of the welfare caseload and the ease with which both experimentals and controls find employment. While it is often held that program impacts will be larger in a strong labor market, a number of studies have found the opposite: greater impacts in a weak labor market, at least in urban areas. In the study of San Diego's job search program, for example, earnings impacts were substantially larger for people entering the program during a severe economic downturn than for a group who entered during a period of economic improvement (Goldman, Friedlander, and Long, 1986). Similar results were found in the National Supported Work Demonstration (Board of Directors, MDRC, 1980).[57] In both cases, this was because improved economic conditions benefited controls as much as they assisted experimentals. MDRC's study of West Virginia's work experience program indicated, however, that in rural labor markets with very high unemployment rates (peaking at 23 percent – the nation's highest – in January 1983), program interventions may have limited success in improving employment prospects (Friedlander et al., 1986). MDRC conducted one other study of a welfare-to-work program in a rural area: in 7 of the 11 agencies in the Virginia study, all of which had stronger labor markets than did the West Virginia study counties. In these rural Virginia counties, there were no significant impacts on any outcome measures, although the authors

---

[57] However, preliminary results from the Minority Female Single Parent (MFSP) Demonstration suggest that impacts were larger when economic conditions improved (Gordon and Burghardt, 1990).

concluded that small sample sizes may have accounted for these results (Riccio et al., 1986).

While results to date do not, therefore, suggest that – except under extreme and/or rural conditions – higher unemployment rates reduce program impacts, there have not been studies of large-scale welfare-to-work programs that were conducted during a severe national recession. It is possible that this could undermine program impacts.[58] In addition, few of the completed evaluations are of very large-scale programs. The impacts of such programs might be more limited if local employers were, for example, saturated by job placement demands from program participants. It is too early to know whether JOBS programs, relative to their local labor markets, will operate at a scale substantially beyond that of some of the larger 1980s WIN Demonstration programs.

Characteristics of the AFDC Program. AFDC grant levels and administrative structures can affect program impacts in several ways. Grant levels influence the characteristics of people on welfare and the extent to which people can combine work and welfare. In low-grant states, caseloads will be more disadvantaged, and even low-wage jobs will lead to case closures. Thus, as shown in Table 4.2, employment rates were lower for both experimentals and controls in Arkansas than in any of the other programs except West Virginia. Further, only 5 percent of experimentals in the Arkansas study combined work and welfare in the third quarter of follow-up, compared to 20 percent of experimentals at the same time in San Diego's SWIM program (Friedlander et al., 1985b; Hamilton and Friedlander, 1989).

With only seven completed studies, however, it is not possible to establish whether there is a clear relationship between grant level, program design, and program impacts. Moreover, a conclusion will depend on the nature of the comparison: On a percentage basis, impacts on earnings and AFDC dependence were largest in low-grant Arkansas and high-grant California; in dollar terms, impacts were much larger in San Diego than in Arkansas.

---

[58] Very depressed economic conditions could also have other results. For example, a welfare-to-work program implemented during a period of extremely high unemployment may be more likely to affect other low-wage workers, who might be displaced by welfare recipients who find jobs as a result of the program. Past studies have not examined this possibility.

In terms of AFDC administrative structure, there is no clear relationship between the magnitude of or variation in impacts and whether a program is state-administered or state-supervised and county-administered. Thus, although Arkansas, Virginia, and West Virginia all had state-administered programs, impacts were quite different in the two Arkansas counties studied, and participation varied substantially across counties in all four states.[59] Participation also varied across counties in the county-administered system in California, where the GAIN study suggests substantial cross-county variation in program objectives and design. County administrative differences may also influence impacts in the ongoing Ohio LEAP, Ohio Transitions to Independence, and Florida Project Independence evaluations, among others.

The Extent of Community Employment and Training Services. The availability of services from JTPA, community colleges, or other facilities will affect welfare dynamics (and outcomes for the control group), program cost, and the ease and extent to which administrators can implement more complex and enriched JOBS programs. While it is often assumed that few WIN-mandatory welfare recipients receive education or training services on their own, the three of the seven completed studies of low- and moderate-cost programs where this was measured suggest substantial activity by members of the control group – and self-initiated activities by experimentals.

Thus, in Virginia, 12 percent of control group members participated in education or training activities within 15 to 28 months after random assignment; in Cook County, 18 percent of controls did so within 9 months of random assignment; and in San Diego SWIM, almost 28 percent of controls participated in community college programs (basic education, continuing education, training, and college-level courses) within 2 to 3 years after random assignment (Riccio et al., 1986; Friedlander et al., 1987; Hamilton and Friedlander, 1989). The SWIM findings illustrate the extent to which controls' access to these programs decreases the service differential between experimentals and controls and, presumably, lowers program impacts. While an impressive 34 percent of experimentals attended community colleges within 2 or 3 years, this was an increase of only 7 percentage points over the control group level.

---

[59] County-specific impacts were not estimated in Maine, Virginia, or West Virginia.

Information from Evaluations Currently Being Conducted

Ongoing studies of broad-coverage programs promise to enlarge the existing knowledge base regarding welfare-to-work programs. The GAIN evaluation in California will provide the first impact data on a mandatory participation, education-based program. GAIN provides a far more comprehensive set of services to its participants than have most previous statewide welfare-to-work programs: Job search, adult basic education, GED classes, English for speakers of other languages, job club, and some training and work experience are available in most counties. The impacts of this bundle of services will be measured in six counties; impact measures will include employment, earnings, welfare receipt, Food Stamp receipt, and, in four counties, registrant survey information on such outcomes as job characteristics (e.g., hours, wages, and fringe benefits), total family earnings and transfer income, efforts to look for work, reasons for not working (where applicable), educational degree attainment, and various attitudinal measures. Impacts on clients' literacy levels will also be measured in some counties.

In addition, as discussed above, California has commissioned an evaluation of intensive case management in the GAIN program. In Riverside County, an experimental design has been implemented to test the effect of GAIN as carried out by high-caseload welfare workers versus GAIN as carried out by low-caseload welfare workers. This differential impact evaluation will be one of the few efforts to isolate the effect of alternative administrative arrangements on participants.

The evaluation of Project Independence in Florida will measure labor market outcomes for adult women on AFDC with children age 3 or older. This group will be eligible for activities that may include job search, education, training, or work experience. Eligibility for particular services will be determined by the application of state "job-readiness" criteria. Job-ready participants are assigned to job search. The evaluation will thus shed light on the consequences of an array of services that are allocated according to guidelines designed to reserve the most expensive services for the less employable welfare recipients.

The forthcoming report on the Pennsylvania Saturation Work Program (PSWP) will provide participation and impact findings for a program that, like San Diego's Saturation Work Initiative Model (SWIM), was designed to test a program model with an ongoing participation requirement. Under the PSWP model, AFDCs with children over 6 and AFDC-UPs received an assessment, which evaluated participants' math and reading skills, vocational interests, job search knowledge, and social service needs. PSWP participants were then referred to activities that could include job-readiness training (including workshops, job clubs, and job search), CWEP, education, and vocational training. Controls in the evaluation were also eligible for many of these services through the existing Work Registration Program (WRP) in Pennsylvania. As a result, the PSWP impact evaluation will provide information about the effects of enhanced case management and an ongoing participation requirement, the two predominant differences between the PSWP program model and the WRP model that was in use for the control group.

The comparison group studies of three programs will provide important information. New Jersey's REACH will analyze a broad-coverage program that emphasizes up-front assessment of participants, followed by a range of services. The ongoing evaluations of Washington's FIP and Massachusetts' ET program will provide findings on broad-coverage, *voluntary* welfare-to-work programs.

The evaluation of Ohio's Transitions to Independence program will provide impact data for two groups of AFDC recipients. For AFDC-UP recipients and for single parents on AFDC who have no children under age 6, there will be a random assignment evaluation of the effect of required participation in work-related activities. These include job club, subsidized employment, education and training, and work experience (CWEP). The study will take place in 15 counties. The second group being studied consists of single parents on AFDC with one or more children under age 6. For this group, there will be a random assignment evaluation in one county (Montgomery) of a program requiring an assessment and vocational counseling, and offering (but not requiring) the work-related activities described above. In addition, this treatment group received an offer of extended transitional child care and Medicaid if they become employed. When the transitional benefits provisions of the Family Support Act took effect, these transitional benefits became available to AFDC recipients in the control group; consequently, this evaluation will measure the impact of the timing and the message associated with transitional benefits. (See Table 3.5.) These studies will increase the knowledge base regarding programs that emphasize work, and the Montgomery County experiment for recipients with preschool children will also provide information on the impact of a treatment that emphasizes significant transitional services that increase the incentives for work (Bell, Hamilton, and Burstein, 1989).

The ongoing, rigorous evaluation of the Food Stamp Employment and Training Program analyzes the effect of a broad-based work requirement for Food Stamp recipients. Enacted in 1985, the federal legislation, like JOBS, gives states considerable flexibility in designing and implementing a mandatory employment and training program for the Food Stamp caseload while setting national participation standards. The study should yield useful information about the design, administration, and operation of the broad-based participation requirement, the choice between low-cost and more intensive service strategies, and the overall impact of the program on recipients' employment, earnings, and welfare receipt. The findings will not be directly generalizable to the AFDC population, however, since participants in AFDC work programs are exempt from participation in the Food Stamp Employment and Training Program. Indeed, only 6 percent of the participants in the Food Stamp study were receiving AFDC benefits, and participants who were on AFDC were more likely to be enrolled in intensive training activities than in the more typical job search activities (Puma, Werner, and Hojnacki, 1988).

Chapter 5

The Knowledge Base: Other Evaluations Relevant to JOBS

Chapter 4 presented what is known about the effectiveness of broad-coverage, usually mandatory, welfare-to-work programs. This chapter focuses on particular services for specific welfare populations. It extends the discussion in two ways. In the first two sections, it focuses on what is known and being learned about the success of certain service components that can be provided as part of a broad-coverage system. It does not repeat the discussion of job search and unpaid work experience, which were tested at scale in the broad-coverage studies. Instead, it covers the substantial number of other rigorous evaluations that have focused not on the entire WIN or JOBS system in a location, but on components of that system or specific services provided through other delivery systems or special demonstrations. These have often involved higher-cost services, have always been tested as voluntary components, and have usually been implemented at smaller scale. For JOBS administrators, these other studies can help get inside the "black box" of the total delivery system and inform trade-offs on critical program design choices, including whether the addition of higher-cost components can increase program effectiveness. Services identified as successful can then be considered for potential broader use within the JOBS system.

The selective-voluntary programs discussed in the first two sections can thus be viewed as possible smaller-scale components within a broad-coverage JOBS program that contains a wide range of activities. Selective-voluntary programs may offer an alternative method of placing welfare recipients in welfare-to-work activities, as compared to some of the fixed-sequence programs discussed in Chapter 4. There are various ways to structure selective-voluntary components within larger systems: Outreach and advertising campaigns can solicit applicants; welfare staff can encourage welfare recipients to volunteer; or an assessment process can be used to assign potential participants to services.[1] The effectiveness of the program may be partly determined by the method of identifying potential participants. States may regard selective-voluntary programs not as models to be compared to low-cost job search programs, but as specific targeting strategies for groups in need of particular services. To further inform this issue, the second section of this chapter focuses on what these studies suggest about the targeting of higher-cost services to particular subgroups of welfare recipients.

In its final three sections, the chapter shifts to cover briefly what is known from broad-coverage or selective-voluntary programs about specific areas of particular relevance to JOBS: education services, services for young AFDC mothers, and support services. The chapter concludes with a discussion of how these different approaches fit together into program-model combinations.

Findings on Selective-Voluntary Programs

There are a number of rigorous evaluations of two types of selective-voluntary programs: enriched, small-scale demonstration programs that test a particular program model; and larger-scale, voluntary services provided by the Job Training Partnership Act (JTPA) and its predecessor, the Comprehensive Employment and Training Act (CETA).

Demonstration Programs

There have been random assignment studies of four selective-voluntary demonstrations: two multi-state programs testing subsidized employment (the National Supported Work Demonstration and the AFDC Homemaker-Home Health Aide Demonstrations), the multi-site studies of an on-the-job training program in New Jersey, and a sequence of activities (including pre-vocational training, work experience,

---

[1] All of the completed evaluations of particular service components have been of activities that were voluntary options chosen by some participants within the usually mandatory WIN system (the mandatoriness of which has varied among states and program offices, as explained in Chapter 2). It is of course possible to evaluate mandatory components, where either entrance to the component (e.g., in a fixed-sequence program) or continued participation in the component is mandatory for those who enroll in it. Some of the current demonstrations discussed in this chapter may fall into this latter group: i.e., initial enrollment is voluntary but, once enrolled, people could be subject to sanctions if they did not continue to participate.

and on-the-job training) in Maine.[2] (None of these studies focused on education and training, key JOBS activities.)

Supported Work enrolled a very disadvantaged group of AFDC recipients (averaging more than 8.5 years on welfare) in a 12- or 18-month program of carefully structured and closely supervised paid work experience with elements of on-the-job training. It led to increases in earnings and reductions in welfare receipt. As seen in Table 5.1, during the third year after enrollment in the program (based on one quarter's data), the experimentals earned an average of $1,076, or 23 percent, more than the $4,703 earned by controls.[3] In contrast to the pattern for the broad-coverage programs that provided mainly mandatory job search, earnings gains in Supported Work were driven primarily by increases in hours worked and hourly wages and less by an increase in employment rates. Researchers in that study concluded that wage increases accounted for 42 percent of the total long-term increase in earnings and that an increase in hours accounted for another 18 percent. While the wage gain is encouraging, the actual amount was not large: Wages rose 12 percent – from $3.69 to $4.12 in current dollars.[4] These earnings gains were accompanied by welfare savings: a reduction of 7 percentage points in welfare receipt and $401 in estimated annual grants.[5] Because reductions in AFDC and other benefits offset a substantial share of the increase in earnings, Supported Work had no statistically significant long-term impact on the

---

[2] See Chapter 3 for a description of the program approaches. Throughout this synthesis, the findings for all of the studies except Supported Work and the Louisville studies are expressed in nominal dollars. Both the costs and impacts of the Supported Work demonstration, which operated during the late 1970s, have been adjusted and are expressed in 1985 dollars, roughly the midpoint in the other studies in Chapters 4 and 5.

[3] In Supported Work, 97 percent of the AFDC experimentals participated (i.e., were employed in program jobs).

[4] Masters, 1981.

[5] The Supported Work earnings gains and welfare reductions shown in Table 5.1 are based on a sample consistent for all years of follow-up. In the original Supported Work study, this was not the case. Impacts for the first 18 months of follow-up were based on the maximum sample of 1,351 individuals. Data for many of these individuals were not available beyond 18 months, and impacts for the 19- to 27-month period were estimated using only an early cohort of 620 enrollees (Board of Directors, MDRC, 1980). A subsequent set of impact estimates (Grossman, Maynard, and Roberts, 1985) – used in this synthesis, with an adjustment to 1985 dollars – incorporated more observations at the end of follow-up, which were available from a final survey wave. For example, 1,069 sample members were used for the 25- to 27-month follow-up period, the last period with data for this full sample. Inflation to 1985 dollars may overstate the actual impacts that would have been achieved had the demonstration been run in the 1980s because it does not take into account erosion of the real minimum wage and real AFDC benefits over time.

**TABLE 5.1 IMPACTS OF THE NATIONAL SUPPORTED WORK
DEMONSTRATION ON AFDC RECIPIENTS**

Outcome and Follow-Up Period		Experimental Group Mean	Control Group Mean	Difference	Percentage Change
Average Earnings	Year 1	$8,360	$1,958	$6,402***	327%
	Year 2	5,159	3,791	1,368***	36
	Year 3	5,779	4,703	1,076***	23
Employed at End of	Year 1	73.3%	30.4%	42.9***	141%
	Year 2	46.6	42.3	4.3	10
	Year 3	45.3	43.3	2.0	5
Average AFDC Payments[a]	Year 1	$3,472	$5,672	-$2,200**	-39%
	Year 2	3,388	4,553	-1,165***	-26
	Year 3	3,501	3,902	-401**	-10
On Welfare at End of	Year 1	70.4%	85.9%	-15.5***	-18%
	Year 2	64.4	73.5	-9.1***	-12
	Year 3	64.2	71.3	-7.1***	-10

SOURCES: MDRC calculations from Grossman, Maynard, and Roberts, 1985; Hollister, Kemper, and Maynard, 1984.

NOTES: All figures are adjusted to 1985 dollars. The data are regression-adjusted estimates that control for the differences of age, sex, race, education, prior work experience, household composition, and prior welfare receipt. Since only control group means and estimated impacts are available, experimental group means were calculated by adding estimated impacts and control group means.

The follow-up period begins with the day of random assignment. Since Supported Work offered up to 18 months of subsidized paid employment, earnings and consequently reduced AFDC payments during the first two years partly reflect wages earned in the program, and not post-program impacts. The annual earnings and AFDC payments impacts for year 3 are based on quarter 9, the last quarter for which there are common follow-up data for all recipients who responded to the final survey.

Averages were calculated for all members of the sample, including those with no employment or transfer payment receipt in the covered period.

"Employed" or "on welfare" at the end of years 1 and 2 is defined as receiving earnings or welfare payments at some point during the last quarter of the year. For year 3, it is defined as receiving earnings or welfare payments at some point during the first quarter of the year.

[a]Includes AFDC, General Assistance, Supplemental Security Income, and other unspecified cash welfare.

Denotes statistical significance at the 5 percent level; and * at the 1 percent level.

percentage of families living below the poverty level. In general, the impacts for Supported Work were largest for those recipients who did less well on their own: older women, women who had not completed high school, those who had been on welfare for a particularly long time, and those with no prior work experience (Board of Directors, MDRC, 1980; Hollister, Kemper, and Maynard, 1984).

The Homemaker-Home Health Aide Demonstrations targeted women who had been on AFDC for at least 90 days and reached a diverse group of welfare recipients, the majority of whom were WIN volunteers (i.e., had children under 6 years old). The program provided four to eight weeks of formal training, followed by up to a year of subsidized employment. It found, on average, results similar to those of Supported Work, with wide variation across the states. (See Table 5.2.) During the third year of follow-up (as defined in the table), there were significant increases in unsubsidized employment in four of the seven states and earnings gains in five. In that year, annual earnings gains averaged $1,121 across the states, with a state low of $132 and a high of $1,944 (Bell, Enns, and Orr, 1986).[6] The factors that produced earnings gains were different in the Homemaker-Home Health Aide Demonstrations than in Supported Work. The Homemaker-Home Health Aide earnings gains came primarily from increases in employment rates, with consistent gains in wage rates in only two of the states with earnings increases.[7] In all, four states showed positive impacts on trainees' hourly wage rates in year 3, and four had positive impacts on the number of hours worked

---

[6] The Homemaker-Home Health Aide study did not present findings averaged across all seven states. The authors of this synthesis volume derived all average numbers from the state results, weighing all states equally. In the Homemaker-Home Health Aide Demonstrations, approximately 84 percent of experimentals participated (i.e., entered training) across all of the states except Texas, where 74 percent participated. Impacts per participant, as a result, are somewhat higher than those shown in Table 5.2. The per-participant impact on annual earnings in year 3 ranged from $144 in New York to $2,592 in Texas, with an average annual earnings impact across the seven states of $1,293. Public benefit savings per participant in year 3 ranged from $12 in Texas to $1,140 in South Carolina, with an average savings across the seven states of $382.

[7] Enns, Bell, and Flanagan, 1987, as discussed in Friedlander and Gueron, forthcoming. The three states with statistically significant gains in hourly wage rates throughout the post-program period had increases of between 29 and 88 cents per hour, or 8 to 19 percent above the average wages for members of the control groups. The evaluators concluded that "productivity [and wage] gains were greatest in the southern and mostly rural states where, in general, wage rates are low relative to the more urban states" (Bell, Enns, and Orr, 1986, pp. 16–17).

TABLE 5.2 IMPACTS OF THE HOMEMAKER-HOME HEALTH AIDE DEMONSTRATIONS ON AFDC RECIPIENTS

Site	Percent Employed in			Average Annual Earnings in			Average Annual Combined AFDC and Food Stamp Benefits in		
	Year 1[a]	Year 2[a]	Year 3[a]	Year 1	Year 2	Year 3	Year 1	Year 2	Year 3
Arkansas	N/A	N/A	19***	$1,536***	$1,392***	$1,116***	-$204***	-$684***	-$540***
Kentucky	N/A	N/A	2	1,980***	1,344***	1,860***	-996***	-1,008***	-432***
New Jersey	N/A	N/A	11***	3,744***	1,848***	1,344***	-1,740***	-1,212***	36
New York[b]	N/A	N/A	-12	240	684**	132	348***	-168	96
Ohio[c]	N/A	N/A	11***	2,844***	2,268***	1,212***	-972***	-1,020***	-564***
South Carolina	N/A	N/A	3	2,976***	912***	240	-1,080***	-1,428***	-1,008***
Texas	N/A	N/A	21***	864**	984***	1,944***	-228***	-468***	12
Cross-State Average[d]	N/A	N/A	8	2,026	1,347	1,121	-696	-855	-343

SOURCE: MDRC calculations from Bell, Enns, and Orr, 1986.

NOTES: All values are experimental-control differences. Experimental and control group means were not available. Impact estimates average net outcomes for all experimentals, including the small share who did not participate in the homemaker-home health aide sequence. The impacts on experimentals who actually started training were somewhat higher in each state and substantially higher in Texas, where nonparticipation was higher.

Total earnings of the experimental group include both demonstration and non-demonstration earnings. Year 1 is the demonstration period and is defined for each state as the number of months from random assignment until the typical experimental left subsidized employment. Year 1 ranged from 7 months in New York to 12 months in South Carolina. Year 2 is defined as the 12-month period following the time when the typical experimental left subsidized employment. Year 3 is based on all months in the follow-up period after year 2. Average annual impacts for each year were calculated by multiplying the average monthly impacts for that period by 12. Since the Homemaker-Home Health Aide Demonstrations offered up to a year of subsidized

TABLE 5.2 (*continued*)

paid employment, earnings and consequently reduced AFDC and Food Stamp benefits during the first two years partly reflect wages earned in the program, and not post-program impacts.

[a]Unlike the reported earnings impacts, employment impacts were reported by the original researchers only for non-demonstration employment. By year 3 the typical experimental was no longer in subsidized employment, however, so the year 3 employment and earnings impacts both reflect post-program employment and are therefore comparable.

[b]Impacts on AFDC and Food Stamp benefits do not include New York City, where no data were available.

[c]Impacts on AFDC benefits only are available.

[d]Cross-state averages were calculated from the original researchers' state-specific estimates, so statistical significance is not available.

** Denotes statistical significance at the 5 percent level; and *** at the 1 percent level.

per month. The year 3 earnings gains led to annual welfare savings in four of the states, ranging from $432 to more than $1,000 and averaging $343 per year across all the states.

The impacts of the Homemaker-Home Health Aide Demonstrations show considerable variation across the states, and there is very little relationship between the states with earnings gains and those with welfare savings. While the reason for this variation is unclear, the authors note that participating states were given substantial flexibility: Within overall demonstration parameters (e.g., eligibility requirements and the basic service components), they could impose their own additional criteria for acceptance of trainees into the program and devise their own training and service provision policies.

The two studies of the on-the-job training programs operated as components of the WIN demonstrations in New Jersey and Maine show employment and earnings results on the high side of those found in the broad-coverage programs. The New Jersey program offered OJT placements in the private sector of up to 6 months, but experimentals could also receive other WIN services. In Maine, there was a fixed sequence of services, consisting of 2 to 5 weeks of pre-employment training in job search and job-holding skills, up to 12 weeks of half-time unpaid work experience in the public or nonprofit sector, and then placement in an OJT-subsidized job in the private sector for 6 to 26 weeks.[8] As shown in Table 5.3, the Maine program led to earnings gains, relative to controls, of $871 in the second year and almost $950 in the third. The New Jersey program led to earnings gains of almost $600 in the second year. (The Maine and New Jersey programs achieved most of their earnings impacts by increasing the wage rate or hours for those employed, rather than increasing employment rates, i.e., by moving people into jobs with

---

[8] Overall, about 90 percent of experimentals in Maine and 84 percent in New Jersey participated in at least one activity within 12 months after random assignment, although a much smaller number – 31 and 40 percent, respectively – were placed in OJT-funded jobs. (The major other activities were pre-vocational training, work experience, and some individual job search, in Maine, and job search in New Jersey.) Participation was also high by controls (who were WIN registrants and had volunteered for the OJT program) – higher than the participation by experimentals in many of the broad-coverage studies presented in Chapter 4. Thus, in Maine, over 50 percent of controls were active in some WIN or JTPA service (primarily individual job search, education, or pre-vocational training) within 11 to 26 months after random assignment; in New Jersey, 73 percent of controls were active in some WIN or JTPA service (primarily job search) within 12 months of random assignment.

TABLE 5.3 IMPACTS OF THE NEW JERSEY AND MAINE ON-THE-JOB TRAINING PROGRAMS ON AFDC ELIGIBLES

Location, Outcome, and Follow-Up Period		Experimental Group Mean	Control Group Mean	Difference	Percentage Change
New Jersey					
Average Earnings[a]	Year 1	N/A	N/A	N/A	N/A
	Year 2	$4,840	$4,249	$591*	14%
Employed at End of	Year 1	54.8%	55.2%	-0.4	-1%
	Year 2[b]	56.1	57.8	-1.7	-3
Average AFDC Payments	Year 1	$3,188	$3,377	-$190**[c]	-6%
	Year 2	1,946	2,184	-238*	-11
On Welfare at End of	Year 1	65.8%	68.6%	-2.8	-4%
	Year 2	45.7	47.5	-1.9	-4
Maine					
Average Earnings[d]	Year 1	$1,466	$1,362	$104	8%
	Year 2	3,183	2,311	871**	38
	Year 3	3,700	2,759	941*	34
Employed at End of	Year 1	52.1%	43.8%	8.3	19%
	Year 2	50.2	43.4	6.9	16
	Year 3[e]	50.4	49.3	1.1	2
Average AFDC Payments[d]	Year 1	$3,419	$3,355	$64	2%
	Year 2	2,609	2,580	29	1
	Year 3	2,191	2,110	80	4
On Welfare at End of	Year 1	81.8%	85.1%	-3.3	-4%
	Year 2	64.4	63.1	1.3	2
	Year 3[e]	55.8	49.8	6.0	12

SOURCES: MDRC calculations from Freedman, Bryant, and Cave, 1988; Auspos, Cave, and Long, 1988.

NOTES: The earnings and AFDC payments data include zero values for sample members not employed and for sample members not receiving welfare. Estimates are regression-adjusted using ordinary least squares, controlling for pre-random assignment characteristics of sample members. There may be some discrepancies in experimental-control differences because of rounding.

"Employed" or "on welfare" at the end of the year is defined as receiving earnings or welfare payments at some point during the last quarter of the year.

Earnings and AFDC payments are not adjusted for inflation.

[a]A year 1 earnings impact is not available in New Jersey for the same sample as the year 2 impact and is therefore not shown. The annual earnings impact for year 2 is based on three quarters of

(continued)

TABLE 5.3 *(continued)*

follow-up. Statistical significance was not calculated for year 2. However, since the earnings impact for quarters 5-7 is statistically significant, the annual impact is assumed also to be significant.

[b]Percent employed at the end of 1 3/4 years.

[c]Statistical significance was not calculated for year 1. However, since the quarterly impacts for quarters 2, 3, and 4 are statistically significant, the annual impact is assumed also to be significant.

[d]For all outcomes, year 1 begins with the quarter of random assignment. The quarter of random assignment refers to the calendar quarter in which random assignment occurred. As a result, "average earnings" and "average AFDC payments" in year 1 may include up to two months of earnings or AFDC payments prior to random assignment. Annual earnings and AFDC payments impacts for year 3 are based on three quarters of follow-up. Statistical significance was not calculated for year 3. However, since the quarterly earnings impacts are statistically significant, the annual earnings impact is assumed also to be significant.

[e]Percent employed and on welfare at the end of 2 3/4 years.

*Denotes statistical significance at the 10 percent level; and ** at the 5 percent level.

higher earnings.[9] An analysis in Maine, not repeated in New Jersey, showed that that program also led to a substantial 9.3 percentage point increase in the proportion of people earning $8,300 a year or more in the final year of follow-up. This pattern of impacts more closely resembled the Baltimore program than the broad-coverage, job search programs.) These gains were accompanied by welfare savings in New Jersey but, surprisingly, not in Maine, suggesting that in Maine, as in Baltimore, part of the earnings gains may have come through getting jobs with higher earnings for people who would have moved off welfare and obtained a lower-paying job in the absence of the program (as shown by the behavior of the control group).[10] (See Auspos, Cave, and Long, 1988; Freedman, Bryant, and Cave, 1988.)

Enrollment in the New Jersey and Maine programs was voluntary, both for women with children over age 6 and the traditional WIN "volunteers" with younger children. While the New Jersey program targeted "employable" WIN participants, the Maine program sought to enroll a more disadvantaged group of women. In fact, both programs screened for motivation and employability and, as a result, enrolled women with a mixture of characteristics. They were quite disadvantaged in terms of their prior welfare receipt and recent work histories, but had relatively high levels of GED attainment and high school completion.

---

[9] In these two studies, as in the broad-coverage evaluations discussed in Chapter 4, employment and earnings came from Unemployment Insurance earnings automated records, rather than surveys, as was the case in Supported Work and Homemaker-Home Health Aide. As a result, while it was possible to determine the extent to which earnings gains came from increases in employment rates versus *either* hours worked *or* hourly wages, there was no information on how much of the change could be attributed to each of the latter two components.

[10] The study, after determining that there was no problem in data quality or program procedures, offered several possible reasons for the lack of impact on AFDC payments. First, Maine was one of a small number of states where the AFDC standard of need exceeded the maximum grant and where the standard of need was used to determine supplemental grants to working recipients. As a result, the amount by which grants were reduced when someone went to work was lowered, and work incentives were increased. Second, any impact for experimentals above the point where earnings were already sufficient to remove them from the rolls would not have led to any further welfare savings. Third, one of the program components instructed participants about the relationship between work and welfare, possibly increasing their effectiveness in assuring that their grants were not improperly reduced when they went to work. Fourth, there may have been welfare savings for those who found employment which were offset by an increase in the time on welfare for other people, e.g., those engaged in longer-term training programs. See Auspos, Cave, and Long, 1988. See also Appendix Table C.1 for more detailed data on the impacts of this program.

This recruitment and screening is typical of past OJT programs and may be similar to the practice in this component in JOBS. Consequently, the results, particularly those for the larger-scale New Jersey program, may be directly relevant to similarly targeted OJT activities in future state JOBS programs.

These demonstrations made greater up-front investments per experimental than did the lower-cost broad-coverage programs, with the expectation that returns would take longer but eventually be larger. The impact findings provide some support for both parts of this expectation. In both Maine and the mixed-strategy Baltimore program, impacts were low in the first year and grew consistently over the period of follow-up. (Obviously, this was not the case in the Supported Work and Homemaker-Home Health Aide demonstrations, which provided jobs with subsidized wages to people while they were in the program.) On job quality, all of the selective-voluntary programs and the Baltimore program appeared to increase the wage rates or hours of those working, rather than having their effect mainly through increasing employment rates, as the job search programs did. (The selective-voluntary programs, in fact, often had relatively small or no effects on the percentage of people working.)

However, the impact findings on selective-voluntary programs point to another lesson as well. While they suggest consistent and relatively large earnings gains, they also suggest clear limits. Increases in total income were still not large. As a result, the programs may have modestly improved people's standard of living, but were unlikely to move many people out of poverty, suggesting the limited potential of even these programs to help most welfare recipients work their way out of poverty, at least within the three years of follow-up. This points to the importance of determining whether programs that make a more conscious investment in increasing human capital can do better, and contributes to the continuing policy interest in complementary policies directed at providing more income to the working poor.

While the selective-voluntary programs' impacts on earnings were relatively impressive, from the perspective of government budgets in a benefit-cost context, the mixed impacts on welfare savings led to very varied findings. The Maine and Homemaker-Home Health Aide demonstrations did not break even. The New Jersey and Supported Work programs produced net savings for the government, the former within three years and the latter over a substantially longer period.

Table 4.6 provides a summary of the estimated impacts for the broad-coverage and selective-voluntary programs, ranking both sets of programs by the net cost per experimental and indicating some of the features of each study that affect the interpretation of its findings.[11] Comparison across studies suggests that Supported Work, the Homemaker-Home Health Aide Demonstrations (and, to a lesser extent, the Maine OJT program) had higher average costs, but also higher average earnings impacts, than the broad-coverage programs.

The section on "Estimating Impacts for Broad-Coverage and Selective-Voluntary Programs" in Chapter 2 outlined a number of reasons why comparisons between the two categories of studies may be misleading:[12] Differences may reflect not only the relative effectiveness of the employment-directed services, but also variations in either targeting or the research design and resulting participation rates. (Also, the selective programs served volunteers, while the broad-coverage ones probably included people who, on average, were less motivated.) On the first point, targeting, the studies unfortunately do not always provide similar data on participants' measured characteristics, so it is not possible to assess the extent to which the programs reached similar or different groups in the caseload. Obviously, the broad-coverage programs involved a heterogeneous group, including people uninterested in program services (some of whom had left welfare). The voluntary programs reached varied and often unspecified subgroups. For example, Supported Work targeted very disadvantaged long-term recipients, while the Homemaker-Home Health Aide Demonstrations[13] appeared to target no clearly identifiable group, but reached a small number of motivated volunteers.[14]

---

[11] All costs and impacts are in nominal dollars, with the exception of Supported Work and the Louisville studies, which were conducted during an earlier period and for which the results are expressed in 1985 dollars (the approximate midpoint of the other studies).

[12] See Friedlander and Gueron, forthcoming, for further discussion of the non-comparability of these two types of studies.

[13] Data from the latter study indicate that fewer than 3 percent of all AFDC recipients contacted by the program (primarily through mass mailings) actually applied for training, and fewer than 2 percent were accepted into the study (Cella, 1987).

[14] The behavior of control group members does not suggest a clear difference in the level of disadvantagedness between people in the broad-coverage and selective-voluntary programs listed in Table 4.6. On the one hand, controls in selective-voluntary programs were more likely to be employed than were controls in broad-coverage programs. (Based

On the second point, in experimental studies of selective-voluntary programs, random assignment is usually conducted very close to the start of program participation, whereas it is implemented much earlier in evaluations of broad-coverage, mandatory systems. As a result, the share of experimentals who actually participated in employment-directed services was much higher for the selective-voluntary than the broad-coverage programs (see Table 4.6). When this occurs (unless, as is not likely, impacts on nonparticipants are comparable to those on participants), average impacts *per experimental* may be lower for the broad-coverage programs, but average impacts *per actual participant in employment and training services* may be much more similar.[15]

The extraordinary accomplishment of the SWIM program for AFDC recipients is also underlined by comparison with the results from the higher-cost, selective-voluntary programs (which also targeted recipients). As shown in Table 4.4, SWIM produced average earnings impacts per AFDC recipient of $889 in year 2 – comparable to the impacts for the smaller, selective-voluntary programs – even though its impacts were averaged across the full spectrum of mandatory recipients and included

---

on the last quarter of follow-up available in year 2, the employment rate for controls in broad-coverage programs ranged from 13.8 percent in West Virginia to 38.1 percent in San Diego I; in selective-voluntary programs, it ranged from 42.3 percent in Supported Work to 57.8 percent in New Jersey.)

On the other hand, controls in selective-voluntary programs were more likely to be on welfare. (Based on the last quarter of follow-up available in year 2, the proportion of controls in broad-coverage programs who were receiving welfare ranged from 36.2 percent in San Diego I to 72.7 percent in Illinois; in selective-voluntary programs, it ranged from 47.5 percent in New Jersey to 73.5 percent in Supported Work.)

[15] For consistency throughout this synthesis, all impacts are shown "per experimental," not "per participant." An example may be useful in illustrating the impact of this distinction across the two types of studies. If we make the extreme assumption that there were *no* impacts on nonparticipants in broad-coverage programs, then the typical participation rate of 50 percent would imply that the impact per participant would be twice the impact per experimental. (This is because the impact per experimental is the average of the impact for the nonparticipating half of the sample, who are assumed to have zero impacts, and for the participating half, who must then have impacts twice the overall average.) Under this assumption, the magnitude of impact per participant for some of the broad-coverage programs in Table 4.6 would be quite similar to the impacts per participant for Maine and the Homemaker-Home Health Aide Demonstrations.

Since it is probable that this assumption is not accurate, i.e., that the threat or reality of sanctioning did have some effect on nonparticipants, the real impact of broad-coverage programs on participants is probably less than that suggested in the prior paragraph. However, the example points to one of the difficulties in using comparisons across the two types of studies to reach conclusions on the effectiveness of the different employment services provided.

nonparticipants as well as participants. These gains are in the same range as the impacts for the four selective-voluntary programs included in Table 4.6, despite their higher participation rates and more intensive average service mix.

SWIM's accomplishments may follow from the unusual combination of providing some low- and some much higher-cost services. They may also, however, follow from a number of different features of this demonstration: the strict enforcement of an ongoing participation requirement, the extensive prior experience of the San Diego staff, or the education and training services available in that county. Given the impressiveness of the findings, it would be particularly important to determine whether the results can be replicated in other locations.

The cost and impact results for the selective-voluntary programs in Table 4.6 can also be used to extend the analysis in Chapter 4's section on "The Effect of the Program Model and Funding." The earlier discussion of the relationship between program cost and impact, which focused mainly on broad-coverage programs, suggested that in addition to average impacts, administrators may be interested in other measures of program effectiveness, including the impact per dollar invested. Since this measure adjusts for variation in cost, it is also more appropriate for comparisons across the different categories of studies in Table 4.6.[16]

The general finding from the broad-coverage programs was that lower-cost programs tended to have smaller *average impacts* on earnings (but not always on welfare savings) than the higher-cost ones, but that their earnings (and somewhat less consistently their welfare) *impact per dollar invested* was often larger. The selective-voluntary demonstrations appear to provide a further indication of the decreasing cost-effectiveness of higher-cost components, using this second measure.[17] This means that lower-cost programs would allow states both to serve more people and (as long as they exceeded the service threshold suggested by the Cook County study) to produce higher aggregate impacts (the total sum of impacts for all individuals exposed to a program) on earnings and, less consistently, on welfare savings for a given budget.

---

[16] See Friedlander and Gueron, forthcoming, for a detailed discussion of these different effectiveness measures.

[17] For example, each dollar spent produced earnings impacts of 75 cents in New Jersey, 47 cents in Maine, 12 cents in the Homemaker-Home Health Aide Demonstrations, and 6 cents in Supported Work (Friedlander and Gueron, forthcoming).

Overall, the findings on selective-voluntary programs would appear to confirm the discussion in Chapter 4 of both the possible trade-offs and the continued uncertainty. On the former, they suggest that, within any particular budget, administrators may have to balance the extent to which they can meet different program objectives: maximizing impacts per person (by providing some higher-cost services) or maximizing total impacts (by serving more people with lower-cost, job search services). If all dollars of earnings gains (regardless of whom they went to or what level of earnings they represented) were valued equally, this might suggest providing lower-cost services to a large number of people. If getting people into jobs with higher earnings – or possibly obtaining more consistent impacts for more disadvantaged recipients[18] – were sought, this might point to providing higher-cost services. Administrators interested in achievements in both directions may favor a broad-coverage program that combines low- and higher-cost components, carefully targeting the latter to maximize impact.[19] Such programs could build on the approaches represented by the Baltimore and SWIM alternatives.

On the second issue – the uncertainties still facing administrators choosing among alternative JOBS approaches – the selective-voluntary programs provide some added information but leave many questions unanswered. While they suggest that higher-cost components may increase average impacts and reach different groups of recipients, they do not address many of JOBS' and FSA's major innovations: e.g., the targeting on (potential) long-term recipients, the strengthened focus on education and training, and the provision of transitional benefits. This suggests the importance of further studies directed at these populations and at specifically testing more substantial investments in increasing recipients' human capital.

---

[18] See the section on "Findings on Subgroups and Targeting" later in this chapter for a discussion of what is known about the relative effectiveness of higher- and lower-cost services in assisting more disadvantaged groups.

[19] Friedlander and Gueron, forthcoming, observe: "Careful targeting of intensive services to long-term welfare groups may be a way to economize on program resources while increasing the rate of success for very disadvantaged program enrollees. By addressing skills deficits, the higher-cost services might increase the ratio of earnings gains to welfare reductions for the most disadvantaged while still yielding the AFDC savings expected for these groups. If these two effects can be demonstrated, higher-cost services may be regarded not as substitutes for job search and work experience but as specific targeting devices embedded in larger programs that rely on lower-cost services to achieve broad coverage."

CETA and JTPA

The other group of selective-voluntary programs, very different in nature from the demonstrations discussed in the preceding section, were employment and training services provided through CETA or JTPA programs. Unfortunately, there were no large-scale random assignment studies of the CETA program. A number of evaluations were conducted using a comparison group design to determine the impact of the program (and different program activities) on the earnings of adult women. While these studies usually found positive impacts for women, they did not provide a useful basis for determining the impact of specific CETA activities – public service employment, classroom training, or on-the-job training – on AFDC recipients because of the wide variation in estimates of those impacts and the fact that virtually none of the studies isolated female welfare recipients (see Barnow, 1987; Burtless, 1989; Job Training Longitudinal Survey Research Advisory Panel, 1985).[20] For this reason, they are not discussed further in this report.

The ongoing random assignment field study of the Job Training Partnership Act (see Chapter 3) will provide reliable estimates of the impact of the JTPA program in 16 sites – and of assignment to job search, on-the-job training, and classroom training – on its AFDC participants. Given JOBS' emphasis on education and training – and on coordination with JTPA – this will be particularly timely. However, as discussed in the following section, the study results will have to be used with caution in making estimates of the likely effectiveness of similar services provided through state JOBS programs. Only a very small fraction of AFDC recipients participate in JTPA,[21] and, more importantly, these are clearly self-selected and program-screened volunteers. Changes in the targeting or scale of these activities can affect the generalizability of these results.

Information from Evaluations Currently Being Conducted

Three evaluations of selective-voluntary programs that include AFDC recipients among participants are now under way: the Minority

---

[20] The one study that did estimate impacts for AFDC women found earnings increases of $600 to $900 per year (Bassi et al., 1984).

[21] For example, fewer than 4 percent of the WIN-mandatory controls in the Cook County study and 4 percent in the San Diego SWIM study participated in JTPA.

Female Single Parent (MFSP) Demonstration, New York's Comprehensive Employment Opportunity Support Centers (CEOSC) program, and the National JTPA Study.

The MFSP programs served minority women who averaged 28 years of age at baseline. Approximately 65 percent of them had children under 6 years of age (40 percent had children under age 3). Over 70 percent of the sample were receiving AFDC or other public assistance at baseline, and approximately 50 percent had a high school diploma or GED. Services included education, employability preparation, job skills training, case management, child care, and other support services. The four sites were operated by community-based organizations rather than public assistance agencies.[22] At 12 months after random assignment – a time when some members of the program group were still "investing" by participating in relatively intensive and long-term program activities, and others had recently left the program – one site (CET) showed relatively large positive impacts on employment rates, hours worked, wage rates, and earnings. In the remaining three sites, experimentals had employment and earnings similar to, or lower than, those of controls. All sites produced significant gains in GED attainment. In one site, there were increases in welfare receipt and welfare payments in the 12-month results; in the other three, there were no impacts on welfare receipt and payments. Researchers working on this study state that the initial findings from the 30-month interviews with part of the research sample "are broadly similar" to the 12-month site results. (See Gordon and Burghardt, 1990.) The 30-month and 60-month follow-up data, when available, will provide valuable information on the trends over time, since the 12-month period is too short to determine the full effects of this relatively long-term investment. Since the four sites in the demonstration varied not only in program configuration (e.g., concurrent and integrated education and training, or sequential), but also in client characteristics and labor market conditions, the results will probably provide numerous important hypotheses about the source of impacts. (These findings are discussed further in the section on "Programs That Test Education Services," later in this chapter.)

---

[22] One of the four community-based organizations, the Center for Employment Training (CET), operated MFSP in several locations in northern California; CET is referred to here as a single MFSP site.

New York's CEOSC program is designed to test the feasibility and impact of a comprehensive employment and training program for AFDC recipients with children under age 6. The CEOSC program serves relatively long-term recipients, with an average current spell on AFDC of 44 months. Sixty percent of participants were never married, and more than 40 percent lacked a high school diploma at baseline. Operating in nine pilot sites since 1987, the CEOSC program allows for both a "customized" approach to participant services and the possibility that some participants may require a number of long-term education, skills training, and support services in order to obtain stable employment. Within the general CEOSC program design guidelines, sites were encouraged to develop innovative approaches to serving the target group. Thus, there were important variations in the design, sequencing, and delivery of services, such as pre-employment, life skills, and/or motivational training; case management; and the emphasis on and duration of education services. Results of an impact evaluation in one site (Albany), using an experimental design and based on 24 months of follow-up, will be available in 1992.

As discussed in the preceding section, the National JTPA Study should provide important new information on the impact of OJT and vocational skills training for selected AFDC recipients and subgroups of recipients. The direct relevance of the findings to state JOBS programs depends on the planned scale and targeting of JTPA activities in JOBS, compared to the 16 JTPA programs studied. With the JTPA system expected to be a major provider of OJT, job vocational skills training, and job placement for JOBS clients across the country, the evaluation will help establish the range of expected results for AFDC recipients referred to outside agencies for these services. For OJT, it is probable that the National JTPA Study sample will include relatively motivated and screened people, who face fewer barriers to participation and employment than the typical welfare recipient; it may not include many very long-term or potential long-term recipients. On the other hand, since OJT programs usually involve substantial screening – whether they are operated within an employment and training services system or another administrative structure – the JTPA results may apply to the JOBS context fairly well. Similarly, because skills training under JOBS will continue to be provided by JTPA vendors in many localities, the study findings about this activity are of particular interest.

Findings on Subgroups and Targeting

The answer to the question "What works best for whom?" is crucial to improving program performance because it allows program operators to target different types of services to the groups that are likely to benefit the most from them. This can help states make the most efficient use of scarce resources and determine how to target higher-cost components. Information on subgroup impacts is particularly valuable in a system such as JOBS, where states may offer a diverse array of components within a comprehensive program based on individual assessments. Several studies have attempted to analyze the effects of a variety of interventions on different subgroups of the AFDC population, and a few used the findings to develop recommendations for targeting strategies to increase the cost-effectiveness of such programs. Nevertheless, many open questions remain. The JOBS evaluation provides an opportunity to answer some of the open issues and to pose new questions, since the program is aimed at segments of the AFDC population that have not previously been mandated to participate, and because states will offer a broader – and potentially more costly – array of services than those typical in previous studies of broad-coverage programs.

Findings on Subgroup Impacts

The general finding from studies of both broad-coverage and smaller selective-voluntary programs is that impacts are larger for more disadvantaged recipients. A more refined review, however, suggests a more complex picture, where the pattern of subgroup impacts varies with the program design and objective.

Because studies of broad-coverage programs have used samples that included a cross section of program eligibles, they are particularly useful for identifying who within the caseload benefited from the program treatment. (This type of analysis cannot be done based on the samples in the selective-voluntary programs because they contained a much more narrow, program- and self-selected group.) As discussed in Chapter 4, there is quite consistent evidence from the completed studies of broad-coverage, mandatory welfare-to-work programs that the most job-ready enrollees (new welfare applicants) did not gain from participating in these programs. Instead, individuals who were more welfare-dependent and had less recent work history tended to benefit more from relatively lower-cost job search or employment-directed programs than did less dependent groups (Friedlander, 1988b). There may, however, be a threshold of disadvantagedness below which there are smaller earnings impacts. That is, the same studies show that the more dependent half of the caseload – on-board recipients, including those who had been on welfare more than two years, did not have recent earnings, and did not have a high school diploma – also appear to have attained below-average gains (see Table 4.3).[23] For welfare savings, the same studies have not yet identified a similar threshold: The largest savings seemed to occur for the more disadvantaged groups, and there were no long-term savings from serving the most employable.[24]

The threshold for earnings impacts from broad-coverage programs may imply that higher-cost services are needed to raise the earnings of the more disadvantaged groups in the caseload. The Supported Work program, which targeted long-term AFDC recipients, provided the most consistent evidence of impacts with this population.[25] Moreover, even among those targeted by the program, Supported Work led to larger-than-average employment and welfare impacts for those women in the sample who were more disadvantaged: e.g., those who had never worked, had several children, were older, or had been on welfare the longest. A reanalysis of Supported Work and the quasi-experimental studies of the impact of WIN and CETA on AFDC recipients also suggested that welfare recipients with little or no recent work experience

---

[23] When bivariate relationships between demographic characteristics – high school diploma status, the absence of children under age 12, the number of children, age, and ethnicity – and impacts were analyzed, they were inconsistent across the programs studied.

[24] The very limited subgroup analysis in the studies of the broad-coverage group and individual job search programs in Louisville indicated that there were larger employment and earnings impacts for the more disadvantaged groups: recipients compared to applicants; people with little or no recent work experience compared to those with recent employment; WIN volunteers with children under age 6 compared to WIN-mandatories with older children. The groups with larger earnings impacts were not, however, the same as the groups with the larger welfare savings. (See Wolfhagen, 1983; Goldman, 1981.) A subsequent, more detailed reanalysis of the Louisville studies found some evidence of a threshold for earnings impacts (Grossman, Maynard, and Roberts, 1985).

[25] As discussed in Chapter 4, the SWIM research has not yet addressed whether that program's quite substantial benefits for AFDC recipients extended to the most disadvantaged subgroups. However, the magnitude of impacts for recipients suggests that they are unlikely to be limited only to the more employable within this group. Planned further analysis will be particularly important because SWIM (unlike Supported Work) was a broad-coverage program and the sample thus included people like those who volunteered for Supported Work programs as well as people who were less motivated.

benefited substantially more, on average, than did those with some recent work experience (Grossman, Maynard, and Roberts, 1985). Subgroup analysis of the short-term impacts (one year after random assignment) of the voluntary Minority Female Single Parent Demonstration (Gordon and Burghardt, 1990) is also consistent with this general pattern. At the one service provider for which there were statistically significant positive impacts on earnings, employment gains were greatest for women with children under age 3 and for those who had received welfare in the prior year.

Findings from the evaluation of the AFDC Homemaker-Home Health Aide Demonstrations show subgroup impacts that varied across sites. Subgroups traditionally regarded as more employable – women with more education or prior work experience, and those rated as having greater potential by intake workers – did not consistently experience larger (or smaller) impacts. The study did find, however, that welfare savings were usually larger for the women with the highest welfare benefits at baseline. The same was not true, however, for women with the longest duration on AFDC (Bell, Enns, and Orr, 1986).

A possible exception to this pattern is the Maine OJT study, which found larger impacts for groups facing fewer employment barriers: women with one child, women who were at least 30 years old, and women who had completed high school. However, impacts were also large for women who had used welfare for more than two years (Cave, 1989).[26]

A very different approach to the goal of identifying subgroups that benefit from welfare-to-work programs was used in two studies that examined program staff's perceptions of and knowledge about clients. In the Louisville group job search study, AFDC recipients who were randomly assigned to participate in job club were rated on job-readiness by their counselors before the job club began. These ratings were based

---

[26] Because of the very small sample, targeting, and screening for the Maine program, and the unusual characteristics of the Maine welfare caseload, it is hard to interpret these results. The authors of the study concluded that the program had reached a relatively highly motivated group of women, who resembled displaced homemakers. This was because, despite an intention to focus on a more disadvantaged group of volunteers, the enrollment process screened out cases with child care or health problems, poor basic skills, transportation difficulties, or other barriers to employment (Auspos, Cave, and Long, 1988). Since less employable participants were not included in the study, its results do not tell us whether they would have benefited from participation in this type of program.

on the counselors' perceptions of their motivation and skills. The study analyzed the relationship between the ratings and subsequent in-program performance, defined as attending job club or dropping out, and as finding a job during job club. The study found that there was almost no relationship between the job-readiness ratings and performance in job club; e.g., some of those who were low-rated had regular attendance in job club and got jobs in the course of that activity.

The second study went further, examining the relationship between staff ratings of clients' employability and two outcomes: in-program performance and post-program results.[27] In the Homemaker-Home Health Aide Demonstrations, intake workers rated applicants' potential for post-program employment by collecting information on their education, work experience, and other personal attributes, and gave an overall rating of job-readiness that combined those factors and other, unmeasured, factors. The study found that program staff based their overall ratings primarily on unmeasured factors (presumably including factors such as motivation). In addition, there was only a very weak relationship between the intake workers' information and ratings and staff members' subsequent assessments of participants' in-program progress. The study also found that the initial ratings were correlated with program *outcomes* (post-program earnings and welfare receipt); however, they were *not* correlated with program *impacts* (the improvement in outcomes over what would have been expected in the absence of the program, as measured by the outcomes for similarly rated people in the control group). In other words, some participants who were rated low on future employability were helped by the program to improve their earnings and get off welfare, while some high-rated participants did no better than they would have done without the program's assistance.

This study thus suggests that intake workers were able to select applicants who had good prospects for employment success, but were not able to identify the applicants for whom the program would have the greatest net impact. The study concluded that the intake workers' ratings were consistent with creaming, rather than with selecting participants so as to maximize program impact (see Bell and Orr, 1988). Both studies suggest that it is difficult for program staff to identify the people who will benefit most from a welfare-to-work program.

---

[27]This further analysis was possible because, in the Homemaker-Home Health Aide Demonstrations, staff ratings were conducted prior to random assignment and thus available for people in both the experimental and control groups.

Guidelines for Targeting

Based on the subgroup results in five states with broad-coverage programs – four with relatively low-cost services and the mixed program in Baltimore – Friedlander (1988b) developed a series of general principles for targeting similar types of programs for adults. Programs of this sort that want to maximize net impacts should not concentrate on serving only the most job-ready portion of the AFDC caseload. To maximize net impacts on earnings, these programs may be well-advised to work with moderately dependent groups such as AFDC applicants who have received welfare in the past (i.e., applicant returnees); then, if resources permit, services could be expanded to include longer-term recipients. To maximize welfare savings, it makes sense to devote increased effort to the more dependent groups. In general, this study advised against targeting too narrowly on the most dependent groups, in part because it is not known whether low-cost job search programs would produce the expected impacts if *only* the more dependent individuals were enrolled.[28] Friedlander concluded that the evidence from the five programs did not provide guidance on targeting specific components to specific subgroups. Given the emphasis in the JOBS legislation on serving long-term recipients, his finding that this group did not always experience earnings gains from lower-cost services takes on added significance. It points to the importance of determining whether more intensive broad-coverage programs will be able to replicate the more promising results for this group found from the targeted, smaller-scale demonstrations (e.g., Supported Work) and suggested by SWIM.

A somewhat different view was taken in an interesting earlier study. A reanalysis of subgroup impacts in Supported Work, the Louisville WIN Labs, WIN, and the Employment Opportunity Pilot Project (EOPP) (Grossman, Maynard, and Roberts, 1985) offered recommendations for targeting job search and employment and training services. Based on the initial results from their subgroup analysis, Grossman, Maynard, and Roberts concluded that there is very little direct evidence that alternative program targeting strategies would be expected to have substantially larger earnings impacts for either job search assistance or subsidized employment and training services. The results did suggest a number of

---

[28] For example, it is not clear that a job club serving only more disadvantaged people would have the same impacts as one that served a more mixed population, including people who are more likely to be successful in obtaining work.

potential targeting strategies that might result in larger welfare savings from more extensive services. These include targeting on high school dropouts without recent work experience, those with no young children, and those who have been on welfare a relatively long time.

Several other subgroups take on new importance because of provisions of the Family Support Act. The act mandates participation by custodial parents under age 20 who have not finished high school, regardless of the age of their children, and prescribes education activities for this population (with some exceptions). Education may also be the prescribed service for adults age 20 and older who do not have a high school diploma and have not achieved a basic level of literacy, although, under certain circumstances, other services may be provided for this group. A few evaluations have studied the effect of voluntary services for subsets of this group, but there are no completed studies on mandatory programs for young mothers, since they were exempt from participation requirements. Because this group has been shown to be at particular risk of long-term welfare dependence (Ellwood, 1986), it will be especially important to get reliable evidence on the effectiveness of education and other services in increasing their earnings and employment and decreasing their welfare dependence. The studies of Ohio LEAP and the Teenage Parent Demonstration should provide important information on adaptations of JOBS' learnfare provisions (discussed later in this chapter).

Summary and Next Steps

In very simplified form, this summary of the results of past research on subgroups and targeting may suggest the pattern of impacts outlined in Table 5.4.

In implementing their JOBS programs, states face difficult choices on the use of more intensive services and the role of job search, especially in light of resource limits and JOBS' emphasis on such groups as long-term welfare recipients, for whom there are only sparse findings of positive program impacts. That there are only a few studies of higher-cost programs and services, which may be needed for this group, adds to the uncertainties. In this environment, further work on subgroups and targeting takes on critical importance. To date, only Friedlander (1988b) and Grossman, Maynard, and Roberts (1985) have examined in depth the impacts of a number of broad-coverage programs across different sub-

TABLE 5.4 SUMMARY OF RESEARCH ON THE RELATIONSHIP
OF IMPACT TO LEVEL OF DISADVANTAGEDNESS
AND TREATMENT

Level of Disadvantagedness	Low- to Moderate-Cost, Broad-Coverage Programs	Higher-Cost, Selective-Voluntary Programs
Less dependent	No consistent earnings gains or welfare savings	Not tested
Middle group	Consistent earnings gains; no consistent welfare savings	Limited number of studies, which did not cover the full spectrum of the caseload and did not systematically isolate groups by level of disadvantagedness. Consistent earnings gains; usually welfare savings
More dependent	Some (but not consistent) earnings gains; more consistent welfare savings	

groups of the caseload. Some information will be gained from further analysis of data from completed experiments – in particular, the planned further analysis of the SWIM data. Here it will be important to determine: What SWIM services were provided to which subgroups? Were the impacts of SWIM uniform across subgroups of recipients? Did SWIM benefit the most disadvantaged groups of recipients? The answers to these questions will help target intensive services on persons who will benefit from them.

The discussion in this synthesis suggests that JOBS administrators may face a trade-off in trying to meet different program objectives: increasing the earnings of particular groups and maximizing welfare savings. But the nature of this trade-off is uncertain. It will remain so until further studies examine the potential of the intensive services that most states will be using under JOBS – particularly education and training – to increase the self-sufficiency of the least employable welfare recipients. This research may identify ways that intensive services can be carefully targeted at very disadvantaged participants to both produce greater earnings gains and generate welfare savings. If such service and targeting strategies exist, programs could reduce the need to trade off success in meeting different program goals.

Programs That Test Education Services

The basic argument for including education services in welfare programs is simple: If welfare recipients can acquire the knowledge and skills needed to get better jobs, that will simultaneously reduce poverty and welfare receipt. An extensive body of human capital research links educational attainment with earnings (Mincer, 1989). Moreover, evidence that the majority of 19- to 23-year-old welfare recipients scored in the bottom fifth of all people their age on the Armed Forces Qualifying Test (Berlin and Sum, 1988) and that 60 percent of California's welfare caseload were determined to lack either the basic educational achievement or high school level credentials judged needed for successful employment (Riccio et al., 1989) demonstrates that the lack of education is a severe problem for many welfare recipients.[29]

Recognizing that long-term welfare recipients typically have much lower levels of education than successful labor market participants, policymakers have reasoned that an increase in education might increase this group's employability. However, virtually all human capital studies have been based on data for people who *voluntarily* decided to acquire additional education. Much of the JOBS population will be under a *mandate* to attend an education program. Moreover, many of them will have previously had negative experiences in school, including school failure and dropping out. It is possible that some members of this population will lack the motivation, confidence, and school-relevant skills possessed by the subjects of existing human capital studies. It is also possible that the mandatory JOBS population will be less likely than others to select the education program that is the most economically promising one for their needs and goals. Education research has also suggested that the previous schooling received by poor and inner-city

---

[29] The limited human capital of welfare recipients is reflected in studies showing that the majority of women on welfare, even if they work full time, are not likely to earn more than they receive from AFDC, especially in high-benefit states (Garfinkel and McLanahan, 1986).

adults (ages 21 to 25) may be of low quality.[30] If participants in the states' JOBS programs receive low-quality education, they may not obtain the human capital, and thus not receive the employment payoffs, that have been found in previous studies.

Because of these possibilities, additional education may not produce improved labor market outcomes for many JOBS participants. The hypothesis that additional education helps welfare recipients leave welfare and become independent is currently awaiting empirical evidence. A review of the research literature indicates that there is currently little solid evidence that education programs for adult welfare recipients can improve their educational attainment or achievement. In fact, there is little education research of any kind on the adult JOBS population, on mandatory education programs for adults, or on the relationship between mandatory participation in adult education and subsequent employment success.

Some insights have come from the Baltimore and SWIM studies and from several selective-voluntary programs: the Minority Female Single Parent Demonstration (which included AFDC adults), the National JTPA Study, the SIME/DIME Manpower Experiment, the Job Corps Computer-Assisted Instruction Evaluation, and JOBSTART (which is discussed in detail in the following section). More evidence will come from the GAIN evaluation, which will provide the first rigorous impact data on labor force participation, educational attainment, and educational achievement for a broad-coverage program that targets many participants for mandatory education combined with other services. The evaluation of Florida's Project Independence, which began in 1990, will provide labor force impact data for a program providing education for recipients who are determined not to be job-ready and whose employability plan includes education. It should be noted that states' JOBS programs will provide education in a wide variety of forms, and this may lead to considerable variation in the measured impacts of educational activities in current evaluations.

Except for the GAIN evaluation, none of the current studies of JOBS-like programs for adults will capture educational achievement

---

[30] "Nearly 50 percent of young adults with 12 or fewer years of schooling who had NAEP [National Assessment of Educational Progress] reading scores in the bottom quartile of the distribution were members of poor or near poor households" (Venezky, Kaestle, and Sum, 1987, p. 39; see also Kirsch and Jungeblut, 1986).

impacts. Educational achievement refers to individuals' performance on standardized tests of reading and mathematics. Such data are useful because they provide a common metric for measuring the skills of individuals who live in different places, attend different schools, and seek work in different labor markets. In contrast, information on individuals' educational attainment (i.e., the years of schooling and degrees they have received) may conceal wide variation in the quality of education that was received and in the skills that were actually learned. The results of the GAIN study of literacy impacts, which will use an achievement test, will provide the first rigorous information on the educational gains that result from JOBS. However, the complexity of the links between education and subsequent employment mean that data from several field experiments will be required in order for analysts to capture the effect of differing education systems within welfare-to-work programs and to understand how lengthy investments in education by welfare recipients affect their employment.

Four selective-voluntary studies that examine education are also relevant to JOBS.[31] The Manpower Experiment in the SIME/DIME (Seattle and Denver) negative income tax experiments offered vouchers for education and training to participants. For low-income female heads of families who were not previously enrolled in school and who received a 100 percent education and training subsidy, participation in education increased, particularly among those 16 to 25 years old. Participants in that age group attended an education activity for an average of one community college quarter, compared to less than .03 quarters for the control group (Hall, 1980). However, there was no consistent pattern of impacts on earnings and employment for single female heads of families, and other groups showed some negative impacts on earnings and employment (SRI International, 1983).

The Minority Female Single Parent (MFSP) Demonstration provided a mixture of relatively intensive education and training to volunteering black and Hispanic adults (72 percent of whom were receiving welfare) in four different community-based programs. (The programs differed in the other services they provided, including counseling, job placement assistance, and child care.) Available results from this random assignment study are limited to the 12 months after enrollment in the demonstration, a period during which program participants are forgoing opportu-

---

[31] The following section, on "Youth-Oriented Services," discusses studies of programs for young AFDC mothers that also include education components.

nities to work and "investing" in education and training in anticipation of future returns, while controls are building human capital through their experience in the labor market. As the increase in impacts between years 1 and 3 in Baltimore suggests, this 12-month period is still too soon to determine which form of investment will yield greater ultimate returns. (The researchers involved in the study note that initial results from a longer, 30-month follow-up for part of the research sample "are broadly similar to the impacts at 12 months after enrollment" [Gordon and Burghardt, 1990, p. 104].)

Results for months 9 through 12 after random assignment show that experimentals have pulled roughly even with controls' employment and earnings at three of the MFSP sites, and moved ahead to show relatively large, positive impacts on employment, wage rates, and earnings at the fourth site, the Center for Employment Training (CET) (Gordon and Burghardt, 1990). At CET in San Jose and other locations around San Francisco, during this fourth quarter, the average monthly employment rate was 9.9 percentage points higher for experimentals than for those in the control group, and average monthly earnings were $133 higher. During the same period, CET experimentals also worked an average of 16.6 more hours per month and received an average hourly wage that was 72 cents higher than that for controls. (All differences were statistically significant.) The CET earnings impacts, if they continue, compare favorably to those for the selective-voluntary programs shown in Table 4.6. There were no impacts on public assistance receipt or payments at three of the four sites (including CET); one site showed increases in these. Finally, all of the sites produced statistically significant gains in GED attainment.[32]

---

[32] In comparing these results with those from broad-coverage programs, it is important to remember the cautions listed in Chapter 2, particularly the high participation rate in CET (84 percent) compared to those in most broad-coverage studies. As explained in Chapter 2, two employment or training approaches may have identical impacts on people who actually *receive services,* but show different average impacts, because participation rates differed. The study with lower participation rates will probably show lower average impacts because it includes more people who do not receive services and whose behavior is not greatly affected by the program's services or mandates.

Thus, the average employment impacts for CET and most of the selective-voluntary programs presented in Table 4.6 were substantially larger than those for most of the broad-coverage programs. As noted elsewhere, SWIM is surprising in having had impacts of the same magnitude as the selective-voluntary programs. (For example, SWIM and CET had similar impacts on employment rates. SWIM increased the employment rate for AFDC recipients – the SWIM group most comparable to the CET group – by 9.4 percentage points in the last quarter of the first year compared to the control group [see Table 4.4].)

The services provided by the four MFSP sites differed. CET provided job skills training to most participants regardless of their educational skills, supplemented by remedial education that was often incorporated into the training, i.e., a concurrent and integrated approach. In contrast, the other three sites placed less emphasis on up-front vocational training and more on education and "general employability training" intended to improve participants' motivation, decision-making, and orientation toward employment so that they could gain access to further training or work (a sequential approach). It may be that the emphasis on up-front job skills training at CET helped welfare recipients make a more rapid entry into the labor force, while improvements in education and general work-readiness may have a more gradual effect on participants' labor market success. Perhaps a greater emphasis on employment as the objective of education helped focus the education services at CET. However, it is also possible that the marked differences between CET and other MFSP sites (e.g., in participants' disadvantagedness, labor market conditions, CET's prior experience with the program approach it operated during the demonstration, the quality of the services provided, CET's linkages to employers, and the availability of on-site child care at CET) may account for the differences between the measured impacts. In grappling with these and other alternative explanations, the researchers note: "It is impossible to isolate the effects of the many factors that we have identified. Short-term findings in a single site simply do not support strong general conclusions" (Gordon and Burghardt, 1990, p. 106). Obviously, the long-term follow-up data on the MFSP Demonstration will be particularly critical. These may alter the initial picture of site impacts, and also provide information on the time path of impacts from education investments.[33]

The Baltimore and SWIM studies also suggest some caution in reaching conclusions on what factors explain the limited results at three of the MFSP sites. Both of these broad-coverage programs sent substantial numbers of participants to education and training which, in general, was sequential. For example, in San Diego, the community college system did not provide any concurrent programs integrating education with training, except for a small amount of English as a Second Language that

---

[33] Findings from the JOBSTART Demonstration will provide further guidance on these issues, since the 13 sites in that project also tested different arrangements for sequential and concurrent education and training.

was provided concurrently with training. The stronger earnings impacts for these two broad-coverage programs (compared to those that provided only job search and work experience) may have been due to their inclusion of these more intensive services. However, as noted elsewhere in this volume, other elements in the programs or environments may have been the critical factors. Thus, while not definitive, the MFSP findings provide an early caution to JOBS administrators on the possible importance of structuring education activities so that they are connected to the job market, if the goal is employment impacts.

The third selective-voluntary evaluation, the National JTPA Study, focuses on persons voluntarily seeking employment services. Some individuals in the research sample (6 to 8 percent of the adults and 16 percent of the youth) were recommended by JTPA operators for education. Data collection at follow-up will not include educational achievement information but will include information on participation and attainment in education. The fact that the point of random assignment in this study was *after* the determination by JTPA operators of "appropriateness of education as a placement" means that experimental-control differences in participation in education *for those who were thought to need it* can be usefully analyzed to determine the impact of JTPA programs on the amount of education received, as well as JTPA's overall impact on employment, earnings, and welfare receipt. These findings will shed light on the role of education in the labor market success of volunteers for training programs.

While impact data on JOBS-like programs emphasizing education are scarce, some information on participation in mandatory education programs is available. Early in the GAIN evaluation, it was found that 14 percent of all GAIN registrants participated in education and that 41 percent of those who participated in any GAIN activity participated in education. (See Figure 4.2.) For adult welfare recipients, the early implementation evidence from California suggests that while some participants may resist having to go to school, others overcome their initial hesitancy and report experiencing at least some success in the program. GAIN's broad education participation mandate, when combined with program management that attempts to maintain participation in education, appears to produce substantial participation in education programs (Riccio et al., 1989).

As noted above, in SWIM, a program that imposed a continuous participation requirement and assigned welfare recipients to job search and unpaid work experience first, some participants were later referred to education or training, after an assessment. (In addition, registrants who were already participating in qualifying education programs at the time of registration were allowed to continue in lieu of other activity.) Participation in community college programs (including adult basic education and continuing education as well as training) was about 7 percentage points higher (representing a 32 percent increase) for SWIM participants than for the control group for both AFDC and AFDC-UP participants. These results indicate that in a program that used up-front job search and work experience to remove job-ready recipients from the welfare rolls, a substantial number of those who did not find jobs participated in education (Hamilton and Friedlander, 1989).

While the lack of research on a range of JOBS-like education programs for adults makes it difficult to discuss the effectiveness of particular education strategies for this population, a recent study of a selective-voluntary program targeted on youth is suggestive. The Job Corps Computer-Assisted Instruction Evaluation (Shugoll Research et al., 1989), which targeted a young, disadvantaged population, including many from AFDC-receiving families, found no impacts of computer-assisted instruction on educational achievement or GED attainment compared to the levels attained by those receiving regular classroom instruction.[34] In this experiment, there was great variation within and between sites in the implementation of the computer-assisted instruction. This finding for a JOBS-relevant population parallels the literature on implementation in elementary and secondary education, which shows that prescribed instructional methods are carried out differently in different classrooms and schools (Berman and McLaughlin, 1978). The implication of these findings for JOBS education programs may be that programs attempting to prescribe particular education techniques thought to be more effective than others are subject to considerable implementation variation that may change the program model.

Youth-Oriented Services

The JOBS program places a priority on serving welfare recipients who are at risk of long-term welfare receipt, including young mothers who have not completed high school. The rationale for focusing on this

---

[34] The Job Corps population in this study included few women with children.

group is clear: If program services can prevent young women on AFDC from dropping out of school (or encourage their return to education programs) and establish them in the labor force, they will not experience the extended period of receipt and the related poverty and costs to the welfare system that have been associated with teen parenting (Ellwood, 1986). The states' JOBS programs may represent a substantial shift from previous programs in their emphasis on serving these groups.

This preventive approach for teen parents on welfare is newer and less tested than the welfare-to-work methods that have been tried and evaluated for adults. For the teen parent population, direct job search and job club are often less appropriate than school-based programs, and thus job search is not used as a screen for more expensive services. The literature on dropout prevention and recovery does not provide clear guidance on services or likely impacts (although it can identify likely dropouts fairly well). Moreover, this literature does not consider mandatory programs with sanctions. While alternative high schools provide a promising approach to the problem of dropout prevention, this innovation has not been subjected to a rigorous impact study. In general, rigorous methods have rarely been used to evaluate dropout prevention programs (U.S. General Accounting Office, 1986; U.S. General Accounting Office, 1987a).

There have been no broad-coverage welfare-to-work programs aimed at preventing long-term welfare receipt among young AFDC recipients until very recently, in Ohio LEAP, the Teenage Parent Demonstration, and Wisconsin's Learnfare. (Wisconsin's Learnfare is not being evaluated using an experimental design.)

The evaluation of Ohio LEAP will provide impact data on the educational attainment, school attendance, earnings, repeat pregnancies, and welfare receipt of teen parents under age 19 who are required to attend school and are subjected to financial rewards or penalties based on their compliance with the attendance requirement. These financial incentives are part of the monthly welfare check received by teen parents (or the adult case heads). LEAP also provides case management, child care, and guaranteed summer jobs. The results of this evaluation will inform policy choices on the design of learnfare models for preventing dropping out of school and for returning dropouts to school. However, it should be noted that other states are using or considering learnfare models that use only financial sanctions (and not financial rewards) as their primary incentive for school attendance; these models are not currently being evaluated using rigorous research designs.

The U.S. Department of Health and Human Services' current Teenage Parent Demonstration uses an experimental design to evaluate the effects of education and other services, and of a continuous participation requirement. Participation is mandatory for a research sample of teen parents on AFDC in Chicago, Illinois, and Camden and Newark, New Jersey, who have one child when they enter the study, and also, in Chicago, for AFDC recipients in the third trimester of pregnancy. The participation requirement includes required school attendance for young teens and brokered or on-site education or training for older teens. Program services are not limited to education, as in some learnfare programs, but also include counseling, parenting instruction, life skills instruction, and other services. The impact evaluation will provide two-year follow-up data on educational attainment *and* achievement (i.e., test scores measuring basic skills).

The Teenage Parent Demonstration will produce important findings on the impact of mandatory education and other services on teen AFDC recipients. The demonstration's use of some on-site education, case management, and other services may create, in effect, an enriched education component, going beyond what is offered by mainstream high school and learnfare programs. The Teenage Parent Demonstration represents a significant model aimed at improving on the discouraging record of dropout prevention and repeat pregnancy prevention programs. In addition, it may be possible to use this data set to analyze links between educational achievement and labor market success.

In addition to the Ohio LEAP evaluation and the Teenage Parent Demonstration, there are several selective-voluntary demonstration projects that include samples of young AFDC recipients. Two of these studies, Project Redirection and the Job Corps evaluation, used a comparison group research design. They are included in this report because they served important populations, because random assignment studies are not available for these populations and services, and because these studies were conducted with considerable effort to identify and compensate for the limitations of the research design. The other two evaluations discussed, JOBSTART and New Chance, use random assignment research designs.

Project Redirection was a four-site, voluntary demonstration for AFDC-eligible mothers under age 18, using comprehensive after-school services intended to prevent dropping out, teach parenting and life management skills, and enhance employability. It produced greater short-term retention in high school, but no long-term differences in educational attainment between experimentals and the comparison group. In this case, program activities alone were not enough to increase high school or GED completion. However, measured five years after program entry, Project Redirection's impacts included an increase of $39 in weekly earnings and a decrease of 12 percentage points in welfare receipt for young women on AFDC at baseline. In addition, Redirection participants showed improved child development impacts, relative to the comparison group. It should also be noted that Redirection participants showed increased childbearing, again relative to the comparison group. (See Table 5.5.) Taken together, these findings suggest not only that the effects of Project Redirection were long-lasting, but also that programs serving a teen population may not show their impacts on employment until participants' children are no longer infants and toddlers. Evaluations that use long-term follow-up appear to be especially important for programs focused on teen parents (Polit, Quint, and Riccio, 1988).

The evaluations of the Job Corps (which serves a population of volunteers including both AFDC recipients and others) found that 42 percent of Job Corps females with children completed a GED or got a high school diploma versus 6 percent of the comparison group. However, the Jobs Corps had consistently lower employment and earnings impacts for females with children than for males or females without children. The Job Corps experience shows that a residential, high-cost, high-intensity intervention can increase the education, and to some extent the employment and earnings, of a young disadvantaged population similar to the young AFDC population (Mallar et al., 1982).

In JOBSTART, a 13-site, voluntary-participation model aimed at disadvantaged youth 17 to 21 years old (and including substantial numbers of young mothers on AFDC), initial impact research results have been obtained for the 12 months following participants' application to the program. These results show that a GED or high school diploma was attained by 27.5 percent of the treatment group versus 9.9 percent of the control group; for females living with their children, the respective figures are 33.1 percent of the treatment group versus 6.4 percent of the control group. Moreover, a pre-post reading test for a subsample of participants showed average reading gains of .7 grade levels from a starting point of approximately seventh-grade level. GED receipt was closely linked to participants' prior basic skills levels. Of treatment group

TABLE 5.5   SELECTED FIVE-YEAR IMPACTS OF PROJECT REDIRECTION FOR WOMEN WHO WERE RECEIVING AFDC BENEFITS AT BASELINE

Outcome	Project Redirection Group	Comparison Group	Difference
Percent with a Diploma/ GED Certificate	47	43	4
Percent Employed	34	24	10
Mean Weekly Hours Worked	13	8	5**
Mean Weekly Earnings	$76	$37	$39***
Mean Number of Weeks Worked during Previous 12 Months	16	11	5**
Percent Receiving AFDC Benefits	54	66	-12*
Percent Receiving AFDC Benefits at Any Point in Previous 12 Months	57	71	-14**
Mean Number of Pregnancies	3.2	3.2	0.0
Mean Number of Live Births	2.3	2.1	0.2*
Mean Home Environment Score	44	39	5***
Percent Who Had Enrolled Child in Head Start	50	34	16**
Child's Mean Vocabulary Score	87	82	5**

SOURCE: Adapted from Polit, Quint, and Riccio, 1988.

NOTES: The impacts are based on analyses of women in the five-year subsample who had been receiving AFDC benefits at baseline (193 young mothers).

*Denotes statistical significance at the 10 percent level; ** at the 5 percent level; and *** at the 1 percent level. The figures shown have been statistically adjusted for important baseline characteristics.

members entering with ninth-grade reading skills, 66 percent received a GED versus 43 percent of entrants who read at the seventh- or eighth-grade level and 20 percent of entrants who read below the seventh-grade level. In addition, sites that emphasized the GED, used frequent practice tests, and offered financial incentives for passing the GED had higher GED attainment than other sites. It will be important to wait for later follow-up data on the employment and earnings of experimentals and controls to gauge the effect of education and training on labor market success.

A potentially significant finding of the JOBSTART Demonstration is that sites that provided concurrent education and training had higher rates of participation in training activities than sites using a sequential program in which education preceded training. Concurrent programs apparently reduced the likelihood that participants would leave the program without reaching the program's training component. For some youth, being able to receive a mixture of education and job-relevant training may increase motivation. At the same time, sequential programs in which up-front education preceded training resulted in participants receiving a considerably higher number of hours of education than did youth in the concurrent education and training sites, perhaps because of the timing of the education activities. One other possible reason for greater education hours in sequential sites was that many youth recruited at these sites were more interested in attaining a GED than in receiving occupational training (Auspos et al., 1989). The longer-term follow-up from JOBSTART will provide an opportunity to see whether, for a group of young AFDC mothers, these variations in service receipt and program structure translate into differences in impacts. (This will be particularly important, given the diverse results from the four sites in the Minority Female Single Parent Demonstration.)

New Chance is a 16-site national demonstration providing comprehensive education and training, and employability, life management, and parenting instruction to young mothers who are 17- to 21-year-old high school dropouts on AFDC. Its experimental design evaluation will provide impact data on educational attainment and achievement, employment, earnings, welfare receipt, and fertility. New Chance builds on the lessons of Project Redirection and other efforts to help young, disadvantaged women make the transition to work and independence. This demonstration is targeted at AFDC recipients who are older than the typical high school or learnfare population but who are appropriate targets for a prevention-oriented approach because they are likely to be long-term welfare recipients (Quint and Guy, 1989). As noted above, this group is one of the JOBS target groups. The results of New Chance will help determine whether an intervention can be effective for these young women.

Programs That Test Support Services

Welfare programs typically provide direct income for recipients, services intended to help recipients leave welfare and enter the labor force, and support services. Support services may include child care during welfare receipt, transitional child care following the period of welfare receipt, medical assistance, transportation to needed services, family planning and life skills assistance, and/or counseling. The rationale for support services includes the belief that they contribute to the ability of welfare recipients to leave welfare and become employed. However, there has been only a modest amount of research on the effectiveness of support services in contributing to reduced receipt and increased employment. Most of this research has focused on the labor market behavior of welfare recipients who receive child care services versus those who do not.

Child Care

Two cross-sectional studies of women with children have found an inverse relationship between child care costs and the women's labor force participation (Stolzenberg and Waite, 1984; Blau and Robins, 1986). It is reasonable to assume that some welfare recipients will not participate in education, training, or work unless they can obtain subsidized child care services, either through the welfare program or from some other source. It can also be assumed that the availability of transitional child care may affect the job retention of former welfare recipients. However, the impact of child care and transitional child care on parents' labor market behavior has not been measured.

The most significant JOBS-related research on child care services is the Expanded Child Care Options (ECCO) Demonstration that began in 1990 in New Jersey. A sample of welfare recipients in the state's REACH welfare-to-work program who have a child under age 3 will be randomly assigned to one of three service groups:

- A control group, whose members will be offered in-program and transitional child care for a period based on the parent's welfare-to-work activities, lasting for up to one year of education and training and for up to one transitional year of post-program employment. The in-program child care will be paid for by the local welfare department at the level set for its clients (and provided at no cost to participants), and the transitional child care will be subsidized at the established, income-conditioned rates used by the local welfare department.

- A group to whom post-program child care will be offered until the youngest child in the family enters the first grade. This group will receive in-program child care paid for by the local welfare department at the level set for its clients (and provided at no cost to participants), and post-program child care subsidized at the established, income-conditioned rates used by the local welfare department.

- A group to whom relatively expensive, high-quality, developmental child care and parenting support will be offered until the youngest child in the family enters first grade. The in-program child care will be provided at no cost to participants, and the transitional child care will be charged to participants at the income-conditioned rates used by the local welfare department for its standard-quality child care. Consequently, the subsidy level for this group will be higher than that used for the other groups to compensate for the higher quality of the care provided.

More than 1,800 children will be covered by these child care offers. Follow-up data on adults and children participating in the demonstration will be collected for at least 15 years after enrollment. In addition to extensive data on children's outcomes, the demonstration will collect impact data on parents' utilization of extended transitional child care, and on parents' earnings, hours worked, use of training and education programs, and welfare receipt. This experimental study of child care services will provide important new information on the role of child care in welfare recipients' decisions to work (New Jersey Department of Human Services, 1989).

In addition to ECCO, there are two state projects that plan to use random assignment designs to test specified transitional child care benefits as part of their welfare-to-work programs. North Carolina received a waiver of applicable federal regulations to permit a test of the effects on mothers' employment (compared to the employment of members of a control group) of a guarantee of child care rather than care on a space-available basis. Texas received a waiver permitting the state to test the effect of offering one year of extended transitional child care and Medicaid eligibility to persons who become employed. When the transitional benefits provisions of the Family Support Act took effect, these benefits were offered to all AFDC recipients; this will affect the evaluation in ways not yet determined. If the North Carolina and Texas evaluations are successfully completed, they will provide useful information on the impact of transitional child care benefits on parents' employment and welfare receipt.

In Massachusetts' ET, a voluntary program that is relevant to JOBS, there is evidence that for voluntary participants who became employed, job retention was greater for users of day care provided by centers, friends, and relatives than for those with no regular child care and those who used babysitters. (Job retention was also correlated with health insurance, provided by the employer or by Massachusetts.) This finding suggests that for those motivated to become employed, regular child care and health insurance are linked to job retention (Nightingale et al., 1989).

The Abecedarian Project, a small, voluntary demonstration, also provides impact data regarding the effect of child care services on low-income teen mothers' employment. Twenty-nine low-income, teenage mothers with infants were randomly assigned; the experimental group received free, high-quality, developmental child care from before the children were three months old until they began kindergarten. Other services, including free medical care for the experimental group children, were also provided. After $4\frac{1}{2}$ years, mothers in the control group had a greater likelihood of being on welfare, more births, and less education than mothers of the children who received full educational day care (Campbell, Breitmayer, and Ramey, 1986).

Studies of broad-coverage welfare-to-work programs for women with school-age children suggest that child care was not a major obstacle to participation. This is probably partly a result of the programs' designs: Activities were often limited to several months and scheduled around school hours. Among program participants during the school year in SWIM, for example, for 33 percent of cases studied, activities usually occurred while the child was in school; in another 17 percent, the youngest child was 14 or older and cared for himself or herself; in 22 percent of cases, a relative provided care; and in 17 percent, a non-relative provided care, usually not in a center. Among a sample of SWIM nonparticipants, only 5 percent showed child care as the reason they were not active (Hamilton, 1988).

There is much more limited evidence on programs for women with younger children, since WIN programs rarely required them to participate (an exception is Arkansas). While the evaluation of California's GAIN program does not involve the experimental manipulation of child care services, it does supply information that supports the widespread belief that program-provided child care services are more important to mothers of young children than to mothers of school-age children. Utilization data show that for welfare recipients who participated in a GAIN activity, 29 percent of those with children age 6 and older received reimbursement from GAIN for child care, and 68 percent of those with children under age 6 received reimbursement from GAIN for child care. Those not receiving GAIN-paid child care either participated in their GAIN activity while their children were in school or made child care arrangements without using GAIN funds. (See Martinson and Riccio, 1989.) The MFSP study also found heavy use of child care (including formal care) by women with young children (Gordon and Burghardt, 1990). These findings suggest that in the states' JOBS programs, the demand for paid child care may be quite high among welfare recipients with children under age 6.

Transitional Benefits

Some analysts have argued that without transitional benefits that compensate for their reduced real income due to medical care costs and the child care services necessary to enable them to work, welfare recipients face a strong disincentive to leave welfare for employment. There are no completed studies that have experimentally varied the transitional benefits provided to former welfare recipients. However, prior to the implementation of FSA's transitional benefit provisions, several states obtained waivers of applicable federal regulations to permit them to enrich services in order to measure the effects of transitional benefits on employment. In Texas's experiment, there will be a comparison between persons offered one year of transitional child care and medical benefits in the pre-FSA period and those not in this enriched services group. (After the transitional benefits provisions of FSA took effect, all AFDC recipients became eligible for these transitional benefits, including all AFDC recipients in the Texas study.) Wisconsin will test the effect of offering one year of extended Medicaid eligibility to persons losing AFDC eligibility because of earnings; this experiment will also include a test of revising the earned-income disregard as an incentive for welfare recipients to leave welfare. (In the experiment, reduced welfare benefits are provided for people entering low-wage employment.) The target group includes AFDC recipients with children three months of age or older. These experiments will provide information on whether transitional benefits encourage welfare recipients to become employed and retain their jobs. (When the transitional benefits provisions of FSA took effect, all persons in the experiments became eligible for them.) In addition, Ohio is testing a program in which the experimental group received an offer of transitional child care and Medicaid if they left welfare for employment, a mandatory pre-employment assessment, and the opportunity to volunteer for welfare-to-work activities (although participation in these is not required). As in the other states, the transitional benefits were extended to all AFDC recipients when the provisions of FSA took effect. The target group in Ohio is AFDC recipients who have children under age 6. Finally, Illinois is testing a program for former welfare recipients earning less than 185 percent of the standard of need. A randomly assigned experimental group will be offered payment for expenses related to training they receive while employed, including transportation, child care, fees other than tuition, and training materials (up to $300). This program aims to prevent welfare recidivism.

Transportation

No rigorous studies have experimentally varied the availability of transportation for participants in welfare-to-work or similar programs. However, surveys of WIN-mandatory welfare recipients who dropped out of job search programs found that approximately 5 to 10 percent cited transportation problems as the reason for ending their participation. Implementation studies of welfare-to-work programs outside of urban areas have found that "[limited] transportation may constitute a formidable constraint in rural areas" (Polit and O'Hara, 1989, p. 190).

Life Skills Instruction and Counseling

Three voluntary demonstrations using rigorous research methods provide impact information suggesting the potential usefulness of life skills instruction and counseling provided by health care workers.

In the Pregnancy/Early Infancy Nurse Home Visitation Program, 400 mothers were randomly assigned to several treatments or to a control group. Participants were recruited if they were under age 19, single, or poor. The treatments involved visiting nurses who provided health care, infant care, and family planning information beginning during the mother's pregnancy and continuing up to three years after the child's birth. Nurses also provided counseling on returning to school or work. Follow-up surveys found that the poor, unmarried mothers who received nurses' visits returned to school sooner (but not more frequently), had a 12-month greater interval between their first and second child, and had twice as many months of employment four years after their child's birth than the control group (Olds et al., 1988).

A replication and expansion of the Nurse Home Visitation Program is currently under way in Memphis, Tennessee (Olds et al., no date). This study will examine the impacts of nurses' home visits to poor, first-time mothers on maternal education, employment, and welfare receipt.

The Johns Hopkins Center for School-Aged Mothers and Their Infants, a hospital-based program, provided comprehensive services and counseling from two weeks after birth until the children reached age 3. One hundred black teen mothers received services and were compared to a matched comparison group who gave birth in the same hospital. Those who received services had a greater rate of school persistence and graduation, and fewer repeat pregnancies, at the final follow-up survey two years after the initial birth (Hardy et al., 1981).

The Teenage Pregnancy Intervention Program conducted a random assignment differential impact study of two treatments: a series of weekly home visits by a nurse for the infants' first six months, or training as a CETA-paid infant care aide in a hospital infant nursery. After two years, both treatment groups had higher rates of returning to school and work, and fewer repeat pregnancies, than controls; these impacts were higher for the infant care training recipients than the nurse visit recipients (Field et al., 1982).

Taken together, these demonstration studies suggest that counseling on school and employment, provided in the context of infant health care support services, can improve school and labor market outcomes for mothers on welfare.

Combinations of Program Models

The review of evaluations in Chapters 4 and 5 divided the relevant research into studies of broad-coverage programs, selective-voluntary programs, education services, etc. Because of budget constraints, however, many states will be designing mixed programs, balancing the pressure to serve large numbers of people against the evidence that more intensive services may be needed to reach long-term and potential long-term recipients. It is probable that some states' JOBS programs will be broad-based, and yet draw on the approaches listed in the other categories of this chapter for serving specific groups of welfare recipients. For example, a broad-coverage JOBS program that has job search as a first component for many people may also include a subsequent choice of OJT, training, education, or other activities for those who do not become employed during the job search activity. (In some programs, participation in these subsequent activities may be voluntary.) In evaluations of this type of program – where different services will be provided for different groups of recipients – comparisons of outcomes (or impacts) across components may not reflect the differential effectiveness of the activities because of differences in the populations served. Moreover, the relevant issue in assessing each component is whether it produces cost-effective impacts specifically for the targeted population, rather than for the broader caseload. This points to the complexity of interpreting impacts for these programs and to the continued importance of in-depth implementation and process studies for understanding the components and strategies that will comprise future broad-based state JOBS initiatives.

Much can be learned about the role of higher-cost and more intensive services from the studies of selective-voluntary and broad-coverage programs already in place. However, new studies are needed to actually determine whether such services – including the kinds of education, training, and support services provided in the selective-voluntary demonstrations – could be expanded in scale and produce greater impacts than the usual mix of activities in broad-coverage programs. It would be particularly useful to implement two types of studies. First are additional net impact studies of large-scale, broad-coverage programs that emphasize education and other human capital development services – JOBS' major programmatic innovation. These would test the impact and cost-effectiveness of these services across the broad group in the caseload that is determined to need education. Second are differential impact evaluations specifically designed to determine the relative effectiveness of competing approaches.[35] These could include studies of the relative effectiveness of:

- High-intensity human capital investment approaches featuring education and training compared to (1) high-intensity approaches stressing participation in the labor force, or (2) lower-intensity approaches featuring job search and placement.

- Different processes to determine who receives more expensive services, e.g., programs that determine services based on an assessment versus those that have a fixed sequence starting with job search.

- Mandatory versus voluntary programs.

- Different types of assessment and case management.

---

[35] Preferably, these would involve the random assignment of program eligibles to two treatment groups and to a control group not given access to JOBS services.

Chapter 6

The Critical Open Questions

The preceding chapters examined the extensive studies of state welfare-to-work programs as well as other studies of employment and support services designed to help low-income people join the labor force. This body of work suggests both that much has been learned and that many key questions remain about how to structure more effective programs. The gaps in knowledge can be seen by comparing the key features of JOBS (Chapter 2) with the current and anticipated findings from existing research (Chapters 4 and 5). Viewed together, the complex JOBS legislation and the evaluation results from previous program models point to the need for new information on two levels: (1) the effects of particular service components on specific populations, and (2) the effects of entire service delivery systems, which include multiple service components and management processes, on the broad welfare population and selected groups within it. JOBS calls for new services, new target groups, *and* new systems. Thus, future judgments of its effectiveness will hinge on closing these knowledge gaps and understanding the trade-offs in meeting different potential policy goals. This concluding chapter briefly discusses the most critical open questions about the potential of JOBS.

1. The Return to the Investment in Education and Training

Chapter 4 pointed out that most past research on broad-coverage initiatives focused on low- to moderate-cost programs that sought to place people rapidly in jobs. Even for programs judged successful and cost-effective, the research shows that many people continued on welfare and that those who left often remained poor. It also suggests that the lower-cost programs that provided primarily job search assistance usually were not able to increase the earnings of the most disadvantaged.

JOBS' emphasis on education (for those with poor basic skills) and on other intensive, usually higher-cost, services represents a very different approach – one that has not been rigorously evaluated. In theory,

238

successful education-based initiatives should increase welfare recipients' human capital and thus their potential for getting better jobs, moving out of poverty, and achieving long-term economic independence. Existing studies clearly show that welfare recipients often have poor basic skills and that education is correlated with higher income. But, as described in Chapters 4 and 5, completed research does not address the question of whether large-scale education programs for welfare recipients can *increase* educational achievement, attainment, and income and *reduce* welfare receipt. This fundamental cause-and-effect relationship between education services and employment-related outcomes has not yet been demonstrated for welfare recipients.

Among the most critical unanswered questions facing states designing their JOBS initiatives, then, are: Will greater investments in education and training services result in greater success, particularly for long-term recipients? Will programs emphasizing human capital development lead to jobs with higher wages and greater stability, to lower rates of job loss and welfare recidivism, to greater long-term self-sufficiency, and to higher incomes and reduced poverty? Will programs emphasizing education result in increases in literacy and quantitative skills? Will additional gains justify the expanded outlays? How should these services be structured and targeted to be most effective?

Complicating JOBS administrators' decisions is information on the effectiveness of lower- and higher-cost services. Chapters 4 and 5 suggested that they may face a trade-off in deciding how to allocate a fixed budget. Together, the studies of the two broad-coverage programs that included education and other more intensive services (Baltimore and SWIM) and the studies of a number of selective-voluntary higher-cost programs (that did not include education) provide some evidence that more intensive activities can lead to higher average earnings gains (but not necessarily higher welfare savings) than lower-cost services. However, the lower-cost services had higher impacts on earnings and welfare savings per dollar invested. This suggests that administrators who focus on raising earnings above a certain minimum level – or possibly reaching more disadvantaged recipients – might favor higher-cost services, while administrators who desire to maximize total program impacts, regardless of their distribution, might decide to serve more people with lower-cost services. Administrators seeking to use fixed resources to reach both objectives might favor a broad-coverage program with higher- and lower-cost components, carefully targeting intensive activities to benefit longer-term recipients.

Unfortunately for JOBS administrators, the many innovations in FSA and the limited number and nature of past studies mean that the relevant parameters of this trade-off, and even its applicability to current JOBS program models, remain highly uncertain. Yet understanding the details of what works best for whom in the new JOBS environment is critical. Every state is facing a choice about the scale and intensity of JOBS services, given the limited resources available compared to the large number of potential enrollees. To structure JOBS initiatives so that the most appropriate services are targeted to groups in the caseload who can benefit from them most – and to balance the pressure to serve more people with relatively few services against the likely return of providing more intensive services to a smaller share of the caseload – additional research is needed.

Some of the evaluations already under way will expand our knowledge in this area. But answering these questions as definitively as central questions of the 1980s were answered will require two types of studies. First, studies will be needed of broad-coverage programs that emphasize education and other human capital development services for substantial numbers of potential long-term recipients; these should include programs that operate across a variety of environments, administrative approaches, and implementation strategies. Second, studies will be needed that determine directly, with rigor and for key subgroups, the relative effectiveness of different JOBS approaches. Specifically, programs that stress human capital investments should be compared to (1) lower-intensity, work-oriented approaches emphasizing more immediate job search and placement, or (2) other work-oriented approaches that stress labor force participation but also include some relatively intensive services, e.g., on-the-job training or education and skills training closely tied to actual jobs. The most conclusive tests would be random assignment, differential impact studies, in which two strategies are implemented and compared in a single site.

Moreover, studies that seek these answers must plan for follow-up data collection adequate to determine the payoff from the greater initial investment in education. While the short-term job search and work experience programs were often studied with very limited follow-up (and sometimes proved cost-effective within two years), the initial impacts for intensive human capital programs may not be apparent until a year or two after enrollment, and a final assessment of their effectiveness will take much longer.

2. The Impact and Cost-Effectiveness of Programs for Mothers with Young Children, Teen Parents, and Long-Term Recipients

The JOBS legislation sharply reduces the population that is exempt from employment programs. It extends the participation requirement to women with children 3 years of age or older (age 1 or older at state option) and specifically targets resources at young mothers. It also requires young custodial mothers without high school diplomas to attend school (the learnfare provision), regardless of the age of their child. While some selective-voluntary programs have targeted these groups, there are many more questions than answers. In particular, we have very little evidence of whether broad-coverage programs can be successful or cost-effective for mothers with preschool children (especially in light of this group's greater child care needs). Regarding requirements for teen parents, two major studies are in place on variants of this approach. They will examine whether the threat of sanctions (or sanctions combined with financial rewards) and the provision of additional services increase school attendance and retention, and thereby increase educational attainment and employment and reduce long-term welfare receipt. We also have very limited information on whether still further outreach, supports, and services are needed to improve teen mothers' school attendance and eventual movement off welfare. Closing these knowledge gaps is particularly important, given the evidence that young, never-married mothers are the group most likely to become long-term welfare recipients – evidence that contributed to their being given priority by JOBS. There is also not a strong research record of employment gains by the most disadvantaged recipients, heightening the importance of determining whether broad-coverage JOBS programs that include higher-cost components can be more successful in assisting this group to move from welfare to work.

3. The Effect of Different Case Management Practices and Mechanisms for Determining the Nature and Sequencing of Services

As suggested by Chapter 4, we know very little about the effectiveness of two other program dimensions highlighted by JOBS: assessment and case management. Both serve in part as mechanisms for determining who is served and what they are offered or required to do, functions that are central in multi-component programs designed to serve people with a range of employability characteristics. These sorting and decision-making processes reflect implicit or explicit targeting policies that are key to allocating services of varying cost and intensity. Thus, the ability of JOBS programs to achieve substantial participation – and potentially convert participation into program impacts – may turn on the effectiveness of these activities.

Past research on broad-coverage programs suggests that the first activity people participate in is crucial, for many do not go into any subsequent activity. Thus, it matters greatly whether a program is structured sequentially – with the order of services based on prescribed and uniform rules – or uses an individualized assessment approach. While most of the broad-coverage programs evaluated to date used a fixed sequence starting with job search, current state JOBS programs often use a structured, intensive up-front assessment, followed by the development of an individualized employability plan and referral to services deemed appropriate by the case manager and/or welfare recipient. Case managers, in addition to helping craft the service plan, play a major role in its implementation, acting to assist, encourage, monitor, and enforce compliance and to link people to services, particularly in more complex, multi-agency programs.

Given the importance of the first component to which people are assigned in determining services received, and the expense of in-depth assessment, it would be particularly useful to understand the relative effectiveness of programs that determine service assignments based on an assessment (and that use different forms of assessment) compared to those that impose a fixed sequence, often starting with job search. Also, it would be useful to learn the relative effectiveness of different assessment approaches: those that use in-depth individual assessments; those that use different definitions of employability; and those that set different criteria for referring people to job search or for entering and exiting basic education (e.g., higher or lower literacy levels).

It would also be important to learn more about the effectiveness of different case management strategies. Welfare-to-work programs use a wide range of case management approaches. In some localities, tasks associated with assessing, assisting, motivating, monitoring, and brokering services for program participants have been divided between welfare agencies and other service providers and, within these agencies, between case managers and other staff. Alternatively, a single case manager may be responsible for every aspect of participation for those assigned to him or her. Caseload sizes and the emphasis of case management activities – e.g., on counseling versus monitoring and enforcing participation – vary as well, and may affect program impacts. The substantial share of JOBS resources that will probably be devoted to these activities, and the central role given this function in some state programs, highlight the importance of further understanding the cost-effectiveness of different intensities of and approaches to case management.

4. The Relative Effectiveness of Mandatory and Voluntary Programs

As indicated in Chapter 4, some people argue that mandatory programs are likely to have larger impacts than voluntary ones, primarily because they may reach people who can benefit but would not opt to participate on their own and because they reach more people overall. Deterrence and sanctioning effects can also contribute to mandatory programs' impacts. Others claim that voluntary programs are likely to be more successful because they may enroll people who are more predisposed to take advantage of program services and who therefore attend activities more regularly, leading to higher impacts and saving the program "compliance costs."

Unfortunately, past studies do not provide clear guidance on this issue. The data for the broad-coverage programs suggest no evident relationship between either sanctioning or participation rates – both of which are possible proxies for the extent to which a program was mandatory – and program impacts. There have been studies of broad-coverage mandatory and smaller voluntary programs, but there are no rigorous studies that directly compare – for similar people – the impact and cost-effectiveness of mandatory and voluntary broad-coverage programs, or of programs that are more or less stringent in imposing program requirements.

The JOBS legislation calls for states to give first consideration to volunteers among the program's target groups, but it allows for a participation mandate for the full non-exempt caseload. In designing their programs, states are likely to move in different directions in response to the complex message of the legislation, their own policy preferences, and the absence of research guidance. This variation will be reflected in several program characteristics affecting mandatoriness:

caseload monitoring strategies, deferral and exemption rules and practices, program "messages," weekly hours of service, and sanctioning procedures. As was also observed in the 1980s WIN and WIN Demonstration environment, states are likely to implement programs that run the gamut from those that serve only volunteers to those that are mandatory and pay a great deal of attention to compliance. There is unlikely to be a clear dichotomy: Many states' programs will probably include aspects of both approaches.

Critical unanswered questions about different approaches include: How effective are mandatory compared to voluntary programs in increasing participation and changing earnings, employment, and welfare receipt, particularly among more disadvantaged recipients? Will stricter enforcement and sanctioning increase program impacts? Do mandatory programs reach people who would not obtain jobs on their own? Do voluntary programs increase services to the group most able to benefit from them (getting them better jobs), or would this group have received services and left welfare for similar jobs on their own? What are the relative costs of operating more and less mandatory programs?

Practices for requiring or encouraging participation will probably affect critical JOBS concerns: targeting, the cost of program management, and success in meeting JOBS' performance standards. This makes it particularly important to clarify how more or less mandatory approaches affect these issues, and how they influence program impact and cost-effectiveness.

5. The Impacts of Programs for Adults in Two-Parent Families

The JOBS legislation contains special provisions for the (usually male) principal earners in families constituting the small AFDC-UP program. These call for involvement primarily in work programs, with an option of education for young fathers who have not completed high school. They set eventual participation standards that are much higher than those for single parents. The dilemma administrators will face when these standards take effect in a few years is how to design programs that are effective and meet the standards, without targeting a disproportionate share of JOBS resources to AFDC-UP cases. Prior research is scanty and has not found effects for work-only models. Determining the cost-effectiveness of alternative approaches for this group is thus of considerable importance.

6. Understanding the Nature and Duration of Impacts on Welfare Recipients and Their Children

Most of the research summarized in Chapters 4 and 5 addressed the impact of welfare-to-work programs on welfare recipients' employment, earnings, and AFDC receipt. Some studies measured effects on welfare recipients' income (but usually not considering household size or the full range of income sources, thus limiting estimates of poverty status), and some looked at effects on wages and job quality. Measures of program effects on educational achievement and on participants' children are almost totally lacking. JOBS' emphasis on education, and the lack of research on whether this translates into employment outcomes for welfare recipients, highlights the desirability of measuring a broader set of outcomes, including literacy and job quality. JOBS' extension of a participation mandate to women with younger children, combined with FSA's assurance of in-program and transitional child care, points to the importance of determining how the program affects participants' children. To address these areas, future studies should be expanded to include job characteristics, family formation, family income and poverty, health status (for mothers and children), educational attainment and achievement, family functioning and parenting, and the well-being, development, and achievement of the children in AFDC families.

A related open question concerns the durability of impacts and their patterns over time. We know that low-cost services have impacts that start soon after program entry and extend for at least the three years measured in recent studies. We have evidence that the effects of more intensive programs will be slower to appear but will also continue for at least this long. However, there is almost no evidence on longer-term impacts or on changes in impacts over time. For example, we do not know whether the impacts of low-cost job search programs will eventually decrease, or whether the impacts of programs that make a more substantial investment in human capital will increase. Longer follow-up will be particularly critical in assessing the payoff of programs that make a substantial investment in education, and those targeting very young mothers and their children. A longer perspective on both higher- and lower-cost services is also essential for determining the relative success of different JOBS strategies in meeting potentially competing program goals, particularly for estimating the parameters of the trade-off described in Chapters 4 and 5 – between average earnings gains and aggregate benefits per dollar spent.

A further open question concerns the relationship between impacts on earnings and welfare savings. State JOBS programs will vary in their emphasis on increasing people's earnings or producing welfare savings, but most will have both as goals. The research summarized in Chapters 4 and 5 showed that programs were sometimes not successful in meeting both objectives. However, it is not clear why results varied widely across sites that tested the same model and across different program approaches. In designing JOBS programs, administrators would benefit from more information on the relationships between program features – e.g., targeting strategies, service models, AFDC grant levels, sanction rates, and various implementation practices – and net impacts on earnings and welfare savings. Similarly, how these program features affect the mix of earnings gains and welfare savings achieved by a program would be invaluable information for JOBS policymakers.

7. The Relationship Between Program Scale or Economic Conditions and Effectiveness

Only a few of the studies summarized in Chapters 4 and 5 were of full-scale, broad-coverage WIN programs. Some studies were limited to a specific program office, county, or segment of the welfare caseload; others were small demonstration efforts. While it is still unclear what "full scale" will mean for JOBS in any given state or, within a state, for individual program components, the financial commitment made by Congress suggests that there will be substantial expansion over the WIN program of the late 1980s. It is not certain whether the impacts from earlier studies can be replicated if JOBS extends services to a much greater share of the caseload.

JOBS' greater scale may affect impacts in other ways. An important issue in all employment and training programs – one that past studies have found extremely difficult to address – is whether employment gains for people in the program represent net increases in job-holding or come at the expense of other (displaced) workers. Further, the multiple provisions in FSA mean that state JOBS programs could substantially change the balance of opportunity and obligation within the welfare system, with uncertain effects on the size of the caseload. For example, new obligations and messages about participation requirements could deter AFDC applications, but new service opportunities and more positive messages about program services could attract people to welfare and lead them to remain longer in order to complete program activities. Some of these effects would not be captured in studies that measure the impact of the program on persons already in the welfare system, rather than on the broader population.

Another unanswered question is the extent to which the effectiveness of JOBS – particularly when it is operated at large scale – will depend on local and national economic conditions. Positive evaluation results in sites facing a range of unemployment levels and labor market changes (but not confronting highly depressed conditions) suggest that these programs can have impacts in relatively strong or weak labor markets, and in improving or deteriorating economic conditions. However, the West Virginia study suggested that welfare-to-work programs may not succeed in rural areas with very weak labor markets. Extreme cyclical variations in the economy may also affect program impacts in ways that are currently unknown.

8. The Feasibility and Replicability of Particular JOBS Approaches and Achievements

The broad-coverage programs described in Chapters 3 and 4 were usually relatively straightforward to implement. They often involved only one or two activities (e.g., job search and work experience), which could often be provided directly by the welfare agency. Even for these programs, however, the evaluations show great variation in implementation strategies and success. The JOBS legislation requires states to design more complex programs involving more activities and extensive coordination among many delivery systems, including JTPA, teen and adult education programs, community colleges, child care agencies, and the welfare system. JOBS also requires states to report on their success in meeting the new and complex participation standards and in serving the JOBS "target groups." These changes may be difficult for states to implement, and they suggest the need for research on the feasibility of different responses to these design and implementation requirements.

There is no body of information available to guide states in making decisions about the structure and implementation of JOBS approaches that is similar to the extensive implementation research on the simpler broad-coverage programs. As noted above, it will be particularly important to understand how assessment and case management practices are implemented. In addition, it will be valuable to know whether the results of individual program models, previously tested in only one site, can be repeated under different conditions: e.g., in states with higher or lower grant levels, different administrative experience, or dissimilar service delivery structures; under the new work incentives created by the Family Support Act; in states with different economic conditions; or where the welfare caseload includes large numbers of people with different characteristics than those previously studied. Most relevant to JOBS administrators will be new tests, under different conditions, of models resembling San Diego's SWIM program and Baltimore's Options, with their different but promising impact results.

9. The Development of Standards to Manage and Motivate the System

During the 1980s, state WIN and WIN Demonstration programs were implemented in a highly decentralized environment, without a clear system of structured federal rewards or penalties. JOBS offers states new resources but also demands new accountability – prominently, through performance standards that link enhanced funding to program participation rates and expenditures on specified target groups. The legislation also calls for the eventual establishment of outcome-based performance standards. The history of the WIN and JTPA programs suggests both the power of focusing staff on performance outcomes and the importance of doing so in a way that supports program goals. The subgroup research summarized in Chapter 4 implies that outcome-based standards in JOBS must be carefully designed if they are to promote cost-effective programming and direct the system toward making the greatest long-term difference in the lives of welfare recipients. More research, across a broader spectrum of the welfare population and program approaches, will be important to refining the lessons from this initial work and determining the feasibility and effectiveness of alternative approaches.

10. The Feasibility, Impact, and Cost-Effectiveness of Support Services and Transitional Benefits

There are no completed studies that measure the impact of subsidized child care on participation in welfare-to-work activities and on subsequent employment. Moreover, as JOBS broadens the traditional target groups to include young mothers participating in alternative education programs and learnfare programs, the current lack of information on the effects of subsidized child care for this group will become increasingly important. More research is needed to determine the feasibility, impact, and cost-effectiveness of a range of child care services and subsidy levels for various target groups in JOBS.

The outcome of states' JOBS programs may also be influenced by FSA's provision that one year of child care and Medicaid are to be offered to welfare recipients who leave welfare to work. Questions about transitional benefits include: Do they provide an effective incentive for people to enter employment? Do they increase job stability and retention and reduce the rate at which people return to welfare? What is the take-up rate for these services? Do they boost the impacts of either low-cost "labor market attachment" (i.e., job search) or higher-cost "human capital investment" program models, or both? Do they change the relative cost-effectiveness of different JOBS approaches, e.g., of programs that tend to place people in lower- or higher-wage jobs? (This change could occur because, in contrast to the past, when any job that made a family ineligible for welfare reduced government outlays, under FSA people may work and receive transitional benefits that can be more costly than cash welfare.)

* * * * *

The JOBS program is being implemented in an unusual research context. There is a large body of rigorous studies that confirm that welfare-to-work programs produce positive impacts and represent a cost-effective investment of public funds. However, many state JOBS initiatives represent major departures from the programs that were tested earlier – in the complexity and nature of the services offered, in their scale of implementation, and in the groups of welfare recipients they target. The key question for such programs in the 1990s is thus not *whether* to implement them, but *how* to design them to be most effective. This necessitates moving from the relatively simple threshold questions of the earlier studies to the more complex issues noted in this chapter.

Some of these questions will be addressed in studies and demonstrations already in place. But others will require additional – and sometimes more refined – designs. Choices will be required, since evaluations, no matter how comprehensive, cannot address all of these questions in equal detail; moreover, some of them go beyond what research can confidently determine.[1] This suggests that new projects should build on one of the lessons from the studies of the 1980s: It is better to answer a few critical questions definitively than many questions partially. Strategic evaluation choices, strong research designs, and the active involvement and cooperation of program administrators and staff in the sites where the research is implemented will be critical in moving from the many remaining questions for JOBS to some clear answers.

---

[1] The JOBS evaluation, funded by the U.S. Department of Health and Human Services (HHS), is being structured to provide information relevant to the open questions described under headings 1, 2, 5, 6, 8, and 9 above, and partial information on the questions under headings 3, 4, and – to a lesser extent – 7.

Appendices

Appendix A
Program Costs[1]

Defining and estimating the costs of the programs discussed in this book is complicated. This appendix describes four ways of defining program costs and presents alternative cost estimates for the primary completed studies of welfare-to-work programs considered in Chapters 3 through 5.

Direct Costs

Direct program costs are those incurred by the agency (or agencies) responsible for administering the program under study. They include the agency's own expenditures on program services and administration as well as the expenses of other agencies that, under formal agreements with the administering agency, deliver services that are part of the program treatment.[2] The total expenditures incurred by these agencies in providing a program treatment to members of an experimental group in a program evaluation constitute the *gross* direct cost of the program.

Expenses may also be incurred by the administering agency in working with members of the control group. For example, control group members in the Baltimore evaluation went through program assessment and orientation and received counseling from WIN staff. Subtracting such expenditures from the gross direct cost leaves the *net* direct cost of the program – i.e., the cost of providing the program treatment to experimentals beyond the cost of services provided to the control group.

Indirect Costs

A program may have two types of effects on the expenditures of *other* programs. One is a complementary effect in which the use of other

---

[1] This appendix was written by David Long.

[2] For the programs covered by this appendix, these agreements were always contracts. However, in other cases, interagency agreements may give an administering agency control over specified funds: e.g., in California, part of the state's JTPA Title IIA funding is used this way for the GAIN program (see Wallace and Long, 1987, Chapter 2).

programs is increased by the program under study – e.g., *indirect* costs are incurred for the experimental group. This effect may arise from program staff's referral of individuals to outside programs, including situations in which individuals are systematically referred to education and training activities in other agencies.[3] It may also reflect increased self-initiated individual use of these other programs owing to the content of the program treatment (e.g., a program treatment that stresses basic skills preparation may cause more welfare recipients to seek vocational training for which such preparation is a prerequisite).

The other potential effect is substitution. Because individuals are enrolled in the program under study, they are not as free to participate in other programs, decreasing the use of those other programs. This effect results in lower indirect expenditures by these programs on members of the experimental group (measured as expenditures on the control group).

In order to get a full picture of the *total* program resource use generated by a welfare-to-work program, both direct and indirect expenditures should be taken into account. Thus, the *gross* direct and indirect cost of a program includes all expenses incurred for the experimental group – not only the direct expenses related to providing the program treatment, but also the complementary expenses incurred by other programs used by experimentals. The *net* direct and indirect cost of a program subtracts from this gross cost all direct and indirect expenses of working with controls.

Applying the Cost Measures

There is no single "correct" measure of program cost. Each of the four measures – gross direct cost, net direct cost, gross direct and indirect cost, and net direct and indirect cost – has particular advantages and applications. Which is the best one to choose depends on how it is to be used. The experience of the SWIM program in San Diego illustrates this. In this program, operated by San Diego County's Department of Social Services (DSS), a welfare recipient was required to participate in job search (operated by DSS); if unsuccessful in getting a job, she was then assigned to work experience (also operated by DSS); finally, if still without a job,

---

[3] As discussed further below, indirect costs associated with such systematic referrals may properly be considered part of the gross cost of the program treatment. However, these referrals do not generate direct costs, since the administering agency has no financial responsibility for or control over the services that result.

she was referred to education and training (DSS made these referrals and provided the support services, but the primary services were delivered and funded by adult schools, community colleges, and the JTPA system). Participation in all three stages of the program treatment was monitored by DSS.

What was the cost of SWIM? As shown in Table A.1, the total cost to DSS of operating the program was $842 per targeted case – the gross direct cost per experimental in the SWIM evaluation.[4] This includes the costs of DSS case managers, job club leaders, work experience placement staff, and other program personnel, as well as the costs of child care (some of which was provided by other agencies under contracts paid by DSS), transportation, and allowances paid when experimentals obtained employment. For budgeting purposes, this is the most pertinent cost figure for a welfare agency that wants to operate a program like SWIM, assuming it can develop similar arrangements with local education and training providers.

The cost to DSS of processing controls, including the allowances they received in connection with their self-initiated employment, was $199 per control.[5] Thus, the net direct cost to DSS of operating SWIM – the additional cost of the program to the agency beyond what it spent on the control group – was $643 ($842 minus $199). This, then, is the additional investment in its welfare caseload made by the administering agency in implementing SWIM.

Like most current JOBS program operators, San Diego DSS relied on existing community resources to provide education and training to SWIM enrollees. Education and training were an integral part of the SWIM treatment, but DSS did not pay for them and had no direct operational control over them. The cost of these services was incurred by adult schools, community colleges, and JTPA programs in San Diego; it amounted to $703 per experimental.[6] When this cost is included, the

---

[4] Here, as elsewhere, cost is expressed per experimental, not per participant.

[5] Table A.1 does not include separate columns showing costs for controls. They may be calculated by subtracting net from gross costs. Thus, in SWIM, the total (direct and indirect) cost per control was $626 ($1,545 minus $919); the direct cost was $199 ($842 minus $643); and the indirect cost was $427 ($626 minus $199).

[6] This includes expenses incurred by the GAIN program, which succeeded SWIM, for members of the experimental group; experimentals who were still enrolled in SWIM when the program ended were transferred to GAIN.

gross direct ($842) and indirect ($703) cost of the program totals $1,545 per experimental. This figure reflects the full expenditure, by all agencies, on the SWIM treatment.

However, on their own initiative, controls in San Diego were free to enroll in education and training, including the activities in which SWIM experimentals were required to participate. As noted earlier, the cost of these (indirect) services was $427 per control group member. Thus, the net direct and indirect cost of SWIM – the gross cost of the treatment minus the direct cost per control of processing and allowances ($199), minus the indirect cost per control for education and training services provided by other programs ($427) – was $919. This represents the net investment of resources made per SWIM enrollee by all agencies.

Costs of Welfare-to-Work Programs

Table A.1 presents the costs of selected programs discussed in this book. Some of these programs did not have their costs measured using all four definitions. For example, indirect costs were not measured for the Baltimore program. There the costs of education and training that were provided as part of the program treatment were incurred by the operating agency under contracts with service providers; thus, they are included in direct costs. However, the costs to other programs – the schools and training programs that did not have contracts with the Baltimore program – were not estimated.

The direct costs reported in the table were all measured using program accounting and enrollment data, and exclude research-related expenses. Indirect costs were estimated using various other data sources. For San Diego I and Supported Work, most of the data were gathered using surveys administered to the research sample members. For other programs in which such data were collected, JTPA, community college, and/or adult school program enrollment and accounting data were used. The data came from automated JTPA and school records covering a broad range of programs in all cases except Virginia, where school data came from paper records and were collected only for a subsample of the overall research sample, and Arkansas, where JTPA data were obtained for selected training programs only.

The costs discussed in Chapters 3 through 5 are the net costs of the program treatments under study – the additional cost of serving experimentals over the cost of serving controls. In most instances, these are the net direct costs shown in the second column of Table A.1.

TABLE A.1 ESTIMATED COSTS PER EXPERIMENTAL OF SELECTED WELFARE-TO-WORK PROGRAMS

Program	Direct Costs Gross	Direct Costs Net	Direct and Indirect Costs Gross	Direct and Indirect Costs Net	Data Sources
Broad-Coverage: AFDC					
Arkansas	$122	**$118**	$162	$158	A,J
Baltimore	1,050	**953**	N/A	N/A	A
Cook County: Job search only[a]	107	102	391	**127**	A,J,C
Cook County: Job search/ work experience	154	149	421	**157**	A,J,C
Louisville Group Job Search	552	**230**	N/A	N/A	A
Louisville Individual Job Search	171	**136**	N/A	N/A	A
San Diego I: Job search only[a]	673	**562**	835	510	A,S,O
San Diego I: Job search/ work experience	761	**636**	875	577	A,S,O
San Diego SWIM	842	643	1,545	**919**	A,J,C,E
Virginia	451	412	611	**430**	A,J,C,E
West Virginia	459	**260**	N/A	N/A	A
Broad-Coverage: AFDC-UP					
Baltimore[b]	643	**552**	N/A	N/A	A
San Diego I: Job search only[a]	699	**586**	809	543	A,S,O
San Diego I: Job search/ work experience	850	**727**	836	672	A,S,O
San Diego SWIM	801	604	1,292	**817**	A,J,C,E
West Virginia[b]	537	**136**	N/A	N/A	A
Selective-Voluntary: AFDC					
AFDC Homemaker-Home Health Aide	9,505	**9,505**	N/A	N/A	A
Maine	2,679	**2,019**	2,813	2,286	A,J
New Jersey	1,197	**787**	1,642	860	A,J
Supported Work	17,981	**17,981**	N/A	17,528	A,S

SOURCES: Direct costs were estimated using program accounting and tracking data (A). Indirect costs were estimated using sources indicated in the last column of the table: program accounting and tracking data (A); surveys of the research sample (S); JTPA data (J), which covers only selected training programs for Arkansas; community college data (C); adult education data (E); and other records (O). N/A indicates that indirect cost estimates are not available. Estimates are calculated from data in Friedlander et al., 1985b (Arkansas); Friedlander et al., 1985a (Baltimore); Friedlander et al., 1987 (Cook County); Goldman, 1981 (Louisville); Goldman, Friedlander, and Long, 1986 (San Diego I); Hamilton and Friedlander, 1989 (San Diego SWIM); Riccio et al., 1986 (Virginia); Friedlander at al., 1986 (West Virginia); Orr, 1987 (Homemaker-Home Health Aide); Auspos, Cave, and Long, 1988 (Maine); Freedman, Bryant, and Cave, 1988 (New Jersey); Kemper, Long, and Thornton, 1981 (Supported Work); unpublished MDRC data for Arkansas, San Diego I, Virginia, and West Virginia.

NOTES: "Direct costs" are those incurred by the operating agency, while "indirect costs" were incurred by other agencies; "gross costs" are the full costs per experimental, while "net costs" subtract from gross costs the costs of serving controls. Cost estimates shown in boldface type best reflect the net cost of services in the intended service sequence; these are the costs cited in this volume (see Appendix A text for details).

(continued)

TABLE A.1 *(continued)*

San Diego I costs are expressed in 1983 dollars; Arkansas, Baltimore, Virginia, and West Virginia costs are in 1984 dollars; Maine costs are in 1985 dollars; Cook County, New Jersey, and San Diego SWIM costs are in 1986 dollars; AFDC Homemaker-Home Health Aide costs, which are presented as a range across states, were measured during the 1983-86 period; and Louisville Individual Job Search, Louisville Group Job Search, and Supported Work costs have been adjusted to reflect 1985 dollars.

The direct costs incurred by Supported Work and the AFDC Homemaker-Home Health Aide Demonstrations include wages paid to participants; those amounted to $8,535 per experimental for Supported Work (in 1985 dollars) and $3,821 per experimental in the AFDC Homemaker-Home Health Aide Demonstrations (averaged across seven states). The direct costs in Maine, New Jersey, and Baltimore include the program's share of on-the-job training wages (employers also paid a share); these amounted to $384 in Maine, $348 in New Jersey, and $10 and $4 in Baltimore for AFDC and AFDC-UP experimentals, respectively.

[a]Costs are presented for both the job search and job search/work experience sequences in San Diego I and Cook County for informational purposes. The participation and impact findings presented in the body of this book for both programs are for the job search/work experience sequence.

[b]Costs for the AFDC-UP programs in Baltimore and West Virginia are presented for informational purposes. The impact results are not presented in the body of this book because the sample size in Baltimore was too small to produce reliable impact findings and the West Virginia study produced uncertain results.

However, in the SWIM, Cook County (Chicago), and Virginia programs, agencies other than the operating agency delivered integral parts of the program treatment (as defined by the operating agency), which were not paid for with program funds. For these programs, the net direct and indirect costs shown in the table's fourth column are used in this book.

Comparing Costs Across Programs

Readers should bear several points in mind when comparing program costs. In comparing gross direct costs, it is important to realize that, because of differences in program treatments and program funding arrangements, costs include different types of services and assistance. The Supported Work and AFDC Homemaker-Home Health Aide treatments included program wages paid to participants ($8,535 per Supported Work experimental and $1,930 to $5,936, depending on the site, per Homemaker-Home Health Aide experimental), and the Maine and New Jersey programs paid for a share of OJT wages ($384 and $348 per experimental, respectively); the other programs (except Baltimore, which paid a small amount of OJT wages) did not incur comparable direct costs. Supported Work's direct costs also included work project operating expenses; many of the work projects also produced revenues that can be considered a partial offset to project expenses.[7] The Baltimore and Maine programs had contracts with education and training service providers to deliver services as part of their treatments, so these expenses are counted as direct costs; other programs relied on other agencies to provide such services with their own funding, so the costs of such services appear as indirect costs. The programs also differed in the extent to which they directly provided child care, transportation assistance, and allowances for other employment- and training-related expenses.

In addition, the costs of the broad-coverage programs (the first two categories of entries in the table) differed from those of the four selective-voluntary programs in two important respects. First, the

---

[7] Supported Work operated work projects in which groups of Supported Workers were assigned to building maintenance, housing rehabilitation, retail operations (such as a gas station), and many other types of work. Many of these projects generated revenues for the program. Supported Work's project revenue amounted to $4,352 per experimental (in 1985 dollars), which is almost a quarter of the program's total direct cost. This revenue was not subtracted from the program costs presented in Table A.1.

broad-coverage programs incurred expenditures associated with processing the AFDC caseload and enforcing mandatory program participation requirements; such costs are particularly noteworthy for San Diego SWIM. The selective-voluntary programs obviously did not have these costs, although some processing and monitoring costs may have been incurred by the local WIN program. For example, some of the individuals who volunteered to be in the New Jersey OJT program were WIN-mandatories, and their involvement in the OJT program satisfied WIN's participation requirements; the costs of monitoring these cases for compliance with these requirements was borne by WIN.

Second, the broad-coverage programs were targeted to large segments of the welfare caseload. Thus, the costs of the programs per experimental are averaged across many nonparticipants as well as participants. The voluntary programs were targeted to welfare recipients who wanted to be in the programs, so most experimentals were also participants. Thus, differences in total program costs reflect not only differences in the costs of employment and training activities per se, but also differences in the costs of administration and monitoring (see the discussion in Chapter 2).

In comparing the net direct costs of programs, it is also important to recognize that the treatment of controls by the administering agencies differed greatly across the evaluated programs. In Supported Work and the AFDC Homemaker-Home Health Aide Demonstrations, the administering agencies did not work with controls at all; thus, gross and net direct costs are the same. In Arkansas, Chicago, and Virginia, the agencies' only contact with controls was for WIN processing, so gross and net costs differed very little. In San Diego SWIM, the direct cost for controls consisted primarily of the cost of processing them but also included allowances for their self-initiated employment. In the other broad-coverage programs – Baltimore, San Diego I, West Virginia, and both Louisville programs – some controls received WIN program treatments of various kinds. For example, controls in Baltimore received counseling and training referrals similar to what was provided in the predecessor WIN program. In the Louisville Group Job Search demonstration, some controls received individual job search and placement assistance, as well as other WIN services. The significance of the services provided to controls is that they define the net cost of operating the program for experimentals (as well as the comparison that yields the net program impact estimates discussed in this volume).

Finally, several issues should be borne in mind when comparing the gross and net versions of direct and indirect costs. Because of the differences in data sources described above and in Table A.1, some of the estimates of indirect costs are based on partial data. For example, the estimates for Arkansas, Maine, and New Jersey are based on JTPA data only (and in Arkansas the JTPA data did not cover all training programs). On the other hand, the data for San Diego SWIM and Virginia cover most of the publicly supported education and training options available to welfare recipients.

Readers should also note that the indirect costs in Cook County (Chicago), San Diego SWIM, and Virginia reflect education and training that was an integral part of the program treatment, even though the services were not paid for by the administering agencies; these indirect costs were sizable. In other programs, indirect costs were smaller and could either be greater or less than zero, depending on whether the program's complementary or substitution effects were relatively greater. For example, total direct and indirect costs for Supported Work are lower than direct costs because the substitution effect dominated: i.e., more controls than experimentals participated in education and training programs other than Supported Work.

Appendix B

Supplemental Tables
for Chapter 4

TABLE B.1   SUMMARY AND QUARTERLY IMPACTS OF THE ARKANSAS WORK PROGRAM ON AFDC ELIGIBLES

Outcome and Follow-Up Period	Experimental Group Mean	Control Group Mean	Difference	Percentage Change
Ever Employed, Quarters 2-12[a]	41.0%	36.2%	4.8**	13%
Average Number of Quarters with Employment, Quarters 2-12[a]	2.44	1.86	0.58***	31%
Ever Employed				
Quarter of Random Assignment	18.0%	12.3%	5.7***	46%
Quarter 2	16.6	11.6	5.1***	44
Quarter 3	18.9	13.5	5.4***	40
Quarter 4	20.4	16.7	3.7*	22
Quarter 5	21.4	17.2	4.3**	25
Quarter 6	21.2	15.8	5.5***	35
Quarter 7	22.8	17.6	5.2**	30
Quarter 8	23.9	20.3	3.6	18
Quarter 9	24.1	18.0	6.1***	34
Quarter 10	25.2	18.3	6.9***	38
Quarter 11	24.9	18.6	6.3***	34
Quarter 12	24.5	18.3	6.2***	34
Average Total Earnings, Quarters 2-12[a]	$3,165	$2,468	$697**	28%
Average Total Earnings				
Quarter of Random Assignment	$111	$80	$31*	39%
Quarter 2	156	98	58**	59
Quarter 3	190	142	48*	34
Quarter 4	217	187	30	16
Quarter 5	229	201	29	14
Quarter 6	294	225	69*	31
Quarter 7	305	243	61	25
Quarter 8	351	288	64	22
Quarter 9	353	250	104**	42
Quarter 10	357	262	95**	36
Quarter 11	352	295	57	19
Quarter 12	360	278	81*	29

(continued)

TABLE B.1 *(continued)*

Outcome and Follow-Up Period	Experimental Group Mean	Control Group Mean	Difference	Percentage Change
Ever Received Any AFDC Payments, Quarters 1-12	75.3%	79.5%	- 4.2*	- 5%
Average Number of Months Receiving AFDC Payments, Quarters 1-12	15.14	17.78	- 2.64***	- 15%
Ever Received Any AFDC Payments				
Quarter of Random Assignment	66.4%	69.4%	- 3.0	- 4%
Quarter 2	65.4	71.5	- 6.1**	- 9
Quarter 3	56.7	63.8	- 7.1***	- 11
Quarter 4	51.0	59.1	- 8.1***	- 14
Quarter 5	48.0	55.6	- 7.6***	- 14
Quarter 6	43.6	52.5	- 8.9***	- 17
Quarter 7	40.1	50.0	- 9.9***	- 20
Quarter 8	38.1	46.0	- 7.9***	- 17
Quarter 9	36.4	44.5	- 8.1***	- 18
Quarter 10	34.8	42.9	- 8.1***	- 19
Quarter 11	35.6	42.4	- 6.8**	- 16
Quarter 12	32.8	40.1	- 7.3***	- 18
Average Total AFDC Payments Received, Quarters 1-12	$2,533	$3,036	- $502***	- 17%
Average Total AFDC Payments Received				
Quarter of Random Assignment	$248	$261	- $13	- 5%
Quarter 2	274	318	- 44***	- 14
Quarter 3	245	292	- 47***	- 16
Quarter 4	231	272	- 41***	- 15
Quarter 5	213	259	- 46***	- 18
Quarter 6	194	244	- 50***	- 20
Quarter 7	193	245	- 52***	- 21
Quarter 8	193	235	- 41***	- 17
Quarter 9	190	240	- 49***	- 20
Quarter 10	186	232	- 46***	- 20
Quarter 11	186	224	- 38**	- 17
Quarter 12	180	215	- 35**	- 16
Sample Size	560	567		

(continued)

TABLE B.1 *(continued)*

SOURCE: Adapted from Friedlander and Goldman, 1988.

NOTES: The earnings and AFDC payments data include zero values for sample members not employed and for sample members not receiving welfare. Estimates are regression-adjusted using ordinary least squares, controlling for pre-random assignment characteristics of sample members. There may be some discrepancies in experimental-control differences because of rounding.

For employment and earnings, the quarter of random assignment refers to the calendar quarter in which random assignment occurred. For AFDC payments, the quarter of random assignment refers to the three months beginning with the month in which an individual was randomly assigned.

A two-tailed t-test was applied to differences between experimental and control groups. Statistical significance levels are indicated as: * = 10 percent; ** = 5 percent; and *** = 1 percent.

[a]Quarter 1, the quarter of random assignment, may contain some earnings from the period prior to random assignment and is therefore excluded from the summary measures of follow-up for employment and earnings.

TABLE B.2   SUMMARY AND QUARTERLY IMPACTS OF THE BALTIMORE OPTIONS PROGRAM ON AFDC ELIGIBLES

Outcome and Follow-Up Period	Experimental Group Mean	Control Group Mean	Difference	Percentage Change
Ever Employed, Quarters 2-12[a]	70.3%	65.5%	4.8***	7%
Average Number of Quarters with Employment, Quarters 2-12[a]	4.10	3.73	0.38***	10%
Ever Employed				
Quarter of Random Assignment	28.0%	26.1%	1.9	7%
Quarter 2	27.0	23.5	3.4**	14
Quarter 3	32.3	27.4	4.9***	18
Quarter 4	34.7	31.2	3.5**	11
Quarter 5	36.3	31.8	4.5***	14
Quarter 6	38.7	33.0	5.7***	17
Quarter 7	38.8	34.9	3.8**	11
Quarter 8	39.5	37.1	2.4	6
Quarter 9	39.5	37.4	2.1	6
Quarter 10	40.8	37.7	3.1*	8
Quarter 11	42.0	38.1	3.9**	10
Quarter 12	40.7	40.3	0.4	1
Average Total Earnings, Quarters 2-12[a]	$7,638	$6,595	$1,043***	16%
Average Total Earnings				
Quarter of Random Assignment	$260	$251	$8	3%
Quarter 2	318	325	- 8	- 2
Quarter 3	466	400	66*	17
Quarter 4	569	495	73*	15
Quarter 5	576	512	64*	12
Quarter 6	668	566	103**	18
Quarter 7	755	630	126***	20
Quarter 8	787	679	108**	16
Quarter 9	777	659	118**	18
Quarter 10	899	741	157***	21
Quarter 11	904	766	138***	18
Quarter 12	919	822	98*	12

(continued)

Outcome and Follow-Up Period	Experimental Group Mean	Control Group Mean	Difference	Percentage Change
Ever Received Any AFDC Payments, Quarters 1-12	95.3%	95.4%	- 0.1	0%
Average Number of Months Receiving AFDC Payments, Quarters 1-12	22.21	22.63	- 0.42	- 2%
Ever Received Any AFDC Payments				
Quarter of Random Assignment	92.4%	92.1%	0.4	0%
Quarter 2	87.4	87.5	- 0.2	0
Quarter 3	77.5	78.3	- 0.7	- 1
Quarter 4	72.0	73.3	- 1.4	- 2
Quarter 5	69.1	70.4	- 1.4	- 2
Quarter 6	64.9	66.4	- 1.5	- 2
Quarter 7	61.3	61.8	- 0.5	- 1
Quarter 8	58.7	59.0	- 0.3	- 1
Quarter 9	55.2	56.7	- 1.6	- 3
Quarter 10	52.8	54.5	- 1.7	- 3
Quarter 11	49.9	52.0	- 2.1	- 4
Quarter 12	48.2	48.4	- 0.2	0
Average Total AFDC Payments Received, Quarters 1-12	$6,361	$6,424	- $63	- 1%
Average Total AFDC Payments Received				
Quarter of Random Assignment	$681	$675	$6	1%
Quarter 2	680	675	5	1
Quarter 3	594	597	- 2	0
Quarter 4	565	571	- 6	- 1
Quarter 5	545	558	- 13	- 2
Quarter 6	519	532	- 12	- 2
Quarter 7	504	511	- 6	- 1
Quarter 8	489	492	- 2	- 1
Quarter 9	480	484	- 4	- 1
Quarter 10	451	463	- 12	- 3
Quarter 11	427	445	- 18	- 4
Quarter 12	425	423	3	1
Sample Size	1,362	1,395		

(continued)

TABLE B.2 *(continued)*

SOURCE: Adapted from Friedlander, 1987.

NOTES: The earnings and AFDC payments data include zero values for sample members not employed and for sample members not receiving welfare. Estimates are regression-adjusted using ordinary least squares, controlling for pre-random assignment characteristics of sample members. There may be some discrepancies in experimental-control differences because of rounding.

For employment and earnings, the quarter of random assignment refers to the calendar quarter in which random assignment occurred. For AFDC payments, the quarter of random assignment refers to the three months beginning with the month in which an individual was randomly assigned.

A two-tailed t-test was applied to differences between experimental and control groups. Statistical significance levels are indicated as: * = 10 percent; ** = 5 percent; and *** = 1 percent.

[a]Quarter 1, the quarter of random assignment, may contain some earnings from the period prior to random assignment and is therefore excluded from the summary measures of follow-up for employment and earnings.

TABLE B.3 SUMMARY AND QUARTERLY IMPACTS OF THE COOK COUNTY WIN DEMONSTRATION ON AFDC ELIGIBLES

Outcome and Follow-Up Period	Experimental Group Mean	Control Group Mean	Difference	Percentage Change
Ever Employed, Quarters 2-6[a]	36.8%	35.8%	1.0	3%
Average Number of Quarters with Employment, Quarters 2-6[a]	1.09	1.05	0.04	4%
Ever Employed				
Quarter of Random Assignment	16.3%	16.2%	0.1	1%
Quarter 2	17.9	17.8	0.1	1
Quarter 3	20.8	20.1	0.7	3
Quarter 4	22.6	21.4	1.3	6
Quarter 5	23.3	22.4	0.8	4
Quarter 6	24.4	23.4	1.0	4
Average Total Earnings, Quarters 2-6[a]	$1,977	$1,921	$57	3%
Average Total Earnings				
Quarter of Random Assignment	$183	$184	- $1	- 1%
Quarter 2	281	286	- 6	- 2
Quarter 3	359	354	5	1
Quarter 4	405	394	11	3
Quarter 5	437	412	24	6
Quarter 6	496	475	21	5
Ever Received Any AFDC Payments, Quarters 1-6	99.8%	99.8%	- 0.1	0%
Average Number of Months Receiving AFDC Payments, Quarters 1-6	14.23	14.45	- 0.22**	- 2%
Ever Received Any AFDC Payments				
Quarter of Random Assignment	99.6%	99.6%	0.0	0%
Quarter 2	92.5	92.6	- 0.1	0
Quarter 3	83.9	85.5	- 1.6**	- 2
Quarter 4	78.9	80.8	- 1.9**	- 2
Quarter 5	75.1	77.1	- 2.0**	- 3
Quarter 6	70.9	72.7	- 1.8*	- 2

(continued

TABLE B.3 (*continued*)

Outcome and Follow-Up Period	Experimental Group Mean	Control Group Mean	Difference	Percentage Change
Average Total AFDC Payments Received, Quarters 1-6	$4,416	$4,486	- $70*	- 2%
Average Total AFDC Payments Received				
Quarter of Random Assignment	$842	$833	$9**	1%
Quarter 2	824	824	0	0
Quarter 3	740	763	- 23***	- 3
Quarter 4	700	726	- 26***	- 4
Quarter 5	675	690	- 16*	- 2
Quarter 6	636	650	- 14	- 2
Sample Size	4,050	3,805		

SOURCE: Adapted from Friedlander et al., 1987.

NOTES: The earnings and AFDC payments data include zero values for sample members not employed and for sample members not receiving welfare. Estimates are regression-adjusted using ordinary least squares, controlling for pre-random assignment characteristics of sample members. There may be some discrepancies in experimental-control differences because of rounding.

For employment and earnings, the quarter of random assignment refers to the calendar quarter in which random assignment occurred. For AFDC payments, the quarter of random assignment refers to the three months beginning with the month in which an individual was randomly assigned.

A two-tailed t-test was applied to differences between experimental and control groups. Statistical significance levels are indicated as: * = 10 percent; ** = 5 percent; and *** = 1 percent.

[a]Quarter 1, the quarter of random assignment, may contain some earnings from the period prior to random assignment and is therefore excluded from the summary measures of follow-up for employment and earnings.

SUMMARY AND QUARTERLY IMPACTS OF SAN DIEGO I (EPP/EWEP) ON AFDC ELIGIBLES

Outcome and Follow-Up Period	Experimental Group Mean	Control Group Mean	Difference	Percentage Change
Ever Employed, Quarters 2-6[a]	61.0%	55.4%	5.6***	10%
Average Number of Quarters with Employment, Quarters 2-6[a]	2.03	1.73	0.29***	17%
Ever Employed				
Quarter of Random Assignment	35.5%	33.1%	2.5	8%
Quarter 2	35.6	28.7	6.9***	24
Quarter 3	40.2	32.3	7.8***	24
Quarter 4	42.4	36.9	5.5***	15
Quarter 5	42.9	37.5	5.4***	14
Quarter 6	41.9	38.1	3.8*	10
Average Total Earnings, Quarters 2-6[a]	$3,802	$3,102	$700***	23%
Average Total Earnings				
Quarter of Random Assignment	$359	$337	$23	7%
Quarter 2	510	369	141***	38
Quarter 3	701	538	163***	30
Quarter 4	810	693	117**	17
Quarter 5	848	729	119**	16
Quarter 6	933	773	161***	21
Ever Received Any AFDC Payments, Quarters 1-6	83.9%	84.3%	- 0.4	0%
Average Number of Months Receiving AFDC Payments, Quarters 1-6	8.13	8.61	- 0.48*	- 6%
Ever Received Any AFDC Payments				
Quarter of Random Assignment	78.3%	80.3%	- 2.0	- 2%
Quarter 2	64.2	67.6	- 3.4*	- 5
Quarter 3	51.8	56.2	- 4.5**	- 8
Quarter 4	45.8	47.9	- 2.0	- 4
Quarter 5	39.5	41.1	- 1.7	- 4
Quarter 6	35.0	36.2	- 1.2	- 3

(continued)

TABLE B.4 *(continued)*

Outcome and Follow-Up Period	Experimental Group Mean	Control Group Mean	Difference	Percentage Change
Average Total AFDC Payments Received, Quarters 1-6	$3,409	$3,697	- $288**	- 8%
Average Total AFDC Payments Received				
Quarter of Random Assignment	$734	$752	- $18	- 2%
Quarter 2	695	765	- 70***	- 9
Quarter 3	582	653	- 71***	- 11
Quarter 4	513	580	- 67**	- 11
Quarter 5	462	501	- 39	- 8
Quarter 6	423	445	- 22	- 5
Sample Size	1,502	873		

SOURCE: Adapted from Goldman, Friedlander, and Long, 1986.

NOTES: The earnings and AFDC payments data include zero values for sample members not employed and or sample members not receiving welfare. Estimates are regression-adjusted using ordinary least squares, controlling for pre-random assignment characteristics of sample members. There may be some discrepancies in experimental-control differences because of rounding.

For employment and earnings, the quarter of random assignment refers to the calendar quarter in which random assignment occurred. For AFDC payments, the quarter of random assignment refers to the three months beginning with the month in which an individual was randomly assigned.

A two-tailed t-test was applied to differences between experimental and control groups. Statistical significance levels are indicated as: * = 10 percent; ** = 5 percent; and *** = 1 percent.

[a]Quarter 1, the quarter of random assignment, may contain some earnings from the period prior to random assignment and is therefore excluded from the summary measures of follow-up for employment and earnings.

TABLE B.5   SUMMARY AND QUARTERLY IMPACTS OF THE SAN DIEGO SWIM PROGRAM ON AFDC ELIGIBLES

Outcome and Follow-Up Period	Experimental Group Mean	Control Group Mean	Difference	Percentage Change
Ever Employed, Quarters 2-9	62.5%	50.7%	11.9***	23%
Average Number of Quarters with Employment, Quarters 2-9	2.72	2.15	0.58***	27%
Ever Employed				
Quarter of Random Assignment	27.9%	25.1%	2.7**	11%
Quarter 2	30.7	24.7	6.1***	25
Quarter 3	33.0	25.6	7.4***	29
Quarter 4	33.6	25.8	7.8***	30
Quarter 5	34.7	26.9	7.7***	29
Quarter 6	34.9	26.7	8.2***	31
Quarter 7	35.6	27.4	8.2***	30
Quarter 8	35.2	28.4	6.8***	24
Quarter 9	34.7	29.3	5.4***	18
Average Total Earnings, Quarters 2-9	$4,932	$3,923	$1,009***	26%
Average Total Earnings				
Quarter of Random Assignment	$274	$271	$4	1%
Quarter 2	365	339	27	8
Quarter 3	486	401	85**	21
Quarter 4	568	456	112***	25
Quarter 5	610	482	128***	27
Quarter 6	677	484	193***	40
Quarter 7	717	545	172***	32
Quarter 8	743	597	146***	24
Quarter 9	766	620	146***	24

(continued)

TABLE B.5 (continued)

Outcome and Follow-Up Period	Experimental Group Mean	Control Group Mean	Difference	Percentage Change
Ever Received Any AFDC Payments, Quarters 2-10	92.1%	92.9%	- 0.8	- 1%
Average Number of Months Receiving AFDC Payments, Quarters 2-10	16.31	17.94	- 1.63***	- 9%
Ever Received Any AFDC Payments				
Quarter of Random Assignment	91.2%	91.4%	- 0.3	0%
Quarter 2	89.7	89.9	- 0.1	0
Quarter 3	79.0	81.6	- 2.5*	- 3
Quarter 4	70.6	76.1	- 5.5***	- 7
Quarter 5	66.0	72.4	- 6.4***	- 9
Quarter 6	60.9	68.3	- 7.3***	- 11
Quarter 7	57.3	64.7	- 7.4***	- 11
Quarter 8	53.8	60.6	- 6.9***	- 11
Quarter 9	51.3	58.7	- 7.4***	- 13
Quarter 10	48.1	55.1	- 7.0***	- 13
Average Total AFDC Payments Received, Quarters 2-10	$8,590	$9,687	- $1,097***	- 11%
Average Total AFDC Payments Received				
Quarter of Random Assignment	$1,194	$1,194	$0	0%
Quarter 2	1,286	1,333	- 47**	- 4
Quarter 3	1,120	1,225	- 105***	- 9
Quarter 4	1,032	1,160	- 129***	- 11
Quarter 5	987	1,112	- 125***	- 11
Quarter 6	922	1,065	- 143***	- 13
Quarter 7	867	1,011	- 144***	- 14
Quarter 8	826	963	- 136***	- 14
Quarter 9	792	922	- 129***	- 14
Quarter 10	758	896	- 137***	- 15
Sample Size	1,604	1,607		

(continued)

TABLE B.5 *(continued)*

SOURCE: Adapted from Hamilton and Friedlander, 1989.

NOTES: The earnings and AFDC payments data include zero values for sample members not employed an for sample members not receiving welfare. Estimates are regression-adjusted using ordinary least square controlling for pre-random assignment characteristics of sample members. There may be some discrepancie in experimental-control differences because of rounding.

For all outcomes, the quarter of random assignment refers to the calendar quarter in which randor assignment occurred. Quarter 1, the quarter of random assignment, may contain some earnings and AFD(payments from the period prior to random assignment and is therefore excluded from all summary measure of follow-up.

A two-tailed t-test was applied to differences between experimental and control groups. Statistic significance levels are indicated as: * = 10 percent; ** = 5 percent; and *** = 1 percent.

TABLE B.6 SUMMARY AND QUARTERLY IMPACTS OF THE VIRGINIA EMPLOYMENT SERVICES PROGRAM ON AFDC ELIGIBLES

Outcome and Follow-Up Period	Experimental Group Mean	Control Group Mean	Difference	Percentage Change
Ever Employed, Quarters 2-10[a]	63.2%	58.9%	4.4**	7%
Average Number of Quarters with Employment, Quarters 2-10[a]	3.18	2.85	0.33***	12%
Ever Employed				
Quarter of Random Assignment	27.3%	26.1%	1.2	5%
Quarter 2	28.3	26.7	1.6	6
Quarter 3	31.3	28.0	3.3**	12
Quarter 4	34.7	31.0	3.8**	12
Quarter 5	35.8	33.1	2.6	8
Quarter 6	35.2	32.1	3.2*	10
Quarter 7	36.4	32.3	4.1**	13
Quarter 8	39.3	33.3	6.0***	18
Quarter 9	38.4	34.1	4.3**	13
Quarter 10	38.7	34.1	4.6***	13
Average Total Earnings, Quarters 2-10[a]	$4,710	$4,222	$488*	12%
Average Total Earnings				
Quarter of Random Assignment	$222	$227	- $4	- 2%
Quarter 2	286	290	- 4	- 1
Quarter 3	384	350	34	10
Quarter 4	459	416	43	10
Quarter 5	505	459	47	10
Quarter 6	530	482	48	10
Quarter 7	596	520	77*	15
Quarter 8	636	528	109***	21
Quarter 9	650	560	89**	16
Quarter 10	663	618	45	7

(continued)

Outcome and Follow-Up Period	Experimental Group Mean	Control Group Mean	Difference	Percentage Change
Ever Received Any AFDC Payments, Quarters 1-11	87.5%	87.4%	0.2	0%
Average Number of Months Receiving AFDC Payments, Quarters 1-11	16.64	16.95	- 0.31	- 2%
Ever Received Any AFDC Payments				
Quarter of Random Assignment	82.9%	83.0%	- 0.1	0%
Quarter 2	76.5	76.2	0.2	0
Quarter 3	66.9	65.7	1.2	2
Quarter 4	59.8	59.4	0.4	1
Quarter 5	56.2	55.1	1.1	2
Quarter 6	52.1	51.7	0.4	1
Quarter 7	48.6	47.8	0.8	2
Quarter 8	44.0	44.9	- 0.9	- 2
Quarter 9	41.1	43.2	- 2.1	- 5
Quarter 10	38.5	41.5	- 2.9*	- 7
Quarter 11	36.6	39.3	- 2.6	- 7
Average Total AFDC Payments Received, Quarters 1-11	$4,329	$4,517	- $188	- 4%
Average Total AFDC Payments Received				
Quarter of Random Assignment	$549	$554	- $5	- 1%
Quarter 2	529	550	- 21*	- 4
Quarter 3	457	484	- 27**	- 6
Quarter 4	426	441	- 15	- 3
Quarter 5	404	407	- 3	- 1
Quarter 6	383	391	- 9	- 2
Quarter 7	358	362	- 4	- 1
Quarter 8	335	355	- 20	- 6
Quarter 9	312	342	- 30**	- 9
Quarter 10	297	326	- 30**	- 9
Quarter 11	279	303	- 24*	- 8
Sample Size	2,119	1,031		

(continued)

TABLE B.6 *(continued)*

SOURCE: Adapted from Friedlander, 1988a.

NOTES: The earnings and AFDC payments data include zero values for sample members not employed and for sample members not receiving welfare. Estimates are regression-adjusted using ordinary least squares, controlling for pre-random assignment characteristics of sample members. There may be some discrepancies in experimental-control differences because of rounding.

For employment and earnings, the quarter of random assignment refers to the calendar quarter in which random assignment occurred. For AFDC payments, the quarter of random assignment refers to the three months beginning with the month in which an individual was randomly assigned.

A two-tailed t-test was applied to differences between experimental and control groups. Statistical significance levels are indicated as: * = 10 percent; ** = 5 percent; and *** = 1 percent.

[a]Quarter 1, the quarter of random assignment, may contain some earnings from the period prior to random assignment and is therefore excluded from the summary measures of follow-up for employment and earnings.

TABLE B.7   SUMMARY AND QUARTERLY IMPACTS OF THE WEST VIRGINIA COMMUNITY WORK EXPERIENCE PROGRAM ON AFDC ELIGIBLES

Outcome and Follow-Up Period	Experimental Group Mean	Control Group Mean	Difference	Percentage Change
Ever Employed, Quarters 2-6[a]	22.3%	22.7%	- 0.4	- 2%
Average Number of Quarters with Employment, Quarters 2-6[a]	0.58	0.62	- 0.04	- 6%
Ever Employed				
Quarter of Random Assignment	8.4%	9.2%	- 0.8	- 9%
Quarter 2	9.2	9.9	- 0.8	- 8
Quarter 3	10.9	11.2	- 0.3	- 3
Quarter 4	12.0	13.1	- 1.0	- 8
Quarter 5	12.7	13.8	- 1.1	- 8
Quarter 6	13.4	13.8	- 0.4	- 3
Average Total Earnings, Quarters 2-6[a]	$713	$712	$0	0%
Average Total Earnings				
Quarter of Random Assignment	$69	$73	- $4	- 5%
Quarter 2	101	95	6	6
Quarter 3	133	112	21	19
Quarter 4	148	155	- 7	- 4
Quarter 5	162	173	- 11	- 6
Quarter 6	168	178	- 9	- 5
Ever Received Any AFDC Payments, Quarters 1-7	96.8%	96.0%	0.8	1%
Average Number of Months Receiving AFDC Payments, Quarters 1-7	14.26	14.46	- 0.21	- 1%
Ever Received Any AFDC Payments				
Quarter of Random Assignment	94.2%	93.2%	1.0	1%
Quarter 2	87.6	86.7	0.9	1
Quarter 3	78.0	79.0	- 1.0	- 1
Quarter 4	70.9	72.5	- 1.5	- 2
Quarter 5	65.5	67.8	- 2.3	- 3
Quarter 6	61.8	63.5	- 1.7	- 3
Quarter 7	57.8	60.7	- 2.8*	- 5

(continued)

Outcome and Follow-Up Period	Experimental Group Mean	Control Group Mean	Difference	Percentage Change
Average Total AFDC Payments Received, Quarters 1-7	$2,681	$2,721	- $40	- 1%
Average Total AFDC Payments Received				
Quarter of Random Assignment	$452	$449	$3	1%
Quarter 2	459	454	6	1
Quarter 3	411	413	- 2	0
Quarter 4	370	377	- 7	- 2
Quarter 5	336	351	- 15*	- 4
Quarter 6	329	337	- 9	- 3
Quarter 7	325	341	- 16*	- 5
Sample Size	1,845	1,834		

SOURCE: Adapted from Friedlander et al., 1986.

NOTES: The earnings and AFDC payments data include zero values for sample members not employed and or sample members not receiving welfare. Estimates are regression-adjusted using ordinary least squares, controlling for pre-random assignment characteristics of sample members. There may be some discrepancies in experimental-control differences because of rounding.

For employment and earnings, the quarter of random assignment refers to the calendar quarter in which random assignment occurred. For AFDC payments, the quarter of random assignment refers to the three months beginning with the month in which an individual was randomly assigned.

A two-tailed t-test was applied to differences between experimental and control groups. Statistical significance levels are indicated as: * = 10 percent; ** = 5 percent; and *** = 1 percent.

[a]Quarter 1, the quarter of random assignment, may contain some earnings from the period prior to random assignment and is therefore excluded from the summary measures of follow-up for employment and earnings.

TABLE B.8 IMPACTS ON COMBINED EMPLOYMENT AND WELFARE RECEIPT STATUS OF THE SAN DIEGO SWIM PROGRAM, FOR AFDC ELIGIBLES

Outcome and Follow-Up Period	Experimental Group Mean	Control Group Mean	Difference	Percentage Change
Not Employed, Received AFDC				
Quarter of Random Assignment	67.1%	69.3%	-2.3*	-3%
Quarter 2	63.6	69.7	-6.1***	-9
Quarter 3	56.4	63.8	-7.3***	-11
Quarter 4	50.4	60.3	-9.9***	-16
Quarter 5	46.5	57.0	-10.4***	-18
Quarter 6	43.8	54.9	-11.1***	-20
Quarter 7	41.0	52.2	-11.1***	-21
Quarter 8	39.9	48.3	-8.4***	-17
Quarter 9	38.6	46.8	-8.2***	-18
Average Rate, Quarters 2-9	47.5	56.6	-9.1***	-16
Employed, Received AFDC				
Quarter of Random Assignment	24.1%	22.1%	2.0	9%
Quarter 2	26.1	20.2	5.9***	29
Quarter 3	22.6	17.8	4.8***	27
Quarter 4	20.3	15.8	4.4***	28
Quarter 5	19.5	15.5	4.0***	26
Quarter 6	17.1	13.4	3.7***	28
Quarter 7	16.3	12.6	3.7***	29
Quarter 8	13.8	12.3	1.5	12
Quarter 9	12.7	11.9	0.8	7
Average Rate, Quarters 2-9	18.6	14.9	3.6***	24
Employed, Did Not Receive AFDC				
Quarter of Random Assignment	3.8%	3.1%	0.7	23%
Quarter 2	4.6	4.5	0.1	2
Quarter 3	10.4	7.8	2.6***	33
Quarter 4	13.4	10.0	3.4***	34
Quarter 5	15.2	11.5	3.7***	32
Quarter 6	17.7	13.3	4.4***	33
Quarter 7	19.3	14.9	4.5***	30
Quarter 8	21.4	16.1	5.3***	33
Quarter 9	21.9	17.3	4.6***	27
Average Rate, Quarters 2-9	15.5	11.9	3.6***	30

(continued)

TABLE B.8 *(continued)*

Outcome and Follow-Up Period	Experimental Group Mean	Control Group Mean	Difference	Percentage Change
Not Employed, Did Not Receive AFDC				
Quarter of Random Assignment	5.1%	5.5%	-0.4	-7%
Quarter 2	5.7	5.7	0.0	0
Quarter 3	10.6	10.7	-0.1	-1
Quarter 4	16.0	13.8	2.1*	15
Quarter 5	18.8	16.1	2.7**	17
Quarter 6	21.3	18.5	2.9**	16
Quarter 7	23.4	20.4	3.0**	15
Quarter 8	24.9	23.3	1.6	7
Quarter 9	26.8	24.0	2.8*	12
Average Rate, Quarters 2-9	18.4	16.6	1.9**	11
Sample Size	1,604	1,607		

SOURCE: Adapted from Hamilton and Friedlander, 1989.

NOTES: Estimates are regression-adjusted using ordinary least squares, controlling for pre-random assignment characteristics of sample members. There may be some discrepancies in experimental-control differences because of rounding.

For all outcomes, the quarter of random assignment refers to the calendar quarter in which random assignment occurred. Quarter 1, the quarter of random assignment, may contain some earnings and AFDC payments from the period prior to random assignment and is therefore excluded from all summary measures of follow-up.

A two-tailed t-test was applied to differences between experimental and control groups. Statistical significance levels are indicated as: * = 10 percent; ** = 5 percent; and *** = 1 percent. The distributed differences are not, however, strictly independent.

TABLE B.9   ADDITIONAL SUBGROUP IMPACTS OF FIVE WELFARE-TO-WORK PROGRAMS ON AFDC ELIGIBLES

Subgroup, Welfare Status, and Program	Percent of Sample[a]	Average Earnings Per Quarter, Quarters 4 - Last			Average AFDC Payments Per Quarter, Quarters 4 - Last		
		Experi-mentals	Controls	Difference	Experi-mentals	Controls	Difference
High School Diploma							
Applicants							
Yes							
San Diego I	61.5	$1,068	$ 923	$146**	$375	$420	- $44
Baltimore	44.9	1,199	1,106	92	337	337	0
Virginia	50.8	939	912	27	175	155	21
Arkansas	55.1	557	397	161**	118	127	- 9
Cook County[b]	46.8	958	957	1	442	457	- 15
No							
San Diego I	38.5	609	534	74	532	547	- 15
Baltimore	55.1	829	593	236***	391	416	- 25
Virginia	49.2	694	559	136*	206	267	- 61**
Arkansas	44.9	313	270	43	143	190	- 47**
Cook County[b]	53.2	461	532	- 71	495	510	- 16
Recipients							
Yes							
Baltimore	42.1	645	598	46	557	546	10
Virginia	38.8	650	569	80	390	378	12
Arkansas	42.0	180	212	- 32	245	309	- 64*
Cook County[b]	30.9	532	467	66*	663	684	- 20
No							
Baltimore	57.9	347	317	30	679	677	2
Virginia	61.2	363	302	61	426	474	- 48**
Arkansas	58.0	129	73	56	311	369	- 58**
Cook County[b]	69.1	269	230	39	761	771	- 10
Number of Own Children							
Applicants							
One							
San Diego I	49.7	887	807	80	346	355	- 9
Baltimore	50.4	1,033	766	267***	299	327	- 28
Virginia	49.6	781	696	85	174	185	- 11
Arkansas	42.5	427	391	36	106	129	- 23
More Than One							
San Diego I	50.3	895	740	155**	525	580	- 56*
Baltimore	49.6	966	891	75	434	434	0
Virginia	50.4	856	780	76	207	234	- 27
Arkansas	57.5	467	305	161**	148	176	- 28
Recipients							
One							
Baltimore	43.1	528	493	35	503	522	- 19
Virginia	42.0	482	426	56	325	341	- 17
Arkansas	34.8	125	173	- 48	192	257	- 65*
More Than One							
Baltimore	56.9	430	392	38	721	696	24
Virginia	58.0	469	391	77	475	504	- 29
Arkansas	65.2	164	108	56	332	390	- 58**

(continued)

TABLE B.9 (*continued*)

Subgroup, Welfare Status, and Program	Percent of Sample[a]	Average Earnings Per Quarter, Quarters 4 - Last			Average AFDC Payments Per Quarter, Quarters 4 - Last		
		Experi-mentals	Controls	Difference	Experi-mentals	Controls	Difference
Ever Married							
Applicants							
Yes							
San Diego I	84.1	$ 908	$806	$102*	$421	$445	- $24
Baltimore	69.9	1,003	821	182**	346	363	- 17
Virginia	74.2	830	705	125*	170	176	- 6
Arkansas	56.9	424	310	114*	112	123	- 11
No							
San Diego I	15.9	805	608	196	511	591	- 81
Baltimore	30.1	980	832	148	413	421	- 8
Virginia	25.8	789	841	- 52	249	308	- 59*
Arkansas	43.1	481	383	98	153	199	- 45**
Recipients							
Yes							
Baltimore	49.1	458	425	33	621	624	- 2
Virginia	65.3	462	376	86*	400	402	- 2
Arkansas	41.8	159	158	1	329	328	1
No							
Baltimore	50.9	487	446	40	633	620	13
Virginia	34.7	497	459	38	432	495	- 63**
Arkansas	58.2	143	112	32	249	353	-104***
Ethnicity							
Applicants							
White							
San Diego I [c]	61.5	949	821	128*	357	369	- 12
Baltimore	33.8	922	767	155	309	318	- 9
Virginia	41.8	801	663	138	128	149	- 21
Arkansas	16.7	403	259	144	72	82	- 11
Cook County[b,c]	21.8	679	709	- 30	353	413	- 61*
Black							
San Diego I	20.7	895	589	306***	532	678	-146***
Baltimore[c]	66.2	1,035	855	180**	395	412	- 17
Virginia[c]	58.2	832	792	40	235	253	- 18
Arkansas[c]	83.3	458	358	100*	141	170	- 29*
Cook County[b]	65.5	741	761	- 20	502	517	- 15
Hispanic							
San Diego I	17.8	693	843	-150	593	556	38
Cook County[b]	12.6	458	608	-150	510	450	60

(*continued*)

Subgroup, Welfare Status, and Program	Percent of Sample[a]	Average Earnings Per Quarter, Quarters 4 - Last			Average AFDC Payments Per Quarter, Quarters 4 - Last		
		Experi- mentals	Controls	Difference	Experi- mentals	Controls	Difference
Recipients							
White							
Baltimore	25.1	$420	$438	- $18	$579	$575	$4
Virginia	26.8	490	398	92	303	305	- 2
Arkansas	8.5	337	55	282**	207	228	- 21
Cook County[b,c]	14.3	517	322	195***	572	604	- 31
Black							
Baltimore[c]	74.9	490	436	55	644	638	6
Virginia[c]	73.2	468	408	60	451	483	- 32*
Arkansas[c]	91.5	132	136	- 4	290	354	- 64***
Cook County[b]	75.3	322	307	15	761	772	- 11
Hispanic							
Cook County[b]	10.4	324	265	59	730	734	- 4
Labor Market							
Applicants							
Urban							
Virginia	78.7	849	769	80	195	213	- 18
Arkansas	64.8	403	302	100	99	126	- 27
Rural							
Virginia	21.3	707	625	82	174	198	- 24
Arkansas	35.2	533	413	120	187	211	- 24
Recipients							
Urban							
Virginia	78.8	521	421	100**	411	450	- 39**
Arkansas	56.5	211	120	91*	250	325	- 75***
Rural							
Virginia	21.2	299	346	- 47	413	383	30
Arkansas	43.5	76	152	- 76	326	366	- 41

SOURCE: Adapted from Friedlander, 1988b.

NOTES: The impact estimates are unconditional, i.e., other subgroup characteristics are not controlled for. Not all subgroups were present in each program. The impacts are estimated for the fourth through last quarter of follow-up.

[a]Percent of applicants and percent of recipients.

[b]The definitions of "applicant" and "recipient" for Cook County are not strictly comparable to those of the other programs. See the text of Friedlander, 1988b, for discussion.

[c]For Baltimore, Virginia, and Arkansas, the category "black" includes a small number of individuals in other non-white groups. In San Diego I and Cook County, "white" includes a small number of non-black, non-Hispanic, non-white persons.

*Denotes statistical significance at the 10 percent level; ** at the 5 percent level; and *** at the 1 percent level.

Appendix C

Supplemental Table for Chapter 5

TABLE C.1 SUMMARY AND QUARTERLY IMPACTS OF THE MAINE ON-THE-JOB TRAINING PROGRAM ON AFDC ELIGIBLES

Outcome and Follow-Up Period	Experimental Group Mean	Control Group Mean	Difference	Percentage Change
Ever Employed, Quarters 2-11	81.8%	80.2%	1.6	2%
Average Number of Quarters with Employment, Quarters 2-11	4.69	4.21	0.48	11%
Ever Employed				
Quarter of Random Assignment	16.4%	24.7%	- 8.2**	- 33%
Quarter 2	23.5	34.8	- 11.3**	- 32
Quarter 3	42.8	39.3	3.5	9
Quarter 4	52.1	43.8	8.3	19
Quarter 5	49.9	41.3	8.6*	21
Quarter 6	47.9	40.7	7.2	18
Quarter 7	50.4	45.0	5.4	12
Quarter 8	50.2	43.4	6.9	16
Quarter 9	50.6	43.4	7.1	16
Quarter 10	50.7	39.7	11.1**	28
Quarter 11	50.4	49.3	1.1	2
Average Total Earnings, Quarters 2-11	$7,344	$5,599	$1,745**	31%
Average Total Earnings				
Quarter of Random Assignment	$71	$109	- $38	- 35%
Quarter 2	173	289	- 116**	- 40
Quarter 3	535	436	99	23
Quarter 4	687	529	158*	30
Quarter 5	716	475	241**	51
Quarter 6	745	572	173*	30
Quarter 7	840	601	239**	40
Quarter 8	882	663	219**	33
Quarter 9	918	669	249**	37
Quarter 10	916	642	274**	43
Quarter 11	933	724	209*	29

(continued)

TABLE C.1 *(continued)*

Outcome and Follow-Up Period	Experimental Group Mean	Control Group Mean	Difference	Percentage Change
Ever Received Any AFDC Payments, Quarters 2-11	98.3%	98.0%	0.3	0%
Average Number of Months Receiving AFDC Payments, Quarters 2-11	19.61	19.19	0.42	2%
Ever Received Any AFDC Payments				
Quarter of Random Assignment	98.6%	99.4%	- 0.7	- 1%
Quarter 2	97.6	98.0	- 0.4	0
Quarter 3	89.9	89.8	0.0	0
Quarter 4	81.8	85.1	- 3.3	- 4
Quarter 5	77.3	77.1	0.2	0
Quarter 6	73.8	71.4	2.4	3
Quarter 7	70.0	68.7	1.3	2
Quarter 8	64.4	63.1	1.3	2
Quarter 9	62.8	60.2	2.5	4
Quarter 10	58.9	52.5	6.4	12
Quarter 11	55.8	49.8	6.0	12
Average Total AFDC Payments Received, Quarters 2-11	$6,768	$6,599	$170	3%
Average Total AFDC Payments Received				
Quarter of Random Assignment	$924	$941	- $17	- 2%
Quarter 2	918	887	31	4
Quarter 3	835	799	36	4
Quarter 4	742	728	14	2
Quarter 5	695	687	8	1
Quarter 6	681	650	32	5
Quarter 7	637	636	0	0
Quarter 8	596	607	- 11	- 2
Quarter 9	578	583	- 5	- 1
Quarter 10	562	516	45	9
Quarter 11	525	506	20	4
Sample Size	297	147		

(continued)

TABLE C.1 *(continued)*

SOURCE: Adapted from Auspos, Cave, and Long, 1988.

NOTES: The earnings and AFDC payments data include zero values for sample members not employed and for sample members not receiving welfare. Estimates are regression-adjusted using ordinary least squares, controlling for pre-random assignment characteristics of sample members. There may be some discrepancies in experimental-control differences because of rounding.

For all outcomes, the quarter of random assignment refers to the calendar quarter in which random assignment occurred. Quarter 1, the quarter of random assignment, may contain some earnings and AFDC payments from the period prior to random assignment and is therefore excluded from all summary measures of follow-up.

A two-tailed t-test was applied to differences between experimental and control groups. Statistical significance levels are indicated as: * = 10 percent; ** = 5 percent; and *** = 1 percent.

References

American Public Welfare Association. 1990. "Early State Experiences and Policy Issues in the Implementation of the JOBS Program: Briefing Paper for Human Service Administrators." Washington, D.C.: American Public Welfare Association.

Ashenfelter, Orley. 1987. "The Case for Evaluating Training Programs with Randomized Trials." *Economics of Education Review*, 6(4): 333-338.

Auspos, Patricia; Cave, George; Doolittle, Fred; and Hoerz, Gregory. 1989. *Implementing JOBSTART: A Demonstration for School Dropouts in the JTPA System*. New York: MDRC.

Auspos, Patricia; Cave, George; and Long, David. 1988. *Maine: Final Report on the Training Opportunities in the Private Sector Program*. New York: MDRC.

Ball, Joseph. 1984. *West Virginia: Interim Findings on the Community Work Experience Demonstrations*. New York: MDRC.

Bane, Mary Jo; and Ellwood, David T. 1983. *The Dynamics of Dependence: The Routes to Self-Sufficiency*. Cambridge, Mass.: Urban Systems Research and Engineering, Inc.

Barnow, Burt S. 1987. "The Impact of CETA Programs on Earnings." *Journal of Human Resources*, 22(2): 157-191.

Bassi, Laurie J.; Simms, Margaret C.; Burbridge, Lynn C.; and Betsey, Charles L. 1984. *Measuring the Effect of CETA on Youth and the Economically Disadvantaged*. Final Report prepared for the U.S. Department of Labor. Washington, D.C.: Urban Institute.

Bell, Stephen H.; Burstein, Nancy R.; and Orr, Larry L. 1987. *Overview of Evaluation Results: Evaluation of the AFDC Homemaker-Home Health Aide Demonstrations*. Cambridge, Mass.: Abt Associates Inc.

Bell, Stephen H.; Enns, John H.; and Orr, Larry L. 1986. "The Effects of Job Training and Employment on the Earnings and Public Benefits of AFDC Recipients: The AFDC Homemaker-Home Health Aide Demonstrations." Draft. Paper presented at the Annual Research Conference of the Association for Public Policy Analysis and Management, Austin, Texas.

Bell, Stephen H.; and Fein, David J. Forthcoming. *Ohio Transitions to Independence Demonstration: Program Impacts in the First Fiscal Year*. Cambridge, Mass.: Abt Associates Inc.

Bell, Stephen H.; Hamilton, William L.; and Burstein, Nancy R. 1989. *Ohio Transitions to Independence Evaluation: Design of the Cost-Benefit Analysis*. Cambridge, Mass.: Abt Associates Inc.

Bell, Stephen H.; and Orr, Larry L. 1988. "Screening (and Creaming?) Applicants to Job Training Programs: The AFDC Homemaker-Home Health Aide Demonstrations." Paper presented at the Annual Research Conference of the Association for Public Policy Analysis and Management, Seattle, Washington.

Berlin, Gordon; and Sum, Andrew. 1988. *Toward a More Perfect Union: Basic Skills, Poor Families, and Our Economic Future*. Ford Foundation Project on Social Welfare and the American Future, Occasional Paper No. 3. New York: Ford Foundation.

Berman, Paul; and McLaughlin, Milbrey W. 1978. *Federal Programs Supporting Educational Change, Vol. VIII: Implementing and Sustaining Innovations*. Santa Monica, Ca.: Rand Corporation.

Betsey, Charles L.; Hollister, Robinson G.; and Papageorgiou, Mary R., eds. 1985. *Youth Employment and Training Programs: The YEDPA Years.* Washington, D.C.: National Academy Press.

Blau, D. M.; and Robins, P. K. 1986. "Fertility, Employment, and Child Care Costs: A Dynamic Analysis." Paper presented at the Annual Meeting of the Population Association of America, San Francisco.

Bloom, Howard; Orr, Larry; Doolittle, Fred; Hotz, Joseph; and Barnow, Burt. 1990. *Design of the National JTPA Study.* Washington, D.C.: Abt Associates Inc. and MDRC.

Board of Directors, Manpower Demonstration Research Corporation. 1980. *Summary and Findings of the National Supported Work Demonstration.* New York: MDRC.

Brooks-Gunn, J. 1989. "Opportunities for Change: Effects of Intervention Programs on Mothers and Children." Paper prepared for the Forum on Children and the Family Support Act, the National Forum on the Future of Children and Families, National Academy of Sciences, Washington, D.C.

Brown, Randall; Burghardt, John; Cavin, Edward; Long, David; Mallar, Charles; Maynard, Rebecca; Metcalf, Charles; Thornton, Craig; and Whitebread, Christine. 1983. *The Employment Opportunities Pilot Project: Analysis of Program Impacts.* Princeton, N.J.: Mathematica Policy Research, Inc.

Burtless, Gary. 1989. "The Effect of Reform on Employment, Earnings, and Income." In Phoebe H. Cottingham and David T. Ellwood, eds., *Welfare Policy for the 1990s.* Cambridge, Mass.: Harvard University Press.

Burtless, Gary; and Orr, Larry. Fall 1986. "Are Classical Experiments Needed for Manpower Policy?" *Journal of Human Resources,* 21: 606-639.

Campbell, Frances A.; Breitmayer, Bonnie; and Ramey, Craig T. 1986. "Disadvantaged Single Teenage Mothers and Their Children: Consequences of Free Educational Day Care." *Family Relations,* 35(1): 63-68.

Cave, George. 1989. "Subgroup Impacts of a Wage Subsidy Program: Randomized Trials of OJT for AFDC Recipients." Paper presented at the One Hundred and Second Annual Meeting of the American Economic Association, Atlanta, Georgia.

Cella, Margot. 1987. *Operational Costs of Demonstration Activities: Evaluation of the AFDC Homemaker-Home Health Aide Demonstrations.* Cambridge, Mass.: Abt Associates Inc.

Cherlin, Andrew. 1989. "Child Care and the Family Support Act: Policy Issues." Paper prepared for the Forum on Children and the Family Support Act, the National Forum on the Future of Children and Families, National Academy of Sciences, Washington, D.C.

Doolittle, Fred; and Traeger, Linda. 1990. *Implementing the National JTPA Study.* New York: MDRC.

Ellwood, David T. 1988. *Poor Support: Poverty in the American Family.* New York: Basic Books.

Ellwood, David T. 1986. *Targeting "Would-Be" Long-Term Recipients of AFDC.* Princeton, N.J.: Mathematica Policy Research, Inc.

Enns, John H.; Bell, Stephen H.; and Flanagan, Kathleen L. 1987. *Trainee Employment and Earnings.* Cambridge, Mass.: Abt Associates Inc.

Family Support Act of 1988. October 13, 1988. 100th Cong., 2d sess. Public Law 100-485.

Field, T.; Widmayer, S.; Greenberg, R.; and Stoller, S. 1982. "Effects of Parent Training on Teenage Mothers and Their Infants." *Pediatrics,* 69: 703-707.

Ford Foundation Project on Social Welfare and the American Future. 1989. *The Common Good: Social Welfare and the American Future.* Policy Recommendations of the Executive Panel. New York: Ford Foundation.

Freedman, Stephen; Bryant, Jan; and Cave, George. 1988. *New Jersey: Final Report on the Grant Diversion Project.* New York: MDRC.

Friedlander, Daniel. 1988a. "An Analysis of Extended Follow-Up for the Virginia Employment Services Program." Unpublished internal document. New York: MDRC.

Friedlander, Daniel. 1988b. *Subgroup Impacts and Performance Indicators for Selected Welfare Employment Programs.* New York: MDRC.

Friedlander, Daniel. 1987. *Maryland: Supplemental Report on the Baltimore Options Program.* New York: MDRC.

Friedlander, Daniel; Erickson, Marjorie; Hamilton, Gayle; and Knox, Virginia. 1986. *West Virginia: Final Report on the Community Work Experience Demonstrations.* New York: MDRC.

Friedlander, Daniel; Freedman, Stephen; Hamilton, Gayle; and Quint, Janet. 1987. *Illinois: Final Report on Job Search and Work Experience in Cook County.* New York: MDRC.

Friedlander, Daniel; and Goldman, Barbara. 1988. *Employment and Welfare Impacts of the Arkansas WORK Program: A Three-Year Follow-Up Study in Two Counties.* New York: MDRC.

Friedlander, Daniel; and Gueron, Judith M. Forthcoming. "Are High-Cost Services More Effective Than Low-Cost Services? Evidence from Experimental Evaluations of Welfare-to-Work Programs." In Charles F. Manski and Irwin Garfinkel, eds., *Evaluating Welfare and Training Programs.* Cambridge, Mass.: Harvard University Press.

Friedlander, Daniel; Hoerz, Gregory; Long, David; and Quint, Janet. 1985a. *Maryland: Final Report on the Employment Initiatives Evaluation.* New York: MDRC.

Friedlander, Daniel; Hoerz, Gregory; Quint, Janet; and Riccio, James. 1985b. *Arkansas: Final Report on the WORK Program in Two Counties.* New York: MDRC.

Garfinkel, Irwin; and McLanahan, Sara. 1986. *Single Mothers and Their Children: A New American Dilemma.* Washington, D.C.: Urban Institute.

Goldman, Barbara S. 1989. "Job Search Strategies for Women on Welfare." In Sharon L. Harlan and Ronnie J. Steinberg, eds., *Job Training for Women: The Promise and Limits of Public Policies.* Philadelphia: Temple University Press.

Goldman, Barbara. 1981. *Impacts of the Immediate Job Search Assistance Experiment.* New York: MDRC.

Goldman, Barbara; Cavin, Edward; Erickson, Marjorie; Hamilton, Gayle; Hasselbring, Darlene; and Reynolds, Sandra. 1985a. *Relationship Between Earnings and Welfare Benefits for Working Recipients: Four Area Case Studies.* New York: MDRC.

Goldman, Barbara; Friedlander, Daniel; Gueron, Judith; and Long, David. 1985b. *Findings from the San Diego Job Search and Work Experience Demonstration.* New York: MDRC.

Goldman, Barbara; Friedlander, Daniel; and Long, David. 1986. *California: Final Report on the San Diego Job Search and Work Experience Demonstration.* New York: MDRC.

Goodwin, Leonard. 1977. "What Has Been Learned from the Work Incentive Program and Related Experiences: A Review of Research with Policy Implications." Report prepared for the Employment and Training Administration. Washington, D.C.: U.S. Department of Labor.

Gordon, Anne; and Burghardt, John. 1990. *The Minority Female Single Parent Demonstration: Short-Term Economic Impacts*. New York: Rockefeller Foundation.

Gordon, Jesse E. 1978. "WIN Research: A Review of the Findings." In Charles Garvin, ed., *The Work Incentive Experience*. Savage, Md.: Rowman and Littlefield.

Gould-Stuart, Joanna. 1982. *Welfare Women in a Group Job Search Program: Their Experiences in the Louisville WIN Research Laboratory Project*. New York: MDRC.

Grossman, Jean Baldwin; Maynard, Rebecca; and Roberts, Judith. 1985. *Reanalysis of the Effects of Selected Employment and Training Programs for Welfare Recipients*. Princeton, N.J.: Mathematica Policy Research, Inc.

Gueron, Judith M. 1990. "Work and Welfare: Lessons on Employment Programs." *Journal of Economic Perspectives*, 4(1): 79-98.

Gueron, Judith M. 1987. *Reforming Welfare with Work*. Ford Foundation Project on Social Welfare and the American Future, Occasional Paper No. 2. New York: Ford Foundation.

Gueron, Judith M. 1985. "The Demonstration of State Work/Welfare Initiatives." In R. F. Boruch and W. Wothke, eds., *Randomization and Field Experimentation*. San Francisco: Jossey-Bass.

Gueron, Judith M.; and Long, David A. 1990. "Welfare Employment Policy in the 1980s." In Louis A. Ferman, Michele Hoyman, Joel Cutcher-Gershenfeld, and Ernest J. Savoie, eds., *New Developments in Worker Training: A Legacy for the 1990s*. Madison, Wis.: Industrial Relations Research Association.

Gueron, Judith M.; and Nathan, Richard P. 1985. "The MDRC Work/Welfare Project: Objectives, Status, Significance." *Policy Studies Review*, 4: 417-432.

Hall, Arden R. 1980. "Education and Training." In Philip K. Robins, Robert G. Spiegelman, Samuel Weiner, and Joseph G. Bell, eds., *A Guaranteed Annual Income: Evidence from a Social Experiment*. New York: Academic Press.

Hamilton, Gayle. 1988. *Interim Report on the Saturation Work Initiative Model in San Diego*. New York: MDRC.

Hamilton, Gayle; and Friedlander, Daniel. 1989. *Final Report on the Saturation Work Initiative Model in San Diego*. New York: MDRC.

Hardy, J. B.; King, T. M.; Shipp, D. A.; and Welcher, D. W. 1981. "A Comprehensive Approach to Adolescent Pregnancy." In K. G. Scott, T. Field, and E. Robertson, eds., *Teenage Parents and Their Offspring*. New York: Grune & Stratton.

Heckman, James J. 1990. "Randomization and Social Policy Evaluation." Paper presented at a conference on "Evaluation Design for Welfare and Training Programs," sponsored by the Institute for Research on Poverty of the University of Wisconsin-Madison and the Office of the Assistant Secretary for Planning and Evaluation of the U.S. Department of Health and Human Services, Airlie, Virginia. Collected papers from this conference will be published in Charles F. Manski and Irwin Garfinkel, eds., *Evaluating Welfare and Training Programs*. Cambridge, Mass.: Harvard University Press. Forthcoming.

Heckman, James J.; and Hotz, V. Joseph. 1989. "Choosing Among Alternative Nonexperimental Methods for Estimating the Impact of Social Programs: The Case of Manpower Training." *Journal of the American Statistical Association*, 84: 862-880.

Hershey, A.; and Nagatoshi, C. 1989. *Implementing Services for Welfare Dependent Teenage Parents: Experiences in the DHHS/OFA Teenage Parent Demonstration*. Prepared for the Department of Health and Human Services. Princeton, N.J.: Mathematica Policy Research, Inc.

Hoerz, Gregory; and Hanson, Karla. 1986. "A Survey of Participants and Worksite Supervisors in the New York City Work Experience Program." New York: MDRC.

Hogarth, Suzanne; Martin, Roger; and Nazar, Kathleen. 1989. *Pennsylvania Saturation Work Program Impact Evaluation*. Draft Report. Harrisburg, Pa.: Department of Public Welfare.

Hollenbeck, Kevin; Hufnagle, John; and Kurth, Paula. 1990a. *Implementation of the JOBS Program in Ohio: A Process Study*. Second Annual Report. Columbus: Ohio State University, Center on Education and Training for Employment.

Hollenbeck, Kevin; Hufnagle, John; and Kurth, Paula. 1990b. *Implementation of the JOBS Program in Ohio: A Process Study*. First Annual Report. Columbus: Ohio State University, Center on Education and Training for Employment.

Hollister, Robinson G., Jr.; Kemper, Peter; and Maynard, Rebecca A., eds. 1984. *The National Supported Work Demonstration*. Madison, Wis.: University of Wisconsin Press.

Interagency Low Income Opportunity Advisory Board, Executive Office of the President. 1988. *Up from Dependency, Supplement 4: Research Studies and Bibliography*. Washington, D.C.: U.S. Government Printing Office.

Interagency Low Income Opportunity Advisory Board, Executive Office of the President. (no date). *Special Terms and Conditions*. Unpublished internal document.

Job Training Longitudinal Survey Research Advisory Panel. 1985. "Recommendations of the Job Training Longitudinal Survey Research Advisory Panel." Report prepared for the Office of Strategic Planning and Policy Development, Employment and Training Administration. Washington, D.C.: U.S. Department of Labor.

Kemper, Peter; Long, David A.; and Thornton, Craig. 1984. "A Benefit-Cost Analysis of the Supported Work Experiment." In Robinson G. Hollister, Jr., Peter Kemper, and Rebecca A. Maynard, eds., *The National Supported Work Demonstration*. Madison, Wis.: University of Wisconsin Press.

Kemper, Peter; Long, David A.; and Thornton, Craig. 1981. *The Supported Work Evaluation: Final Benefit-Cost Analysis*. Princeton, N.J.: Mathematica Policy Research, Inc.

Ketron, Inc. 1980. *The Long-Term Impact of WIN II: A Longitudinal Evaluation of the Employment Experiences of Participants in the Work Incentive Program*. Wayne, Pa.: Ketron, Inc.

Kirsch, Irwin S.; and Jungeblut, Ann. 1986. *Literacy: Profiles of America's Young Adults*. Princeton, N.J.: National Assessment of Educational Progress, Educational Testing Service.

Lalonde, Robert; and Maynard, Rebecca. August 1987. "How Precise Are Evaluations of Employment and Training Programs: Evidence from a Field Experiment." *Evaluation Review*, 11: 428-451.

Long, David; and Bloom, Dan. 1989. *Design of the Project Learn Evaluation*. Unpublished document prepared for the Ohio Department of Human Services. New York: MDRC.

Mallar, Charles; Kerachsky, Stuart; Thornton, Craig; and Long, David. 1982. *Project Report: Evaluation of the Economic Impact of the Job Corps Program, Third Follow-Up Report*. Princeton, N.J.: Mathematica Policy Research, Inc.

Malone, Margaret. 1986. *Work and Welfare*. Report prepared for the Subcommittee on Employment and Productivity of the Senate Committee on Labor and Human Resources and the Subcommittee on Social Security and Income Maintenance of the Senate Committee on Finance. 99th Cong., 2d sess. S. Prt. 99-177.

Manpower Demonstration Research Corporation. 1989. Unpublished internal documents.

Manpower Demonstration Research Corporation. 1988. *Research Design for a Special Study of Case Management in the Riverside County GAIN Program*. Unpublished internal document.

Martinson, Karin; and Riccio, James. 1989. *GAIN: Child Care in a Welfare Employment Initiative*. New York: MDRC.

Masters, Stanley. Fall 1981. "The Effects of Supported Work on the Earnings and Transfer Payments of Its AFDC Target Group." *Journal of Human Resources*, 16(4): 600-636.

Mathematica Policy Research, Inc. 1988. *REACH Welfare Initiative Program Evaluation: Technical Proposal*. Princeton, N.J.: Mathematica Policy Research, Inc.

Maxfield, Myles, Jr. 1990. *Planning Employment Services for the Disadvantaged*. New York: Rockefeller Foundation.

Maynard, Rebecca; Maxfield, Myles; Grossman, Jean; and Long, David. 1986. "A Design of a Social Experimentation of Targeted Employment Services for AFDC Recipients." Paper prepared for the U.S. Department of Health and Human Services. Princeton, N.J.: Mathematica Policy Research, Inc.

Mead, Lawrence M. 1990. "Should Workfare Be Mandatory? What Research Says." *Journal of Policy Analysis and Management*, 9(3): 400-404.

Mead, Lawrence M. 1986. *Beyond Entitlement: The Social Obligations of Citizenship*. New York: Free Press.

Mincer, Jacob. 1989. "Human Capital and the Labor Market: A Review of Current Research." *Educational Researcher*, 18(4).

Moffitt, Robert. 1990. "Evaluation Methods for Program Entry Effects." Paper presented at a conference on "Evaluation Design for Welfare and Training Programs," sponsored by the Institute for Research on Poverty of the University of Wisconsin-Madison and the Office of the Assistant Secretary for Planning and Evaluation of the U.S. Department of Health and Human Services, Airlie, Virginia. Collected papers from this conference will be published in Charles F. Manski and Irwin Garfinkel, eds., *Evaluating Welfare and Training Programs*. Cambridge, Mass.: Harvard University Press. Forthcoming.

New Jersey Department of Human Services. 1989. *Child Care Plus: A Demonstration of Enhanced Child Care Options for Low-Income Families*. Draft Report. Trenton: New Jersey Department of Human Services.

Nightingale, Demetra Smith; and Burbridge, Lynn C. 1987. *The Status of State Work-Welfare Programs in 1986: Implications for Welfare Reform*. Washington, D.C.: Urban Institute.

Nightingale, Demetra Smith; Burbridge, Lynn C.; Wissoker, Douglas; Bawden, Lee; Sonenstein, Freya L.; and Jeffries, Neal. 1989. *Experiences of Massachusetts ET Job Finders: Preliminary Findings*. Washington, D.C.: Urban Institute.

North Carolina Department of Human Resources. (no date). *Child Care Recycling Fund Demonstration Project: Pretest and Evaluation*. Unpublished internal document.

Olds, David L.; Belton, Jann; Cole, Robert; Foye, Howard; Helberg, June; Henderson, Charles R., Jr.; James, David; Kitzman, Harriet; Phelps, Charles; Sweeney, Patrick; and Tatelbaum, Robert. (no date). *Nurse Home-Visitation for Mothers and Children: A Research Proposal*. Unpublished document. Rochester, N.Y.: New Mothers Study, Department of Pediatrics, University of Rochester.

Olds, David L.; Henderson, Charles R., Jr.; Tatelbaum, Robert; and Chamberlin, Robert. 1988. "Improving the Life-Course Development of Socially Disadvantaged Mothers: A Randomized Trial of Nurse Home Visitation." *American Journal of Public Health,* 78(11): 1436-1445.

O'Neill, June. 1990. *Work and Welfare in Massachusetts: An Evaluation of the ET Program.* Boston, Mass.: Pioneer Institute for Public Policy Research.

O'Neill, June A.; Wolf, Douglas A.; Bassi, Laurie J.; and Hannan, Michael T. 1984. *An Analysis of Time on Welfare.* Final Report to the U.S. Department of Health and Human Services, Office of the Assistant Secretary for Planning and Evaluation. Washington, D.C.: Urban Institute.

Orr, Larry L. 1987. *Evaluation of the AFDC Homemaker-Home Health Aide Demonstrations: Benefits and Costs.* Cambridge, Mass.: Abt Associates Inc.

Polit, Denise; and O'Hara, Joseph J. 1989. "Support Services." In Phoebe H. Cottingham and David T. Ellwood, eds., *Welfare Policy for the 1990s.* Cambridge, Mass.: Harvard University Press.

Polit, Denise; Quint, Janet; and Riccio, James. 1988. *The Challenge of Serving Teenage Mothers: Lessons from Project Redirection.* New York: MDRC.

Porter, Kathryn H. 1990. *Making JOBS Work: What the Research Says About Effective Employment Programs for AFDC Recipients.* Washington, D.C.: Center on Budget and Policy Priorities.

Puma, Michael; Werner, Alan; and Hojnacki, Marjorie. 1988. *Evaluation of the Food Stamp Employment and Training Program: Report to Congress on Program Implementation.* Cambridge, Mass.: Abt Associates Inc.

Quint, Janet C.; and Guy, Cynthia A. 1989. *New Chance: Lessons from the Pilot Phase.* New York: MDRC.

Quint, Janet; and Guy, Cynthia. 1986. *Interim Findings from the WIN Demonstration Program in Cook County.* New York: MDRC.

Rein, Mildred. 1982. *Dilemmas of Welfare Policy: Why Work Strategies Haven't Worked.* New York: Praeger.

Riccio, James; Cave, George; Freedman, Stephen; and Price, Marilyn. 1986. *Virginia: Final Report on the Employment Services Program.* New York: MDRC.

Riccio, James; Goldman, Barbara; Hamilton, Gayle; Martinson, Karin; and Orenstein, Alan. 1989. *GAIN: Early Implementation Experiences and Lessons.* New York: MDRC.

Shugoll Research; Battelle Human Affairs Research Centers; and Kearney/Centaur Division, A. T. Kearney, Inc. 1989. *Job Corps Computer-Assisted Instruction Pilot Project Evaluation.* Report prepared for the U.S. Department of Labor. Bethesda, Md.: Shugoll Research.

SRI International. 1983. *Final Report on the Seattle-Denver Income Maintenance Experiment, Volume 1: Design and Results.* Menlo Park, Ca.: SRI International.

Stolzenberg, R. M.; and Waite, L. J. 1984. "Local Labor Markets, Children and Labor Force Participation of Wives." *Demography,* 21: 157-170.

Urban Institute. 1989. *Evaluation Design for the Family Independence Program: Third Draft.* Prepared for the Legislative Budget Committee, State of Washington. Washington, D.C.: Urban Institute.

U.S. Congressional Budget Office. 1987. *Work-Related Programs for Welfare Recipients.* Washington, D.C.: U.S. Congressional Budget Office.

U.S. General Accounting Office. 1987a. *School Dropouts: Survey of Local Programs.* Washington, D.C.: U.S. General Accounting Office.

U.S. General Accounting Office. 1987b. *Work and Welfare: Current AFDC Work Programs and Implications for Federal Policy.* Washington, D.C.: U.S. General Accounting Office.

U.S. General Accounting Office. 1986. *School Dropouts: The Extent and Nature of the Problem.* Washington, D.C.: U.S. General Accounting Office.

Venezky, Richard L.; Kaestle, Carl F.; and Sum, Andrew M. 1987. *The Subtle Danger: Reflections on the Literacy Abilities of America's Young Adults.* Princeton, N.J.: Educational Testing Service.

Wallace, John; and Long, David. 1987. *GAIN: Planning and Early Implementation.* New York: MDRC.

Werner, Alan; and Nutt-Powell, Bonnie. 1988. *Evaluation of the Comprehensive Employment Opportunity Support Centers, Vol. 1: Synthesis of Findings.* Cambridge, Mass.: Abt Associates Inc.

Wilson, Julie B.; and Ellwood, David T. 1989. "Welfare to Work Through the Eyes of Children: The Impact on Children of Parental Movement from AFDC to Employment." Paper prepared for the Forum on Children and the Family Support Act, the National Forum on the Future of Children and Families, National Academy of Sciences, Washington, D.C.

Wolfhagen, Carl. 1983. *Job Search Strategies: Lessons from the Louisville WIN Laboratory.* New York: MDRC.

Zimmerman, David R.; Wichita, John A.; Wills, Michael; Rynders, Paul; and Skidmore, Felicity. 1983. *Final Report on Job Search and Participation Requirements and Their Enforcement in the Employment Opportunities Pilot Project.* Madison, Wis.: Mathematica Policy Research, Inc.

Subject Index

Page numbers in *italics* refer to tables and figures. The symbol *n* refers to notes. The main table summarizing the completed evaluations appears as both Table 1.1 and, with minor additions, Table 4.6. The two tables are jointly cited in this index: *15-20 (168-174)*.

tional Medical Benefits Study, *118,* 120, 233-234

Wisconsin Learnfare, 225. *See also* Mandatory education; Young custodial mothers' school requirement

Work experience, 11, 97, 132, 189-190; broad-coverage programs, *85-92,* 97-98, *130-131,* 134; impacts, 27, 29, 165-166, 165*n,* 189-190; implementation, 166; as JOBS option, 56; mandatory requirements, 166; selective-voluntary programs, 106. *See also* Broad-coverage programs; Community work experience programs; Subsidized employment

"Workfare," defined, 21, 54, 97. *See also* Work experience

Work Incentive (WIN) Program, 182, 248; evaluations, 21, 69*n,* 84*n,* 93, 93*n,* 127; history, 7-8, 52-55, 54*n;* JOBS predecessor, 2, 21-22, 45, 48, 55-56, 127; participation, 54, 73*n,* 105, 185; requirements, 54, *see also* Participation requirements; services, 14. *See also* individual programs and topics; Welfare-to-work programs; WIN Demonstration Program

Working poor, policies regarding, 5-6, 11, 203. *See also* Poverty reduction

Work-only programs, impacts, 46

Work supplementation, as JOBS option, 56. *See also* Grant diversion; On-the-job training

WRP. *See* Pennsylvania Work Registration Program

Young custodial mothers' school requirement, 34, 42, 55, 57, 109, 110, 216, 225, 226, 248-249. *See also* Ohio Learning, Earning, and Parenting (LEAP) Program; Teenage Parent Demonstration; Wisconsin Learnfare

Young fathers, JOBS provisions, 34, 46. *See also* AFDC-UP; Youth-oriented services

Young mothers. *See* JOBS target groups; Long-term welfare receipt/recipients, potential long-term recipients; Mothers of preschool children; Young custodial mothers' school requirement; Youth-oriented services

Young parents. *See* Young custodial mothers' school requirement; Young fathers; Youth-oriented services

Youth-oriented services, 80, 82, 110-114, *111-113,* 224-230. *See also* Job Corps; JOBS education and training provisions/focus; JOBSTART Demonstration; Mandatory education; New Chance Demonstration; Ohio Learning, Earning, and Parenting (LEAP) Program; Project Redirection; Support services; Support services tests; Teenage Parent Demonstration; Young custodial mothers' school requirement

Author Index